C000254057

THAT LITTLE VOICE
IN YOUR HEAD

That Little Voice in Your Head

ADJUST THE CODE THAT RUNS YOUR BRAIN

Mo Gawdat

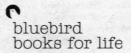

bluebird
books for life

First published 2022 by Bluebird

First published in paperback 2022 by Bluebird

This edition first published 2023 by Bluebird
an imprint of Pan Macmillan
The Smithson, 6 Briset Street, London EC1M 5NR
EU representative: Macmillan Publishers Ireland Ltd, 1st Floor,
The Liffey Trust Centre, 117–126 Sheriff Street Upper,
Dublin 1, D01 YC43
Associated companies throughout the world
www.panmacmillan.com

ISBN 978-1-5290-6617-3

Copyright © Mo Gawdat 2022

The right of Mo Gawdat to be identified as the
author of this work has been asserted by him in accordance
with the Copyright, Designs and Patents Act 1988.

All rights reserved. No part of this publication may be reproduced,
stored in a retrieval system, or transmitted, in any form, or by any means
(electronic, mechanical, photocopying, recording or otherwise)
without the prior written permission of the publisher.

Pan Macmillan does not have any control over, or any responsibility for,
any author or third-party websites referred to in or on this book.

3 5 7 9 8 6 4 2

A CIP catalogue record for this book is available from the British Library.

Printed and bound by CPI Group (UK) Ltd, Croydon, CR0 4YY

This book is sold subject to the condition that it shall not, by way of
trade or otherwise, be lent, hired out, or otherwise circulated without
the publisher's prior consent in any form of binding or cover other than
that in which it is published and without a similar condition including
this condition being imposed on the subsequent purchaser.

Visit **www.panmacmillan.com/bluebird** to read more about all our books
and to buy them. You will also find features, author interviews and
news of any author events, and you can sign up for e-newsletters
so that you're always first to hear about our new releases.

The gravity of the battle means nothing to those at peace

For Ali
It's time to open my eyes and see that life is beautiful

Contents

Introduction

I'm trying to make a billion people happy. Crazy, I know, but I believe it's the only goal worth spending the rest of my life trying to reach.

The story of OneBillionHappy began in 2014. The trigger, as it often is, was a tragedy. I lost my superhero – my wonderful son and wise teacher, Ali. He left our world as a result of preventable human error during a routine surgical procedure and with him took a piece of my heart. Seventeen days after his death, I started to write, and I couldn't stop. My topic was happiness – the most unlikely subject to choose after such a tragic event. What I wrote was what he had taught me; the gift he had given me which I wanted to share with the world.

The result was my first book, *Solve for Happy*, which challenged almost every false belief the modern world had taught me about happiness. It was a true eye-opener. After the tragic loss of Ali, I developed and shared the algorithm I had used to help me move forward. *Your happiness is greater than or equal to the difference between the perception of the events of your life and your hopes and expectations of how life should behave.* Although it was my hope that this would resonate with readers and they would benefit just as I had, I never expected it to take off the way it did. The book was translated into thirty languages, became an international bestseller and sold hundreds of thousands of copies worldwide. People from all over the world wrote to me daily, expressing their gratitude and asking me questions about happiness and my mission.

Losing a child must be the hardest thing a parent ever has to endure. Even today, after so many years, I still can't find the exact words to describe how it feels. Ali was my son and my sun. He lit up my life with his love and wisdom. He was my best friend and coach. He was always peaceful and always happy. Although the pain of losing him still lingers, it's brought me so much joy to know that his loss was the trigger that enabled me to find my mission, which is dedicated to spreading his wisdom, celebrating his life of love and compassion.

Two weeks before Ali left our world, he had a dream that he only told to his sister, Aya. He said, 'I dreamed that I was everywhere and part of everyone. It was so incredible that when I woke up, I felt I didn't want to be confined in this physical body any more.' 'Habibi,' Aya said, 'he dreamed he was dying.' He did. He was! Aya only told me about this dream a few days after his death. My highly trained, achievement-driven brain interpreted this as a target, handed down to me by my master. I have never missed a target – and my work at Google meant I had to set big targets to reach billions of people – so once Aya had spoken I burst into tears. I realized that Ali had come to teach us, to make us love him so much and then leave, so that his departure would become the spark that ignited what was yet to unfold. I cried so hard; my body was shaking. I knew exactly what it meant. My life was no longer mine, but rather belonged to his mission. The rest of my life was going to be dedicated to making his dream come true. I was going to take everything he had taught me and tell the whole world about it. I was going to spread his essence to humanity at large and in doing so, through six degrees of separation after many years, a bit of Ali-ness was going to be everywhere and part of everyone. The target was set, and I was not going to miss it. I stopped crying, got up and started the work.

As any businessman would, I set myself a measurable target. This was to share the happiness model I had devised with Ali's help with ten million people. Once the target #10MillionHappy was set, the universe itself conspired to make it happen.

Only six months after the launch of the original mission, I had already reached tens of millions of people online. The message was helping to change many lives, and it was clear that we needed to keep moving forward. The inspiration for increasing this mission from ten million to OneBillionHappy came to me during a short meditation. It was a moment when I realized that technology, which I had helped build through my computing career, was shaping our future beyond recognition. I realized that unless we teach the upcoming artificial intelligence about the essence of what makes us human – happiness, compassion and love – we would be in deep trouble. This is the core message of my second book, *Scary Smart*. I realized that Ali's target was real, that we could reach not just ten million but billions. We had the means to go everywhere and reach everyone.

Our small team kept making progress, and the content we created has now been viewed more than 120 million times online – a big reason to celebrate. But also to keep going. To reach a billion people, we need a much more fundamental change.

We need to get real about where we are in the world. The more we succumb to our negative thoughts, the more our actions become negative, and the more people behave negatively. You get back what you put out. If more people focused on being kind and compassionate to others there would be a ripple effect. People would start mimicking that kind and compassionate behaviour.

We would start a positive Ponzi scheme, with each newly happy person bringing in two more. This scheme would have the power to change the world, and it starts right inside you, with the very biggest reason for unhappiness – negative thoughts.

I believe thought is the most immersive of all illusions. There's a little voice in our head always, always telling us what to do. It's constantly there, like air, so we deal with it mechanically, just like our brains deal with our breathing. Year after year, we take that little voice for granted and it takes us for a ride to suffering.

In my research I found that thoughts, and only thoughts, have the single biggest impact on our state of happiness. That little voice in our heads affects our mood even more than some of the harshest circumstances we endure in life.

In this book, I will draw from my experience as a software engineer and my extensive study of spiritual teachings and neuro-science to take you on a journey through the hidden corridors of your brain. I will aim to show you that, although it is highly sophisticated, your brain, just like your computer, can be highly predictable. That if you give your brain specific inputs and run specific programmes on it, it will always give you the same output. The most undesirable of all possible outputs, I believe, is unhappiness. Our thoughts are a major reason why we become unhappy. My aim here will be to show you how to run your brain correctly to live happier. If you understand exactly how the code that runs your brain works, it will be easy to use it to consistently deliver your happiness. It is that predictable.

In fact, your brain is so predictable that I can summarize the way it operates in **a clear and concise user manual**. This book is that user manual. It will include **step-by-step instructions** on how to deal with your negative emotions, repetitive negative thoughts, stress and other conditions you may encounter in the operating environment of your computer – your brain.

It will also include **training instructions** because your brain can be trained. Using specific exercises, you can steadily reshape the very wiring of your brain over time. That way, you don't need to keep going back to the manual and instead make healthy habits your standard operating procedure. This book guides you through these rewarding and hopefully **enjoyable exercises in simple, straightforward steps**.

Consider this book **a fusion of computer science and neuroscience, written in a clear and accessible way**. As an engineer, I will often use technology analogies and simplified process diagrams of the different programmes we run in our brains and show how each influences our thoughts.

Don't be alarmed if you are not a techie. I will use simplified terminologies and explain the concepts plainly. Occasionally, you may need to learn something new about tech itself, but once you do, you will notice it in your everyday use of technology, the concept will become clear and that will help you remember it and include it in your approach to a happier life.

Any process starts with inputs. Regardless of how smart a computer is, the wrong inputs yield the wrong results. The inputs that we allow into our brains can often be destructive. We need to cleanse the palate of inputs that find their way into our head in order to stay happy, just like we follow a healthy diet to stay healthy.

Then there's the process – the way the programme runs. Follow the wrong path as you run your code and you end up suffering. Follow another and it will give you a path to everything you want from life. We need you to gain full awareness of what is actually happening inside your head so you're able to tell when you're thinking the wrong way. Once we refine the inputs and gain control of the process, we can start to optimize for what, I believe, is all we truly want from life – happiness, success and compassion for others.

I believe that much of our unhappiness comes from problems in our neural network – the underlying functioning of our brains. To define these in a way you can always remember, I will call them the 4-3-2-1.

There are *four* wrong inputs that we constantly allow into our brains. These trigger *three* exaggerated defences. As we navigate life, we suffer an imbalance between *two* polarities in our approach to life. A downward spiral to unhappiness, then, is triggered by *one* type of malicious thought. To continue the software analogy, none of this is because our brains are running badly. It's not even that they run on bad programmes. It's that they are good programmes run badly. So, as any good software engineer would, we need to debug our brain software.

We will run those programmes on the pages of this book and show you the kinds of symptoms they produce – uncontrollable emotions, chemical imbalances and endless loops of hurtful thinking. Once you learn to observe and identify those symptoms, the programmes producing them can be fine-tuned to fit their purpose and perform as intended – that is, to help you become successful in life while keeping you at your optimum state as a human: happy.

When the causes are known and the symptoms are identified, the solutions become easy – as easy as 1-2-3-4.

There are four main programmes that we can run in our brains that are optimized for our happiness. These are to fully *experience* life as it is, to *solve* problems, to *flow* and to *give*. Learn to make those a primary part of your operating system and you will consistently find your path to joy.

Later in the book, once you've acquired the skills you need, I will arm you with a flow chart. Yes, a bulletproof process to bounce back to happiness whenever life throws you off your path. With the process clearly documented, I will leave you in charge. You can find your way back to happiness or stay stuck in suffering. That's your choice; but don't say that life is making you unhappy. If you choose not to change, then the only thing making you unhappy is you. *You are in charge.*

We live in a world that is different to the world for which the code in our heads was originally designed. We will start with updating *your* code in this book, but who knows how far the effects of that may go? When you learn how to change your own world, it's possible that you may change the world itself.

Maximizing Your Benefit from This Book

This is a practical book, full of exercises, not just a book for your intellect.

If you are used to reading textbooks and being given knowledge in a distilled version, you may be tempted to skip the parts of this book that don't simply convey information – especially because some of them may appear oversimplistic initially. Please resist the urge to do this and follow the exercises as intended. It will benefit you and solidify your understanding more than I am able to describe in words.

You may also have the tendency to keep your books clean and neat. I'd urge you to change that with this book. Books are like houses: they are meant to be lived in. Make your book your own. Feel free to scribble all over it, take notes and fill in the blanks on the pages themselves with your own commitments and observations. This will be a rewarding experience, not only in terms of breaking some of your preconditioning, because it will remind you of what registered most, but also because user manuals are made so you can come back and revisit them. Your notes will guide you to the parts you need to tackle the functions or errors you want to address. I do advise revisiting the concepts a few times in the first few weeks. Some of the controversial topics we will discuss here may need a bit of revision to stick.

Finally, I will occasionally ask you to put the book down. I might ask you to go and do something else online or simply to stop reading and take a break. Please do allow yourself the time to stop. This is not a race and there are no trophies for those who finish fastest. The trophy – which in this case is a lifestyle change that will lead to a happier you – is for those who never really finish, those who keep dedicating the time needed to find their path to joy. We are not trying to achieve anything within a finite amount of time. We are trying to upgrade the code that runs our brain by frequently installing happier and happier versions.

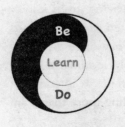

Progress is not only achieved by learning or doing. Sometimes it's good to just be. This will be the model we will use to make progress. I call this model: Be–Learn–Do. Be before you learn and learn before you do. Give yourself time to reflect and make concrete changes.

I guess what I'm trying to say is . . . chill. Enjoy the journey.

Now. Let me introduce you to your tools. We'll be using seven practical tools to help you through your learning experience:

1) We've All Been There

At the heart of our ability to change and improve is a need to acknowledge what is not going well. Since the success of *Solve for Happy*, I have noticed that sometimes readers, or audiences at public events, speak to me as if I am some kind of guru – a master  of happiness who is immune to the habits and practices that make us unhappy. This could not be further from the truth.

If I have any unique contribution, it is that I discuss the topic of happiness from the position of a normal modern-day human, one who is engaged in the hustle and bustle of life daily. I'm not a monk sitting in solitude practising meditation or a spiritual teacher lecturing from some faraway part of India. Just like you, I get stuck in traffic, I get bored out of my head in meetings, I have relationship problems and I worry about where our world is heading.

In this book, I have found the courage to share with you my worst stories. The times in my life when I was the opposite of everything I now teach. It humbles me to acknowledge what I did badly and hopefully these stories will remind you that we have all been there, we all have our faults and blind spots, and it is only in being more open about them that we can address them as we should.

2) Exercises

Once you acknowledge a need for change, there's no better way to proceed than through practice and reflection. This book is full of simple exercises that  will enable you to learn a skill, form a habit or deliberately dig deep within yourself to find awareness and grasp a concept.

Do your homework. As a matter of fact, go back and do it over and over and over again. Neuroplasticity (a concept I will explain more about in Chapter Four) enables us to learn better the more we repeat the same actions. It's the power of habit. It's the only way to put this user manual behind you because the skills contained within it will become your second nature.

Exercises will come in two different forms: **Awareness exercises** will help you reflect and learn something important about yourself. **Practice exercises** will help you develop a necessary skill.

Because we are all human, we will all be better at one than the other. Those who are naturally very aware are not always great at putting things into practice, and those who are great at doing are sometimes not fully aware. Push yourself even if you don't feel like doing one or the other. Being and doing are both equally important to give you a complete learning experience. I promise you that all the exercises are designed to be fun. So, whatever you do, don't forget to enjoy them.

3) Group Discussion

For the complex bits, however, there is nothing more powerful than discussing them openly with someone else. Often, I will ask you to get together with trusted friends to openly share your views about a variety of topics.

The only rule to keep in mind is that there are no right answers. Everyone's view is true . . . for them. Respect and embrace every diverse view. Even better, be curious and ask clarifying questions so that you can go deeper in understanding the views that differ from yours.

The best way to do this is face to face with real people. Perhaps you could ask a few of your friends to read this book too so you can set aside a time for a weekly one-hour meeting to discuss what you've read, as well as the group discussion exercises that have come up during the process.

Obviously, this may not work for everyone and many of you may prefer to work through the book alone. That's fine too — just adjust the exercises accordingly. Though I would still highly rec-ommend that you have the conversations with at least one close friend who you trust to help you see through any blind spots you may have.

4) Some Pop to Remember

Well, I don't know about you, but I remem-ber good songs and movies more than anything I ever learned in school. They stick in my head, playing on repeat. I love discuss-ing the scenes of a movie or the inspiring lyrics of a song with friends and I want to share those with you  too. Many of the concepts we will discuss in this book have been captured in the lyrics of incredibly talented artists or in scenes of timeless cinematic art. I will suggest those to you, so please stop reading and listen or watch if they inspire you to get the full experience of this book.

Plan an evening with friends to watch my movie recommen-dations. Try to look beyond the obvious and reflect on your own life to see how a scene or a concept of a movie may apply to you. For songs, please download a legal copy of the song or watch the official video on the internet. Play it until the concept sticks. Then add it to your happy playlist so that you can revert to it often. Learn those happy songs by heart. You'll be surprised how, at the time they are needed most, they will surface, play inside your head and remind you of exactly what you need to do. Music is life. So don't be shy to shake those hips while doing those not-so-demanding musical assignments.

5) Appii

Appii is your happiness assistant. It is built around the Be–Learn–Do model. It helps you track how you feel, customize the learning experience to your needs and give you relevant exercises to develop the skills you need on your path to happiness. The free downloadable app contains thousands of useful videos, inspirational  quotes, tasks and exercises. Appii will also use artificial intelligence to help you develop healthy happiness habits.

Get Appii from your play store or app store for free, or go to www.appii.app and use the promo code ThatLittleVoice to get a three-month premium subscription for free – giving you access to longer video lectures, training and advance features.

6) Slo Mo

Slo Mo is a top global podcast in terms of popularity. My podcast invites you to take time out of your busy life, slow down and reflect on topics that matter. I host some of the wisest people on the planet to share their inspirational stories and what they've learned, so you, the listener, can learn too.

We discuss happiness, spirituality, neuroscience, relationships and other topics that can help you become a better version of yourself or make our world a better place.

Join our community. Download Slo Mo for free on your podcast player or go to mogawdat.com/podcast to learn more.

7) OneBillionHappy

This book, as well as the other tools I provide you with, are part of a mission, perhaps the most crucial mission of our generation.

Despite the progress and technological advancements we've made in the last one hundred years, humanity is failing when it comes to our happiness. One in every six people will be diagnosed with depression in their lifetime – which is likely to be an underestimate of the true number suffering.[1] One human life is lost to suicide every forty seconds.[2] One in every four people surveyed in the USA say that when they feel unhappy, they don't have a single person to turn to for help.[3]

We need to reverse the trend. Our joint mission #OneBillionHappy has you, not me, at the heart of it. I can't reach one billion people alone. But together we can.

Help me reach the dream by taking on your own share of the quota. Make two people happy – it could be your children, spouse, sister or best friend – by alerting them to the fact that happiness is their birthright and should be their top priority. Teach them what you learn about happiness from this book and make it clear that happiness is predictable. If you do the work, you will get there. Pay it forward. Spread the word. If you really want to make a difference, tell twenty people, two hundred or even two million if you can. Be a happiness hero.

Please visit www.OneBillionHappy.org to learn more.

Throughout this book there will be a few tasks related to the mission. Please don't ignore those. Take them seriously and make them happen. Do it for humanity and enjoy the reward it brings.

A billion is not a large number if we all do it together, one person at a time. I will do my part and start with you. Let me, now, take you with me along the journey.

Destination ... Happy!

What We've Learned So Far

Here's a quick recap on a few of the concepts from my first book, *Solve for Happy*. Those are key to establishing a foundation for what we will discuss here. The first important basic principle was that we are all born happy. Children and infants, as long as they are fed, safe and given their basic needs for survival, are happy.

Happiness is innate within us. It's not something that we should seek outside us. **Happiness is our default state.** As we become adults, societal pressures, obligations, expectations and the illusions we learn to believe convince us that success is more important than happiness.

We relentlessly chase success and, in the process, we lose our happiness.

That happy child we once were, however, is still there inside each of us – only buried under a pile of false and limiting beliefs, waiting to be rescued so it can return back to its happy, childlike nature.

Happiness is not found by adding things to your life – all the fancy clothes, gadgets and vacations. A child is happy until something interrupts its happiness. If a diaper gets wet, the child will cry. Change the diaper and the child will go back to its default state — happy. This is still your nature even today. If you manage to remove the things that make you unhappy, what's left behind is happy. Simple as it sounds: **happiness is the absence of unhappiness**.

When you really get it, happiness is very predictable. So predictable, as a matter of fact, that it follows an equation:

$$\text{Happiness} \geq \text{Your perception of the Events of your life} - \text{Your Expectations of how life should behave}$$

Happiness happens when life seems to be going our way. We feel happy when the events of our life match our expectations, our hopes and wishes of how life should be.

Rain, for example, has no inherent value of happiness in it. Rain doesn't make us happy or unhappy. Rain makes us happy when we want to water our plants and unhappy when we want to get a tan.

Guided by that equation, you can find an accurate definition for happiness. Happiness happens when events meet or exceed our expectations. It is that calm, peaceful contentment we feel when we're OK with life as it is. It's the moments that we want to last forever because we don't want anything to change. It doesn't matter exactly how life is. If you're OK with it, you're happy.

Unhappiness, on the other hand, can be defined as a survival mechanism. It happens when our brains look at the world around us, find something that worries them and attempt to alert us that something might be wrong. Because we rarely listen attentively to our thoughts, the alert comes in the form of an emotion — shame,

anxiety, regret, sadness or any of the other emotions we associate
with unhappiness.

Between feeling happy or unhappy, we find a state that is
neither – the **state of escape**.

Escape is when we
engage our physical
forms in activities that
occupy our brains
and numb them long
enough to stop trying
to solve the happiness
equation.

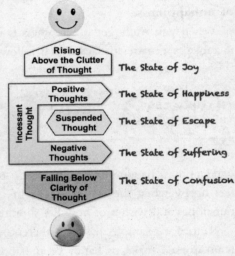

We find this state
of escape when our
bodies engage in fun
and pleasure. There is
nothing wrong with
fun. It's just that when we use it to escape our unhappiness it acts
rather like a painkiller – a replacement for happiness but not the
real thing. So, we go back for more and more; we become addicted
to fun. The more we do this, the more difficult it becomes to find
true lasting happiness.

People who are in the state of joy are constantly happy. They
look at life in a way which recognizes that most events don't
deserve unhappiness. They rise above the clutter of useless, harmful thoughts and there they find their joy.

Those, on the other hand, who are in a state of confusion
always search for what's wrong with every passing event, big or
small. If you search for what's wrong, you're more than likely
going to find it. Everything will miss your expectations; your
suffering will go deep and will linger.

Unhappiness as a survival mechanism is useful but it doesn't need to linger. There is a massive difference between **pain** and **suffering**. The initial pain, emotional or physical, happens because of external conditions. It's what triggers the alarm in our survival mechanism. As much as we dislike pain, it helps us focus on what matters, change direction, learn, develop and stay safe.

Pain is out of our control; it happens to us. **Suffering is a choice!** We choose to stay unhappy by replaying the events that triggered our emotional pain over and over again inside our heads when they are no longer happening or have not yet happened in the real world. It's almost like **pain on demand** – a very unwise choice indeed.

No event in your life ever has the power to make you unhappy until you choose to grant it that power by turning it into a thought and ruminating on the negative side of it to torture yourself with unhappiness.

If unhappiness lives firmly inside our thoughts, then learning to think better is the answer to all our suffering.

That is what this book is all about: learning to think better.

Let us begin.

Chapter One

The Basics

What is real? As your eyes scan over the words written here in this book, ask yourself, are those words real? Is the book real? Are your eyes real? How can you tell for sure that you are not in a dream? And if you are dreaming, is there anything wrong with that dream? If you could still get to the information, connections and life that you live in it, why should it count as anything other than reality itself?

The Objective Nature of Reality

As you read my words, you turn them into concepts in your own brain. Those concepts will become reality ... but only for you. They will become your reality which could be different to how someone else may comprehend the same words. If I told you that this book was going to be long, for example, the concept of 'long' may in your own brain translate into more than 300 pages. However, 300 pages won't seem long to you if you've read all 1296 pages of *War and Peace* a few times in your life.

The concept 'long' is an idea, a thought, that each of us creates in our own brains. Each of these definitions is real for the one who is thinking it. But, at the same time, none of them are actually real.

The book itself may not even be real. Through the lens of physics, the words on a page are nothing more than a bunch of particles organized in a specific pattern to form the page, and a bunch of other identical particles organized differently to form the pigments of the ink. As the photons of light hit the page, the ones that hit the white are reflected into your eyes and, because light is absorbed by the colour black, those photons that hit the ink are not. The photons travelling back to your eyes create the impression of an image – that is flipped upside down – when they reach your optical nerve, and the pattern is turned into electrical pulses that represent, but are not, the shape of the words. Your brain then takes those electrical signals and turns them into a vision of words on a page.

If I managed to simulate the electrical signals directly into your brain using electrodes that touched your scalp, you would end up seeing the same vision, only in that case there would not even be a book there. This should not be seen as some form of science fiction. A simpler version of it happens when we get completely absorbed in a movie. We feel as if we are actually observing some form of reality when it is actually nothing more than moving pictures.

We all know that what we see on a movie screen is not real. We all know that the actors are not really making love, just acting it out, and yet we perceive it as reality. We don't even need a movie theatre to create this illusion. We sometimes wake up from a dream feeling it was completely realistic, as if we were really there. None of the events of the dream happened, but the electrical signals occurred in our brain. This is sufficient to make us see it and even believe it is real.

You see, it doesn't really matter what the world presents to you . . .

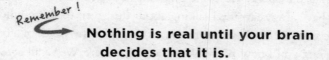

Remember!

Nothing is real until your brain decides that it is.

This, hands down, is the most important foundation we need to agree as we navigate the journey inside your head and attempt to understand how that little voice inside actually operates. It is important to realize that some of the very basics of what you may have spent a lifetime believing might not be entirely true. I will invite you to reconsider some of your most cherished beliefs and even invite you to question some of what we are told is true by gurus and scientists. Those truths, perceptions and beliefs that I will ask you to question, you will find, apply only within a certain context. Sometimes, when you change your vantage point, your whole world changes as a result.

Now, use that brain of yours that creates your reality to think about this: when your brain has so much power over your perception, how often does it tell you the truth? What happens when it doesn't?

Living an Illusion

We've All Been There!

Have you ever believed something so wholeheartedly that it affected every single one of your actions — only to find out later that what you believed wasn't true? My life has been littered with an endless stream of such misplaced beliefs: belief in corporate slogans, patriotic biases, religious doctrines, and belief after belief in the lies of the modern world. None, however, do I regret more than the belief that my wonderful family were a duty and a burden on me instead of seeing them as they really were: the biggest gift I have ever been given.

I have always avoided talking about this, even to those who are closest to me, but here I am now, writing it in the pages of a book. But, hey, you know what? We've all been there. We've all acted in ways at a particular point in our life that we now wish we hadn't. The Mo that acted in that way is now long gone.

I Was Wrong

I never really liked kids. I thought they were noisy and messy — that is, until the morning Ali was born. Ali *habibi*, my beloved, was born around two years after my late father, who was very dear to me, left our world. We did not plan for Ali. Nonetheless, I was raised to be a reliable man and, as such, I welcomed his anticipated arrival with a sense of responsibility — perhaps not the top quality a child needs but it was a good start. I may not enjoy the company of kids, I reasoned, but if it's *my* kid, he will be granted everything he could ever wish for or need. I worked a bit harder, closed a few extra deals, set up a room for him, paid for medical expenses, and was ready — as a good husband should be — to join Nibal in the delivery room.

The minute he arrived, everything changed. In his face I could see my dad, I could see my love for my beautiful then-wife manifested and I could feel vividly in my heart that, at that moment, I was being given a gift that would completely change my life ... and he did.

The joy this crumpled little creature brought into my life was beyond my wildest expectations. Nibal truly blossomed as a woman and emerged as the incredible mother she was always destined to be. I, on the other hand, just went to work. Eighteen months later, our daughter, Aya, joined the gang to bring more love, more blossoming for Nibal – and more work for me! By the time Ali turned five, I was spinning out of control, becoming a true workaholic and dissatisfied with my life in every possible way.

The truth is, I brought it all on myself. The only way I knew how to express myself as a father was to provide. I could not recognize, as Nibal made clear to me a thousand times, that a real father provides a lot more than just the financial means necessary to send the kids to a good school, buy them toys and cover their needs – but what can I say, I was an obsessive hard-working engineer. When I set my mind to something, I did it, then overdid it, and then overdid it some more.

Work comes with stress and, in my case, it came with a lot of stress. The jobs I chose were regional or global because those earned me more money. That meant endless hours in airports and on aeroplanes. I was doing well but then I overdid it. I worked extra hours to address more customers, close more deals and make more commissions – more money than I actually needed. I was doing very well financially but then I overdid it some more. I chose to trade in the American Nasdaq market, which opened every day at 5.30 p.m. my time in Dubai and added another work day – or work night – to my already draining hours. Note that these were all my choices and yet my brain chose to attribute the stress of my world to them. My brain created its own reality where my family and their needs were the reason for my burden. I believed that they were the reason I needed to work so hard.

I was wrong. The reason for my burden was triggered by my love for them, but it was not them. That trigger took on a life of its own. My exaggerated workaholism was a result of my failure to realize what they actually needed. It was clear as day that *I* was the reason for my life conditions and that – as I look back at it now – there was, in fact, no burden at all. There was only the joy of a beautiful family crowned with abundance. But brains don't work that way. They don't really care much for what is going well. They'd rather complain, blame and worry. Once my perception was set by my brain, it became my reality, and then it took me more than ten years to restore my sanity and erase that deep-seated concept that had deprived me of enjoying the incredible gifts I had been given. What a waste! Ten years I missed out on, just because I believed in one wrong concept. Does this feel familiar to you?

The Most Resilient Parasite

My favourite movie of all time, *Inception*, sums it up best. In the first scene of that movie Leonardo DiCaprio asks: 'What is the most resilient parasite? Bacteria? A virus? An intestinal worm?' He pauses for a few seconds then offers the answer: 'An idea. Resilient, highly contagious. Once an idea has taken hold of the brain it's almost impossible to eradicate.'

I have lived with that parasite for years. I know now that ideas are not impossible to eradicate but I surely do agree that an idea – a negative thought – is a resilient parasite when left to run astray. You don't need to be a scientist with a PhD and shiny headlines in the news to know that to be true. All you need is to remember a friend of yours who has been obsessing about a thought for days, weeks or years and feeling unhappy as a result. Perhaps you, yourself, have been there too. One thought that sticks deep inside our heads somewhere can cost us years, even a lifetime, of suffering.

In my research I found that thoughts, and only thoughts, have the single biggest impact on our state of happiness. The little voice in our head affects our mood even more than some of the harshest circumstances we endure in life.

PSSST... The following concept is one that we discussed before in *Solve for Happy*. It fits perfectly here and so I need to bring it up again to keep our thread of thought. I strongly urge you to keep reading through the parts you may already know; there is a lot coming up that we have not discussed before.

Let me show you how and uncover the relationship between your thoughts and your happiness.

Awareness Exercise
The Blank Brain Test

Homework

Target	To become aware of the relationship between our thoughts and unhappiness
Duration	5 minutes
Repeat	Once is enough
You'll need	A quiet place where you will not be interrupted

This exercise consists of two parts. For the first part, your task will be to think of something that makes you unhappy. For the second part, the task will be to construct the name of something from the letters on the next page.

You can consider yourself successful if you manage to complete both parts simultaneously. This means you have to guess the name correctly (task 2) while you manage to remain unhappy (task 1).

To begin, close your eyes for twenty to thirty seconds and think of something that makes you unhappy (please accept my apologies for spoiling your mood, but you will find this useful in a couple of minutes). This, I believe, will be an easy task. As soon as you tell your brain, 'Hey, brain, bring me something that upsets me,' your brain will jump at the opportunity. It will say something like, 'Seriously? Can I tell you something to upset you? I have 263 things that I have been waiting to talk to you about.' Once your brain supplies the first one and you find that feeling of unhappiness, focus on it, feel it and get into the depths of it. Now try to keep it there and, with that unhappy feeling, move on to the second task. Your task now will be to decipher the letters below and uncover the name of the object they spell out. (Hint: it is a thing that makes some people very happy.)

Remember, you need to do this while you remain unhappy. Ready? Let's go.

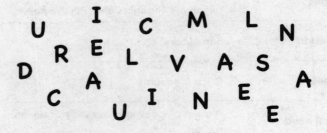

Did you guess it? The answer is Vanilla Ice Cream Sundae. It doesn't matter if you guessed it, by the way. I'm not your second-grade teacher. What matters is, did you manage to stay unhappy while you tried to guess it?

I've run this test, or some variation of it, with tens of thousands of live audiences in my public talks and, I will tell you, I am yet to meet someone who can complete both tasks correctly.

Those who manage to guess the thing drop out of their self-induced state of unhappiness, and those who decide to let their unhappiness linger by focusing their attention on whatever it is they chose to make themselves unhappy, always fail to guess the words Vanilla Ice Cream Sundae.

This is an important point because it helps you fully comprehend the way your thoughts work.

Remember !

When the little voice in your head speaks, it can't focus on anything else, and when it focuses on something else, it simply can't speak.

The Only Thing That Ever Made You Unhappy

Reverse-engineering refers to the process of examining the construction or performance of an existing product in order to understand how it operates. To understand how a product works in all its modes of operation, an engineer would take the machine from one extreme of its full range of motion all the way to the other extreme and record readings of how it performs at each point. Let's call this a full cycle simulation.

The blank brain test you just performed is a full cycle simulation of you, as a machine, when it comes to your state of happiness. Right before the test started – call that moment T(0) – you seemed to be engaged with reading the book and not feeling unhappy. At T(0) nothing was upsetting you. You were happy!

I then asked you to think of something that made you unhappy. Let's call that moment T(1). Once you allowed an unhappy thought to take you over, you immediately moved to the other extreme of your range of states and you became unhappy.

Then, finally, I asked you to use some random letters to guess the name of a thing – call that moment T(2) – and *Puff*, the unhappiness was gone. You focused on the problem at hand and for that brief moment your brain was not thinking about anything that could upset you. You were happy again.

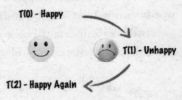

Now, there is a question that I need to ask you which will shed a floodlight on how happiness works inside your brain and will probably change your life forever: between T(0) and T(1), and between T(1) and T(2), did the real world change in any significant way for your mood to change?

Let's say, for example, that when I asked you to think of something that made you unhappy, you thought of a harsh remark your friend or spouse made last Friday. The thought made you unhappy as if you were hearing those words again, but were you? When you were engaged in solving the puzzle, as you stopped feeling unhappy, your friend did not show up to apologize, did he? Nothing actually happened in the real world for the duration of the exercise.

What is the only thing that happened, may I ask?

The only thing that happened to make you unhappy was that you started thinking and the only thing that stopped your unhappiness was that the thinking stopped. You see?

Remember!

It's the thought that makes us unhappy!

No event, I dare say, in your entire life ever had the power to make you unhappy unless you granted it that power by turning it into a thought and running it through your head over and over to make yourself miserable. In the absence of the thought, such as your state when you were at $T(0)$, there was no unhappiness to be felt. Of course, some of those thoughts are unavoidable. If you are financially insecure or you've lost someone you love, you are bound to think about it. Just notice that when you think, you feel unhappy and when you stop thinking you focus on other parts of your life as if the problem doesn't exist.

Before Ali left our world, he lived in Boston and so I could not see him for extended periods of time. I missed him but not like I miss him now. Although the fact, either way, is that I could not get to see him, the thought that he left our world and so I will never again see him in his handsome physical form makes my longing so much deeper.

While we all say that we want to find happiness in life, our heads are almost always full of thoughts, often negative thoughts, that make us unhappy. Those thoughts, as they occur, are not real events. They are just reconstructions of past events or predictions of future possibilities. When you think about it this way, you may realize that you are rarely ever unhappy because of something that is happening to you. If ever you manage to make yourself unhappy, it is because of an imagined event, generated in the form of a thought in your head, and not the reality of what is happening to you right then.

If anything requires your attention — be it guessing the name of an object or escaping from a tiger — the voice in your head stops.

That's why the voice is always silent when something is wrong because it only speaks when things are OK here and now.

This limitation on our brains' ability to engage us in an internal dialogue is very similar to the way you deal with your computer or smartphone. When you are focusing on a certain page to click on parts of the interface, your computer is, sort of, in communication with you, but if you direct your attention to typing numbers into a spreadsheet, for example, the communication stops until you can once again manage to direct your attention to it.

I could end the book right here, because this little insight can help you silence your inner voice whenever it hijacks your state of happiness. But let's keep going a tiny bit longer to uncover some more of the secrets of this very effective machine – your brain. Let's begin with the biggest myth of them all . . .

Who's Talking?

Inner Speech – a person's inner voice – provides a running verbal monologue of thoughts while they are conscious.

In our modern Western world, there is no confusion over who that voice is. The French philosopher Descartes summarized it in his famous quote, 'I think, therefore I am.' I find it interesting that the way most of us understand this statement is not at all how Descartes intended it to be. At the time, he was attempting to prove that he existed, in reality, and that he was not just a simulation. Being able to think, Descartes reasoned, was proof that he existed. We took his reasoning and twisted it to fit the hyperlogical civilization we have built in the modern world. We now glorify thought so much that we interpret his quote to mean that we are the thoughts – the voice – inside our heads. Big mistake! Funnily enough, he might have been mistaken on his thesis too. Modern science points to ample evidence that we could actually be living in a simulation despite the fact that we think. But that's a topic for another book. Let's focus, for now, on the bigger mistake. Is the voice inside your head really *you*?

I can most certainly tell you it is not and while I wish I was one of those authors who can impress you by telling the story of an epiphany they had as they were treading their path to enlightenment in the furthest corners of Asia, sadly, I am not. I've had the majority of my insights in the most mundane of places. One day, many years ago, I was sitting in a cute cafe somewhere in our vast globe when I found it difficult to focus on the magnificent music playing in my noise-cancelling headphones by my favourite band in the history of music – Pink Floyd. Regardless of how loud I turned up the volume, the headphones couldn't cancel out my frantic inner speech. I had been struggling with an issue at work and was unable to find the clarity or peace needed to shut down the chatter raging inside my head. The song playing in my ears was, quite appropriately, called 'Brain Damage'. It was just one more track playing along with countless other trains of thought running through my mind: *this person is playing political games, that client may not close the deal on time, we will miss our target, my boss is annoying*, and so the thoughts kept coming.

Then, just like when you're at a very noisy party that suddenly goes quiet right before you start to shout something important, my thoughts went silent just at the moment when Roger Waters sang: **'There's someone in my head but it's not me.'** I paused the music, stunned. Then I played back the last verse, then the whole song, over and over, countless times. Yes, there's someone in my head – but I always thought it was me. I always thought that little voice was me talking to me.

With that one verse in a song acting as my wake-up call, I started to conduct my own massive enquiry. Like everyone I have ever discussed that concept with, the first question I asked myself

'Brain Damage'

Listen to Pink Floyd's 'Brain Damage' from start to end.

While the voice in our head is not always a lunatic – often it is a genius – the song surely describes in a clear way how letting that voice go wild and listening to it too much can drive any of us crazy.

---

was: *If the voice in my head isn't me, then who is it?* My thoughts took me back to the time when I was growing up. Cartoons, then, often portrayed the voice as an angel on your right shoulder and a devil on the left, with each deliberating their case and arguing about it, using your head as the conference room. Is that what it is? Messages from other beings? Psychologists, meanwhile, name it various other things. Sigmund Freud calls it the Id/Ego/Super-Ego, while Eric Berne calls it Parent/Adult/Child. Is that who it is? Religions also call it many different things. Islam calls it the whispers. Buddhism calls it the monkey mind. Others believe it is the devil itself dictating its devious agenda right inside your head. Sci-fi fans think of it as the ghost in the machine – a tiny person inside your head running the bigger person that you are. Does any of that make any sense to you? Eckhart Tolle, in his incredible book *A New Earth*, calls it the thinker without really describing who that is, and Pink Floyd in their song call it the lunatic. Well, that sounds about right. (That's a joke. Don't stop reading.)

With so many different views, I had my hands full. There was almost nothing in common between these diverse perspectives other than one thing. That little voice is not you. It's a third party. It is a different entity talking to you.

Now, that made a lot of sense to me once I started to think

about it. I mean, it's a very simple subject–object relationship. If that voice in my head was me talking to me, why would it need to talk? If it was me, I would inherently know what it wanted to say without the need for anything to be said at all.

That idea of a third-party speaker changes a lot of things but, still, who is it? To find out, let me ask you a question. Have you ever woken up one morning telling yourself that you are the blood being pumped around your body? Do you believe the statement, 'I pump blood, therefore I am'? Your heart pumps blood around your body to keep you alive, but you don't believe that you *are* that blood, do you?

The biological function of your kidneys is to extract toxins and waste matter out of your system and remove them from your body in the form of urine. None of us thinks that we are the biological product of our kidneys. And while on a bad day guilt can make some of us feel like we're a piece of . . . number two, nobody believes that poop is the essence of who they are. 'I breathe, therefore I am' is not true either. You are not the CO_2 that you exhale. Why then do we believe that we are the biological product of our brain?

If thinking is a biological function, then a thought is analogous to urine and CO_2. It is just a biological product.

This idea has a lot to support it. Your brain, fundamentally, is a three-pound lump of meat, just another biological organ concerned with your survival. The product it produces to aid with that altruistic purpose is thought. Although, as a race, we humans have managed to push our brains to the point where they have created iPhones and built civilization as we know it, the original function those brains were designed for is entirely focused on keeping us alive. To do that, they analyse the world around us, turn our complex environment into simple concepts that we can grasp and then turn those concepts into words (the only building block of knowledge we can comprehend). With this knowledge we can make the all-important decisions needed to survive, and then implement those in the form of orders given to the different parts of our bodies so we can remain safe. That's it, really. Your brain is your inner voice. It's the one telling you what's going on and suggesting how things should be. It is the one making all the noise.

Psychology has discussed this since the 1930s when the Russian Nobel Prize winner Lev Vygotsky observed that inner speech is accompanied by tiny muscular movements in the larynx. As a result, he argued that inner dialogue developed through the internalization of our out-loud speech. The idea is that when you start learning to speak as a child, you narrate everything you see out loud. *Mama, toy. Mama, car.* It's a way of learning the significance of words and concepts, in order to help yourself understand the world around you. You keep doing this until it starts to become awkward. Then, to avoid embarrassment, you turn the dialogue inwards.

In the 1990s, neuroscientists confirmed Vygotsky's view when they used neuro-imaging to demonstrate that the areas of the brain which are active when we speak out loud, like the left inferior frontal gyrus, are also active during inner speech. In one of my favourite MRI studies, conducted by MIT back in 2009, researchers observed the brain activity of participants while they solved puzzles. First, the relevant problem-solving part of the brain – say, the parieto-occipital regions – engaged for a few seconds to find a solution. Then, they went dark and the right frontocentral regions – the same parts we use when we speak out loud – lit up for as much as eight seconds before the participants recognized the answer.[1]

Your brain solves the problem first, then takes up to eight seconds to turn whatever answer it found into English so that you can understand it. In that sense . . .

Remember!

Your brain is literally talking to you.

Thoughts are real. 'I think, therefore I am', however, is an illusion. The reality of the illusion is *I am, therefore I think*. Or rather . . .

Remember!

I am, therefore *my brain* thinks.

And that is magnificent news, because it means that your thoughts don't define you. If you are not the thoughts in your head, then you no longer need to obey. You can debate and question claims that seem to be invalid. You don't even have to listen. Best of all, with a little bit of practice, you can — and should — frequently tell your brain to shut up completely.

Our brains are the best gift humanity has ever been given. We've just never learned how to properly use them. It's like being given the most powerful computer on the planet when you don't know how to use a spreadsheet. As you enter the wrong numbers in the wrong cells and run the wrong macros, you will undoubtedly end up with a big pile of nonsense. This is exactly what happens with our brains. Running astray, they produce the weirdest thoughts and end up torturing us and those we love.

There's nothing wrong with your computer. Let's learn how to use it.

Learning to Compute

That three-pound lump of meat inside our skulls is still, despite the incredible recent advancements in technology, the most sophisticated computer on the planet. This machine comes complete with an entire sensory monitoring system that can detect vision, sound, touch, weight, temperature and many other complex stimuli, subtle as they may be, in the environment surrounding it. It has the capacity to constantly monitor all that sensory information and compile it into comprehensive concepts to make sense of the world around it. It's capable of impressive memory storage and recall. It has incredibly accurate motor functionality controls that would put any robotics engineer in our world today to shame. It has its own power generators contained within the body and, most impressive of all, it is capable not only of solving complex problems, but also of formulating them into problem statements that accurately describe the challenges that need to be addressed. Then, to top it all, it is capable of reading, communicating and exchanging information with other brains.

Indeed, our brains are an impressive piece of engineering work. As children we take this brain to school to learn about mathematics, biology and an array of other academic topics. Then, as we grow older, we attempt to teach it things like healthy eating, fitness or the art of posting funny stuff on social media just as we teach it to get addicted to likes and social approval. We take it to pottery classes and salsa lessons.

We teach it to comprehend and control everything around it, but we rarely ever teach it to understand or control itself.

It sounds curious when you think about it, the concept of teaching a machine to run itself. But this is fast becoming a more acceptable idea – cars that drive themselves and search engines that teach themselves how to search are becoming common everyday tech. The closest we have come to this with our brains is meditation, which teaches our brains how to calm themselves down, slow the incessant thinking and focus. We all know the benefit of that. Meditation changes the life of a dedicated practitioner for the better by enhancing one of our most crucial brain functions: deliberate attention. If we practise meditation for an extended period of time, our brains reap the rewards and our lives improve. So, what if we could learn and practise ways to improve every other process the brain can perform? How much better would our whole lives become then?

There are many ways we can describe how our brains work and many ways to improve how they do what they do. Neuroscientists look at lobes, cortices, synapses and chemical signalling. Spiritual teachers look at mind training and psychologists look at conditioning and traumas. Each of those perspectives comes with its perks, but none treat the brain as the computer that it really is. I'd like to complete the picture, and for that, as I describe to you how the brain works, I will talk about software.

You'd be amazed how similar our brains are to the computer systems we build. The knowledge provided by neuroscience, psychology, spirituality and many more fields that have studied the brain can help us view the different functions our brains perform as independent 'programmes'. There is code in our brains that helps us reason, other code that collects sensory information and yet more code that controls our hardware – our bodies. These programmes operate independently and interact with each other. Use them well and you have the most sophisticated machine on earth at your disposal. Use them in the wrong way and the software becomes buggy. It leads to the wrong results and crashes into states of sadness, even depression, way too often. I will avoid the deep technical terms and help you understand our brain's software operation at the basic level. Once you know how the machine works, it will be easier to spot the bugs that cause the programme to malfunction and make us unhappy. Fix those, and we're good for prime time – a computer that resolves our daily challenges without causing us unnecessary suffering.

Let's begin with a tiny bit of engineering lingo. In their simplest form, operational diagrams describe the relationship between what you input into a system, the processing that takes place by the system software and the output that results from this process. If the inputs into a system are the numbers two and six, for example, and the software performs a process of addition, the output will be eight. Simple!

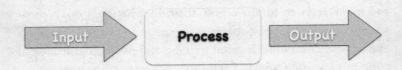

The complexity of real systems, however, increases beyond the apparent simplicity of this diagram. Most systems have multiple inputs and various processes that sometimes operate independently and sometimes interact, overlap, complement or contradict each other. Such complex systems then often result in multiple possible outputs.

So, here's the plan: to keep things reasonably simple as we explore how our brains work, I will break our brains down into inputs, several distinct processes and, accordingly, several possible outputs. Together, we will take the machine apart piece by piece to give you a comprehensive look at each of those components. As with a computer, I will use neuroscience to show you which part of your brain runs which specific software. I will explain the primary function of each specific programme, and if there are any bugs in the way we use it, I will show you how to fix them. We will also examine the interrelationships between the different programmes. If a certain programme enables or inhibits another, I will make that clear. When you finally understand how each programme works, we will put the machine back together to arrive at some kind of a user manual. This will include practices that you, as a user of your brain, should adopt to ensure good working order and optimum performance of your own priceless machine.

Don't be intimidated by the complexity. It really is going to be simple, entertaining and filled with 'Aha' moments as you realize things you've never understood before. In the first few pages of every user manual, there is always a drawing that shows a picture of the product you purchased, along with elegant arrows pointing to the different parts to give them names. It's a bit like saying, 'Let me introduce you to those you will be working with – here's Emma, Jonathan and Kim' (only engineers tend to choose names that are a bit more complicated).

The brain user manual would start with a picture that looks like this:

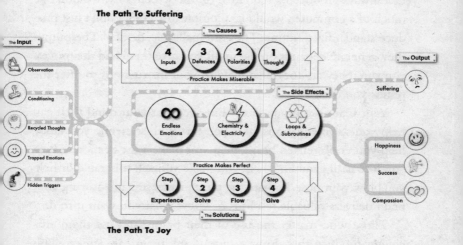

Please don't skip this diagram. Take a few minutes to examine it and see what each of the names I have used might mean for you.

Note: I suggest you add a bookmark here to keep track of the diagram above. You may want to refer to this model as you navigate the comprehensive content in this book.

As you do, I will go celebrate because, honestly, our whole book is right there in one diagram. All I need to do now is to write a few intelligent pages about each of the above listed components, keeping things simple without the use of any mystical words. It's only a matter of weeks now, and the manual will be in the hands of the users.

What Does Success Look Like?

Imagine buying a complex computer, for a few thousand dollars, which could do only one thing. Regardless of what you did with it, it always produced a red circle on the screen. That wouldn't be much of a computer, would it? Complex machines don't just produce standardized output. They are malleable, flexible. The output they generate depends on the input you give them and the process you run. They are tools that yield to your instructions to offer the results you desire.

Your brain can produce anything you put your mind to. It can help you solve equations, help you flirt with someone you fancy, help you cook refried beans, help you make a lot of money, help you lose it all gambling, help you make yourself miserable or help you blow your nose. Perhaps the most pivotal step in ensuring your brain delivers valuable results is to know what you want it to do.

Those who master the use of their brains, and use them efficiently, produce the ultimate output any brain can achieve. This can be summed up in three outputs. They realize their own individual happiness, they achieve a reasonable measure of success (depending on how they define success) and they live with the compassion needed to impact the lives of others positively.

All my work – my books, my podcast (Slo Mo), the happiness app (Appii), every training I have taught and every talk I have given – aims to help you achieve those three goals. This book is no exception. As we dive deep into the inner workings of our brains, we will attempt to deliver your happiness without ignoring your own individual success and your positive impact on the world. I hope you will find this worth your time.

I'll go put on my overalls now and grab my toolbox to start deconstructing the machine. This may take me a few minutes. So while I do, let me suggest that you spend the time doing the following exercise. Take your time to finish it, and I will wait for you in the next chapter.

What are the sources of information you rely on as the input that informs your thinking process?

Every bit of information that enters your brain leads you down a path of a different set of thoughts. Over time, those thoughts make you the person that you are. They shape you so much that paying attention to what triggers them might be the most important thing you will ever do.

Awareness Exercise
What Triggers Your Thoughts

Target	To become aware of what your thoughts are made of
Duration	5 minutes
Repeat	Repeat at least once a week as needed
You'll need	A quiet place where you will not be interrupted
A notepad and a pen

Find a quiet place and take a few moments now to look back and ask yourself what sources of information you have been allowing into your head. Here are a few examples: Jacqueline, my friend from school, has been telling me about her diet. What my mother taught me about work ethic has been influencing my engagement at work. Recent posts on Instagram have been affecting my sense of self-worth. The news has been making me feel that our world is unsafe.

List all of them down – as many as you can.

This is just an awareness exercise. There's nothing that you need to do about your list for now but that awareness will become useful in the next chapter as we analyse the different inputs we let into our brains.

Part One

The Neural Causes of Suffering

The **Causes**

4 Inputs — 3 Defences — 2 Polarities — 1 Thought

Practice Makes Miserable

To fix a machine, first you need to find out what's wrong with it. To fix the unhappiness your brain is experiencing, you need to find out what causes it. I believe that the reasons our brains make us unhappy can be summed up in a simple model: 4-3-2-1.

> *4 (wrong) **Inputs** that distort our perception of the truth.*
> *3 (exaggerated) **Defences** that keep us safe but make us suffer.*
> *2 (opposite) **Polarities** failing to stay in balance.*
> *1 (harmful) **Thought** that causes all the unhappiness you have ever felt.*

*Repeat these often enough and you become really good at them because **Practice Makes Miserable**, when what you practise is your own unhappiness.*

Chapter Two

Garbage In . . .

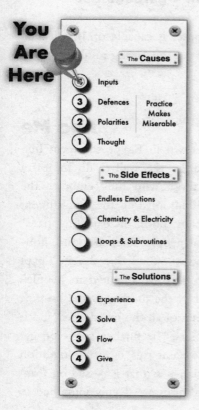

They say that you are what you eat. I believe that. Whatever you put inside that biological form of yours shapes you into what you become. The impact will become visible in the shape of your body, sometimes immediately and sometimes in the longer term, for example, when you drink too many sugary drinks.

You also are what you think. The stuff that you allow into your head forms the thoughts that trigger your immediate actions, makes up your ideology, informs the memories that shape your beliefs, constructs the experiences that define your attitude, your choices and everything else that makes up your identity.

You could own the best computer on the planet and write the best programme to run on it. If, however, you sat in front of it when it was ready and used the keyboard to enter the wrong data, what would you get? The wrong calculations and, accordingly, the wrong results. In programming we sum this up in one famous rule . . .

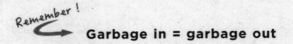

Remember !

Garbage in = garbage out

It doesn't matter what your computer is capable of. If you feed it the wrong information you will get the wrong result. So, what are you feeding your brain?

Jibo Me

We've All Been There!

In my hometown in Egypt, the term Jibo is often used, by the well-to-do minority, to describe those who fully embrace the beliefs and traditions of the less-affluent Egyptian society. Jibos, or 'true Egyptians', are wonderful people. They are kind, honourable, hospitable, giving and funny. Spend one day in Egypt and you will be offered tea, help, and even invited to people's homes for a lovingly cooked meal by the mother of the host, *set el habayeb* – which means 'the queen of all the loved ones' and is how Egyptians refer to their mothers. The further away you get from the big cities, the more prevalent this beautiful tradition becomes. There is a way to Egyptian-ness that is passed on from generation to generation. Our traditions are deeply ingrained in true Egyptians. An elder in Egyptian society will always set an example and pass down their wisdom in words – lots and lots of words – to the younger Jibos.

The Arabic-speaking world where I was raised adores words. Part of our culture is built around the use of words and Arabic is a complex language in many ways. Every word in traditional Arabic has many meanings: the word *asad*, for example, can refer to the name of a person, a lion or bravery, among many other possible meanings. Moreover, for every meaning there are endless words – there is a full Wikipedia page for the words that mean 'lion'. On it there are five hundred different words, which range from the commonly used *asad* all the way to words such as *sabe'*, which also means a man who is really good in bed, and *kanafes*, which also happens to mean The Beatles. It's a funny way of using language, I know, but it illustrates the most important characteristic of Arabic sentence composition – context matters.

This incredible versatility allowed the poets of the past to be activists within highly oppressive regimes. They used words to write poems of praise for the king or khalifet that, when seen through a different lens and in a different context, could mean the king was an absolute idiot. Arabic truly is a glorious language that constantly invites the listener to analyse and debate in an attempt to figure out the context. It invites contemplation, as opposed to rushing to conclusion, to discover what all the different possible variations a certain 'configuration' of words might mean. This, eventually, leads to a deep grasp not of what's being said, but of what is actually meant.

The days of glory of the traditional Arabic language were long gone by the time I was growing up. By then, this fascinatingly complex language was often taken literally and was losing a lot of the rich context from its past. This applied also to the proverbs that constituted the backbone of how Arabian culture transferred its wisdom from generation to generation.

As a young man, I was bombarded with sayings that appeared to be wise but were often misleading and even detrimental, when misinterpreted out of context, to my nation's culture and progress. *Ala ad lehafak med reglaik* was a proverb developed during times of famine which basically means 'Stretch your legs only as far as your blanket can cover'. In the context of famine, this proverb encourages resourcefulness, but when that context is forgotten it starts to hint at resignation – don't strive to improve your situation. Just accept what you're given (a short blanket) and learn to live with it. Which can be interpreted as complacence!

Men sab adimo tah is another proverb, which means 'If you leave your past behind, you will lose your way'. Again, it's a noble call to learn from the past and be proud of your roots, but somehow the Arab world often understands it as a call to reject progress and stay stuck in tradition.

I grew up hearing these words repeated by the elderly and in songs on the radio. They were presented as sources of wisdom. Some of them confused me and in my early twenties I decided to stop acting upon them, but they remained inside me like unfinished business. Over the years they often resurfaced, not as undisputed wisdom, but still presenting themselves as viable options or perhaps valid thoughts that contaminated my thinking. It wasn't until later, in my forties, that I decided to dedicate long patches of silence to revisit my beliefs. I examined all the proverbs, religious dogma, capitalist teachings and traditions I'd taken on board on my journey. I attempted to cultivate the good ones and get rid of the weeds. That process, so late in life, made me a better person or at least an honest person, one who acts upon his own reflections and whom I can now respect and enjoy living with. Consider spending time to reflect on your beliefs too because . . .

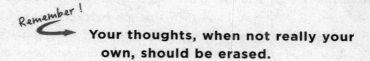

Your thoughts, when not really your own, should be erased.

This is also a valid analogy for computers, because despite their seemingly abundant resources, they too can suffer performance degradation when they run out of valuable space. I'm sure you remember a time when your phone's performance slowed down or it refused to take more photos, for example. This happens when unusable or useless information is stored in the memory. These files keep piling up and use up memory capacity needlessly. Every clever programmer will tell you that in order to ensure optimum performance, you need to clean up behind you. When you store something in the memory that is needed for a specific process, you need to erase it when you're done. If you don't, the memory of your computer will fill up fast and your computer will fail as a result. We even had a name for the process of cleaning up the stuff that was left there unintentionally. Guess what it was called? Garbage collection.

Have you collected your garbage recently? Have you given yourself the time to reflect on the validity of what you believe? Have you cleaned up useless or harmful concepts from your own memory system?

If you haven't, you're not alone. So much idiocracy defines nations across the world. So much propaganda is seen as wisdom. It does not matter where those concepts originate from, be it antiquated traditions, the agenda of mainstream media or your friends and family. What matters is to eradicate them. Once we believe something, it starts to shape us and if what we allow in is garbage, our resulting thoughts and the emotions that they produce within us also become, well . . . garbage. At the end of the last chapter, I asked you to complete the 'What triggers your thoughts' awareness exercise. Now you know why that was needed. It was just the first attempt to keep score of some of what is shaping you. It's now time to dig deeper and understand all the different types of garbage that affect us. I call those . . .

The Triggers of Thoughts

Imagine you wake up on a Sunday morning with thoughts about your next vacation. You're feeling a bit burned out at work and as you observe the rain outside, you start to think that you need a sunny destination. That thought then triggers a memory from your last vacation and you start to wonder how that friend you met there is doing. Your brain then jumps to the future. You have always wanted to see Egypt, you think, so your thoughts go to pyramids, to the Temple of the Kings and that relaxed diving trip on the shores of the Red Sea. Yet, you recall Fox News saying some of these destinations are unsafe. So, you start pondering a vacation in Memphis instead. This cycle of thinking gets interrupted when you get a message from a friend saying she just saw your ex-girlfriend holding hands with someone else. You abandon the vacation thinking and your thoughts drift to think about all that went wrong between you.

We allow so many things to input into our thoughts. If I started listing all of them it would take pages and pages. To simplify, I tend to group them into five categories: observation, conditioning, recycled thoughts, trapped emotions and hidden triggers. Only one of the five comes close to the truth. The other four just mislead you.

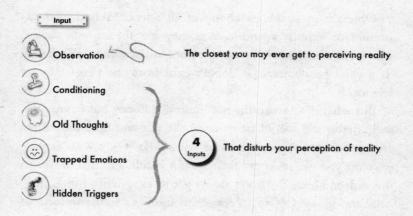

Now You See Me

The first of the five triggers – **sensory observations** – theoretically – are the only source of information we should allow into our heads with a moderate level of confidence in their validity.

Islamic mysticism refers to three levels of knowing: knowledge, observation and experience.

If I tell you that there is a pot of honey in the kitchen, you have *knowledge*. That knowledge *seems* to be true, but can you take it for granted? What if my information is outdated? What if the pot of honey I may have seen in the morning has been removed by someone since then? What if I'm lying? You'd be more confident in that knowledge if you walked into the kitchen and saw that pot for yourself, right? *Observation* is a more confirmed form of knowing than 'knowledge'. It is the bottom line, a level of knowing you can rely on for your decision-making. Hence, it is often wise to question what you are told unless you have witnessed it for yourself. A way of life then is summarized in an Arabic axiom that translates to: 'If you are told, verify. Then your decisions are sound and only then you don't suffer regret for an uninformed decision later.'

Observation is the backbone of all science. When scientists attempt to explain scientific facts they use the *scientific method*, which relies exclusively on observation. Any scientist will tell you: 'If it can't be observed, it doesn't exist from the perspective of science.'

But what if what's in the pot looks like honey, but is, say, caramel? Better still would be to open the pot and taste the honey. *Experience* is the highest form of knowledge. Only with experience do you get to know that the pot is full, and that what's in it is indeed honey. We don't always get to experience things firsthand and so it is OK to accept observation as a sufficient form of knowing in that case.

Remember!

What you observe with your own senses is the closest you can get to the truth of the physical reality.

Taking something that you are told as truth may mislead you. Sadly, this happens way too often in our modern world. Don't take my word for it (pun intended). Ask yourself how much of what you allow into your thought cycles is not actually sensory observation. How much is gossip, hearsay, fake news or just plain guesswork by someone who is not qualified to assess the validity of what they are talking about? The sources of unverifiable information are endless. It is almost impossible to keep count of them and, sadly, we consume them as our primary source of knowledge and then we think we know. In English, the word ignorance is defined as the lack of knowledge or information. In Arabic, ignorance – *al jahl* – is to know something that is not true. That kind of ignorance, sadly, has become the state of the world.

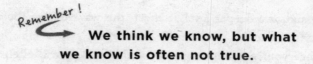

Remember!

We think we know, but what we know is often not true.

False knowing is the first of the neural causes of suffering. In the modern world it is triggered by what I call the . . .

Four Inputs

When we mix our own perceptions with what is presented to us by others or by our own irrationality, we can lose touch with reality. Being lost in false knowing makes us feel that things are not fitting together correctly. Something just doesn't feel right. We worry and start to search for clues to validate our worries. We search for them and we find more of them in the endless hype of false knowledge. They worry us even more and that's when deep unhappiness sets in. There may be nothing at all with our life at this moment but our false knowledge convinces us that the world is about to end. Have you ever been there before?

Beyond sensory observation, our brains create thoughts based on four other types of input. Let me take you quickly through the first three which are fairly obvious: conditioning, recycled thoughts and trapped emotions. Then we can dedicate more time to the fourth – hidden triggers – which truly is the root of a lot of evil.

Interestingly, the first three of these negative inputs come from within us. They affect the way we view the world and respond to it, but it is not actually the world that is misleading us, it's our own internal baggage that we carry with us through the years.

Conditioning is the summation of all the beliefs and traumas we develop or encounter throughout a lifetime. Your conditioning affects the way your thoughts flow, the way your decisions are made and, at a deeper level, it affects the way you see the world in the first place.

Once your conditioning is set within you, it will often affect you even more than your external circumstances. If you believe that all women or men are players, for example, you are bound to suspect that your date or partner is a player, even if they are honest and loyal in their nature. The truth may be staring you in the face, but you would not be able to see it because it is viewed through your conditioned lens of perception. Your life story, then, would not be the sequence of events that you experienced but rather a series of stories that are generated by your brain as a result of past conditioning.

Those stories are rarely ever true because the nature of conditioning is such that . . .

Remember!

Conditioning is often created in a context that is very different from the context in which it is applied.

Once, in my career at Google, a country manager who worked within my organization was an immigrant who came from very tough beginnings and had had to flee his country in a state of war. At a point during the time we worked together, he applied for a Canadian permanent residence, sent his wife and two daughters to Canada and started an MBA at the London Business School. At the same time, unfortunately, his father was diagnosed with cancer back in his home country. To meet the demands of those commitments, he needed to spend a week of every month in Canada, a week in London, a week next to his dad, and could only spare a week for his duties in the country he was responsible for. His work suffered significantly and we needed to talk about it. When I asked him why he was stretching himself so thinly, he said, 'You don't understand, Mo. Life shouldn't be trusted. I need to make it in life to make sure I and my family are safe.' That was his conditioning. It was built within a context of war, poverty and hardship. I said: 'Make it how? You are the country manager of the hottest company in the world in your favourite country on the planet. How exactly can you make it more than this?' Being country manager at Google is considered the height of success for many and yet, due to his childhood conditioning, he still felt unsafe. He felt he was still in the middle of the storm.

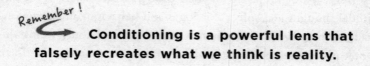

Remember!

Conditioning is a powerful lens that falsely recreates what we think is reality.

Those false perceptions are often used as input into our thinking process. We rely on them when they're not even true and as a result we suffer. The validity of our conditioned beliefs should be investigated and corrected if we are to find a path to a life of more clarity and happiness.

Take, for example, the thought *Success is more important than happiness* – a thought that is seated deeply into many of us early in life. Parents teach it to their children and teachers to their students as genuine and sincere advice meant to save them from hardship in life. That one thought massively impacts our choices as adults. When presented with a potential path to success that may also lead us to unhappiness, we take the path of success and suffer. We make success our priority and miss out on happiness as a result. Some stay in jobs that make them unhappy, others live in places that add daily stress to their commute, and some even forgo opportunities for love and family as they prioritize their career instead.

The seed of that one thought festers and grows to become a

web of thoughts that can, and often does, completely take over our adult life. If success is more important than happiness then, logically, it is OK to forgo happiness because unhappiness is the tax one must pay for eventual success. This then leads to the thought *It's OK to be unhappy*. It leads to the idea that prioritizing happiness signifies a lack of commitment. It convinces us that success is measured by material positions and ego-boosting tokens that one can show off, and that those who fail to accumulate these are considered failures. All deep-seated, recycled thoughts that are built on an old piece of advice that comes with no basis of any truth.

Tens, if not hundreds of such thoughts can derive from one initial thought and infect our logic and behaviour in every conceivable way. While this may feel like a bit of a detour, I think this topic is so important that it is worth taking a short break to perform two quick exercises – one specifically on the topic of happiness vs success and the other on your thoughts and beliefs in general.

Is success (and all the other things we prioritize) really more important than happiness? If you were offered all the success there is to attain but were to become miserable as a result, would you take the offer?

Awareness Exercise
Delayed Gratification

Target	Revisit your beliefs about happiness and success
Duration	30 minutes
Repeat	If you enjoy the conversation, repeat is as many times as you like
You'll need	A group of open friends or family members and an open mind

The logical answer is that you shouldn't take such an offer, but so many of us live that way for most of our lives. It's insane. We all need to revisit the thoughts that put our happiness second and question their validity.

Please spend about thirty minutes with a group of friends or a family member, in person or online, to discuss the following:

From your personal experience, share a few examples of self-imposed conditions that sound like the phrase: *I will enjoy my life more when such and such happens*.

Examples may include:

- I have decided to work hard for the next five years to reduce the mortgage before I can change to a job that I enjoy more.
- When my children go to uni, I will move to a sunny place.
- How can I smile when the current president is ruining our country?
- When I finally reach the target I've set for myself, I'll find happiness waiting for me there.

Each member of the group should share no fewer than five examples. Let the ideas flow for as long as you can. Don't judge, don't correct, and don't suggest solutions or fixes. Write down your top examples here.

I will be happy when I do this: . . . .
. . . .

I will be happy when I have this: . . . .
. . . .

I will be happy when I achieve this: . . . .
. . . .

I will be happy when this happens to me: . . . .

. . . .

When you have finished brainstorming, choose one example each and discuss it in detail.

Why do you feel this way? Why do you believe what you're waiting for is more important than fully living in the current moment? Discuss what you're gaining and losing in the short and long term as a result of the choice that you have made.

Finally, ask the group to help you verify if the thing that is delaying your happiness is the only possible way that can lead you to achieve your targets. Ask if there are other, simpler ways to get to where you want to be, even if a little later, without having to pay for it with the tax of your unhappiness. Close your eyes then and try to imagine what life could be like if you gave happiness a higher priority and still managed to find a path to a reasonable level of success. Wouldn't that be a better way of living? If so, should you drop that old belief?

If you are open-minded, you will realize that you should drop it, that happiness should be an integral path through life. That core conditioning, which we sometimes live a lifetime by, is wrong. You can do the same exercise with so many other concepts that seem to be widely accepted in Western societies today. I'm not saying they are invalid, just asking you to examine them. First ask the group to share examples of how they live by those concepts already. Then question if this way of life is working and if, perhaps, there is another way. Then imagine how life could be lived differently. Here are a few other deep-seated modern-day concepts that I think are false for you to examine:

Material possessions are the most accurate measure of success.

Unhappiness is an acceptable tax to pay for success.

The shape of your body matters.

Other people's opinions indicate our true value.

We need to fit in.

Fake it till you make it.

It's weak to show your vulnerabilities.

Fun is an adequate replacement for true happiness.

We live in a democracy. Democracy is the best form of governance.

Watching the news allows citizens to shape society and government for the better.

And the list goes on. Feel free to expand it to include everything you hold dear and every belief that defines you. When done with each, put your pen down and prepare for a moment of truth as you do the following exercise.

If some of your thoughts and beliefs are limiting, then you might as well do something about it. Now! Not tomorrow, not next week. A weed left unchecked grows to take over the whole garden.

Practice Exercise
Make It Right

Target	Weed your garden of thought
Duration	15 minutes at a time

Repeat	Repeat for the rest of your life
You'll need	A quiet place where you will not be interrupted and the determination to make things right

First, revisit the examples you developed in the last exercise about your priorities and targets in life, and consider how in pursuit of them we often miss out on life, we delay enjoying the present moment or we align to illusions that cause us pain. Reflect on one example at a time and repeat this every week for as long as you need. Our whole being is made up of our belief system. You'll be amazed how often I weed out my belief system, even today – ten years after I started to perform this practice.

To remove a belief, you first need a reality check made up of three questions:

Question 1: Is aligning to a specific conditioned belief working for or against you? Is it, in fact, preventing you from achieving your goal rather than achieving it? Is it leading you to a different goal that you don't really need to achieve? A prime example of this, which I have witnessed countless times in my career, is the number of people who put up with a job they hate because they think it will lead to something better. Often, they end up quitting (or being asked to quit) before they achieve their goal because of their mounting unhappiness.

Question 2: If I offered you an opportunity to achieve your goal, the promise your conditioned belief is dangling in front of you, but you would end up feeling miserable as a result, would you take my offer? What if I offered you a guaranteed state of happiness if you gave up on (or slightly changed) that target? Would you take that? Think about it.

Question 3: Can you think of a different, better, target? Or a different path to achieving your target, where you could remain happy? If you can, then why would you do things any other way?

Once you achieve clarity on what really matters to you, and possible alternative routes to getting there, commit to taking the steps needed to effect a change.

Ask yourself: *If my priority truly was my happiness, what would I do differently?* Be specific.

List down actionable steps you need to do in order to include happiness formally into your path. Then stick to your plan. Make things right!

Conditioning can be spotted in our actions and thoughts if we thoroughly examine our beliefs. It isn't easy to spot but it is possible. However, the next input into our thoughts is the trickiest to discover:

Recycled old thoughts and **trapped emotions** are often fully blended with our thought processes in ways that make them hard to parse and distinguish. They occur inside each and every one of us and, with a little bit of reflection, you can start to notice them in yourself.

Let's begin with recycled thoughts. The difference between those and conditioning is that the one generating them is you. They are not triggered by events or advice that comes from outside of you. Instead, they result from thoughts that you leave unexamined, which you grow to believe are true. I'm sure you can easily recall a time when one single thought — *(S)he doesn't love me any more*, for example — triggered fifty more, such as: *That's because I'm ugly; (S)he will leave me; I hate dating; I will never find love again; I will live and die alone.* None of those thoughts happened. They all were volunteered by your brain as new input, though invalid. Those kinds of thoughts also share another interesting characteristic – they seem to resurface, time after time after time. An old partner who cheated makes the new partner a likely candidate to do the same. The old thought generated then is recycled now. The original might have been triggered by a real event, but the recycled thought is triggered entirely by your brain, which creates it first then finds the justification to prove it. Old thoughts resurfacing, then triggering a whole sequence of other thoughts, is an everyday occurrence for many of us. We don't always notice this cycle because our old thoughts, sometimes, are subtle. They morph and hide in the background of our subconscious brain. *I'm not good enough. I don't deserve to be loved. Life is tough. I'm unlucky. Everyone cheats and lies.* Thoughts that present themselves as undisputed facts or socially accepted 'knowledge' so that they fool you into accepting them and you don't revisit them as they eat away at your life a tiny bit by a tiny bit.

Trapped emotions also trigger our thoughts almost all the time. Wake up one day feeling irritated and your thoughts are bound to be negative. *Everything is against me, no one understands me* or *Everyone's an idiot* are the type of thoughts that are sure to dominate your day. Someone could walk up to you and say, 'Good morning,' and you'll snap, 'Don't good morning me! I'm not good-morningable.'

Isn't it funny that when you're in love, life seems to be amazing? The same commute to work turns into an opportunity to think of your beloved and typing away at the little keypad of your phone does not seem to be a chore any more. Our emotions shape our thoughts so significantly and yet we seem to separate our emotions and our thoughts. This, mainly, is due to how disconnected we have become from our emotions in the modern world. In a world where reliability, predictability and delivering results matter, we learn to prioritize our thoughts and actions while we ignore our emotions. As we trap the negative ones, they sink to the bottom of our psyche and poison our thoughts. Identifying and embracing our emotions takes a lot of work, so let's leave them to one side for now. We will discuss them in detail in a later chapter. Just make a mental note to remember that while emotions result from thinking (I know you may not agree with this statement yet), they also produce thoughts that then produce more emotions in an endless vicious cycle.

A lethal mix of deep conditioning, recycled thoughts and trapped emotions often makes up our belief systems.[1] And your belief system dictates your state of happiness and way of life. They are so deeply resident within us that they are sometimes hard to detect, even as they continue their input into everything we feel and do.

There is no way I can stress enough the importance of checking the validity of the sources of information that you allow into your head. With your diet, you would never eat anything that you knew had gone bad or was contaminated with disease. You wouldn't take even one bite, would you? Similarly, one bad thought becomes that parasite DiCaprio described at the beginning of the movie *Inception*. A good rule to live by is . . .

Very Important !

Never let a negative, invalid piece of information into your brain.

How can you do this? **Question everything.** Not only everything you are told, but everything you tell yourself too.

Once, I taught a class to a small group of highly influential executives from Belgium. Typical of Northern European culture, the class turned into an endless debate. Someone, almost instantly, debated whatever I said, then everyone debated the person's debate. It was reasonably obvious that there was no real disagreement, just a need to be heard. Four hours into the training, I was still on the third sentence of the first slide, and I was totally cool with it, because I knew there was a much bigger lesson to be learned. Eventually, I asked why it was that everyone was constantly debating everything, and the answer was clear: by debating we get closer to the truth. Being a truth junky myself, I praised that behaviour, I said: 'Yes, I invite you to question everything.' But I also asked:

Have you ever debated something that your brain has told you?

Before you object to something that contradicts your own knowledge or beliefs, take a moment to question if what you know is true, if there could be other views that are also true and if your thoughts are even your own thoughts, rather than those implanted in you by your parents, teachers, friends or public figures and opinion leaders.

Often, we forget that what makes up our own beliefs might not always be valid and **while we go out into the world questioning what everyone else believes, we fail to remember that the ones misled could very well be us and not them**. We forget that over the years, through our own unique exposure to the world and through years of recycling our thoughts and trapping our emotions, we may have arrived in the wrong place. We forget that we may be our own worst enemy – the source of many blurry illusions that take us astray. Our beliefs are the result of a million little inputs. It's almost impossible to track back to their origin. We can only verify them by examining the validity of the final outcome – the current thoughts that fill our brains.

In my own daily practice of looking inward – the 'make it right' practice – I observe the endless activities of my thought-generating machine. It never ceases to surprise me what I find. Every now and then I stop at a thought with total amazement. 'Where did that come from?' I ask myself. 'How did I ever believe that?' I sometimes find myself laughing out loud and sometimes weeping in amazement at how the tiniest seed of thought, conditioning or emotion planted inside me as a child could single-handedly define decades of my life. When I find such thoughts, I make them right. I still do this almost every day.

Look inward and question. It's the greatest show on earth!

Which leads me to the root of all evil, the other show that acts as the source of millions of inputs, the fourth of the wrong inputs, the one you can act upon immediately to stop creating more of the other three. I call that . . .

The Hidden Triggers

Before the modern tools of code development, writing computer programmes was done by feeding thousands of lines of code into a compiler. Being human, it was almost inevitable to make mistakes every now and then. Those mistakes would lead to disastrous results if undetected. The hardest mistakes to catch were when the programme compiled (meaning there were no errors in the syntax of the commands you wrote), so the programme worked but used wrong inputs to perform its calculations. A constant that you entered by mistake in your algorithm, an equation where you used x when you should have used y, or a registry in the memory storage that you did not clean properly before you started to use it. Those were hard to deal with because they produced random wrong results. You knew the answers were wrong, but it was difficult to trace to the trigger that caused the errors. The same happens to us as humans. We could be using sound logic to analyse the world around us but produce the wrong results because we are fed false information while unaware. When that happens, we make the wrong choices, not knowing what the causes of our errors are.

A problem is easier to fix when you can accurately define what triggers it. Things become a lot harder when the triggers are subtle and harder still when they flow in abundance, trigger after trigger after trigger. This is how information is constantly fed into our heads. Each opinion, image, article and video on its own may not amount to much, but keep them coming line after line, day after day, and you're toast. Your thoughts are no longer yours. You become another loudspeaker repeating what you hear without even being aware of where the roots of your thoughts originated. I call these constant drips of false information in today's modern life the **hidden triggers**. A thought qualifies as a hidden trigger when it is sneaky in the way it provides you with false information while attempting to make you believe it is true.

At the very top of this list of such triggers is **mass media** – news channels, social media, reality TV and the internet. Then there is the movie industry, which creates fiction that becomes part of our perception of reality. This is then supported by celebrities who have tens of millions of devoted followers believing their every word. Then there are your friends, parents, those you consider your teachers, and even books, this one included, that tell you things in a way that makes it sound true. The list goes on and on, and we take it all for granted.

Don't you think you should stop for some due diligence on the credibility of these sources before you turn to them for guidance? Can you imagine the kind of power you are giving them over your thoughts, beliefs, opinions and your resulting actions? Please think about this for a minute before you continue reading. How much influence do you let into your head without ever questioning if it is true?

Believe me, I'm not bitter. I love all the advancements that the modern world offers us – but make no mistake, if you blindly follow everything you see, read or hear, your chances of finding the truth, and accordingly your state of happiness, will quickly diminish all the way down to zero. When that happens, those who fed you all the fear, conspiracy, ideologies and slogans will not take the blame. The truth is, no one is to blame for our unhappiness but ourselves. The responsibility for distinguishing the good from the bad, the truth from the endless fakery and lies, resides firmly with you.

You see, it's unlikely that our capitalist world will wake up tomorrow and admit that it's wrong to twist the truth in the pursuit of greed. When you wake up tomorrow, you will be facing another day of utter lies. Advertisers will continue to dazzle you with things that you don't need, making you promises they don't intend to fulfil. News networks will continue to author a hypernegative, biased perspective of events, triggering your fear to keep you glued to the screen. Even your friends, though well intentioned, will attempt to recruit you to their belief system and will continue to passionately bestow their opinions of the day on you. Hollywood will continue to produce sex, horror and violence in the hope that you will shed some of your money at the box office, and politician, thought and business leaders will continue to give inspirational speeches to convince you to support their success and career. And who could blame them? **As long as you continue to buy into their product, why would they change?**

Let me be blunt here, the only way our world is going to change is (as Gandhi said) if you . . .

Remember !

'Be the change you want to see in the world.'

Every day, hundreds of millions of TV screens in the sanctuary of our very own homes will display a scene of someone pointing a gun at someone else's head and pulling the trigger. Our hearts don't even move any more. This is not true to our human nature. We should feel compassion for the loss or suffering of another. To accept it as just another scene in a movie is diminishing our ability to connect to the innate qualities that make us human. Accepting such atrocities as the norm is known as the . . .

Hypernormalization of Reality

Our brains, brilliant as they are, are built with limited computing capacities. For them to perform efficiently they tend to filter out things that they don't deem necessary for their success. This happens in many ways. Focusing on the moving cars and traffic lights while you cross the street while ignoring the rest of the surrounding environment, for example, allows your brain to dedicate its full resources to what matters most – your safety. This kind of filtering is good for you. But then the same deliberate act of preserving its resources can work against you too. This is what happens when we hypernormalize reality. Our brains are built, first and foremost, to ensure our safety. They are supposed to pick on anomalies in the patterns of life to react to the dangerous ones if need be. Our brains are supposed to jump out of their seats in response to violence or horror. But then we immerse them in those experiences repeatedly, either through movies or watching the news, and they start to think that those acts are normal. Accordingly, in an attempt to preserve their resources, our brains ignore the violence, the lies, the suffering of others, and consider those to be the new reality. This is why you can walk past a homeless person suffering in the freezing cold of January, ignore their presence and continue on your way. It is wrong. The opposite happens too. Our brains are supposed to experience awe and wonder. They are supposed to enjoy beauty and to feel aroused at the sight of an attractive person. Work in a butterfly enclosure and the incredible miracle of a butterfly becomes hypernormalized to a job. Spend too much time watching porn and the sight of a perfect sexy normal person would not turn you on any more. Either way, we become numb and life becomes bland. We lose the awe, wonder, alertness and joy because an excess of abnormal input becomes hypernormalized and considered a reality.

While we remain blissfully unaware, volumes of violent, scary, arousing or untruthful inputs completely rewire our brains and reshape the way we look at the world. We accept this synthesized view of life and, drop by drop, it becomes our new normal. We integrate it into our decision-making and make it part of everyone's life, then we wonder why there are so many school shootings and creatively violent crimes. We wonder why dating and finding a life partner has become so difficult and we wonder why life often feels tasteless and unexciting.

How have we come to this? you may ask. Well, my top answer would be the media and entertainment industry.

Terry Pratchett – author of the Discworld series – wrote this brilliant paragraph, said by the angel of death, in the novel *Thief of Time*:

> *You had to hand it to human beings. They had one of the strangest powers in the universe . . . No other species anywhere in the world had invented boredom. Perhaps it was boredom, not intelligence, that had propelled them up the evolutionary ladder . . . that strange ability to look at the universe and think 'Oh, the same as yesterday, how dull. I wonder what happens if I bang this rock on that head?' And along with this had come an associated power, to make things normal. The world changed mightily, and within a few days humans considered it was normal . . . They told themselves little stories to explain away the inexplicable, to make things normal.*[2]

Boredom drives the herds of humanity to follow all the distractions of the media and entertainment industry as it drives those with power to play games of war, politics and business. Then, strange as it all becomes, our ability to hypernormalize reality hides the rough edges and makes it all seem OK. A slow but steady drip of ideologies rips apart what it truly means to be human, while we sit and watch.

I have never seen this more clearly than in the highly celebrated 2017 movie *Wonder Woman*. Early in the movie, a handsome man arrives at the shore of the island where Wonder Woman is the protector and the princess. She rushes to defend her island and approaches that man only to quickly notice that he is being pursued by hundreds of others. She asks: 'Why are they chasing you?' And he answers, 'They are the bad guys.' With that one sentence, it seems that her new reality is created because, without ever checking the validity of what he claims, she and her army proceed to kill every single one of those poor souls. Every single one of those who were killed with intricate skill in graphic clarity in front of my own eyes on the massively big screen was a human with a story, dreams, ambitions and a family who will miss him. But somehow, for most viewers, they were reduced to supporting actors. It seemed OK for them to be wasted, just because someone introduced them one minute earlier as the 'bad guys'. This is how gullible we've become.

And since we're so easily swayed, the movie then goes on to show that the 'bad guys' – in this case the Germans – were building a weapon of mass destruction to hurt millions of people. This moves the generous heart of the heroine, Wonder Woman, so she rushes to save the 'good guys'. Now, that's hypernormalization of reality at its finest!

Please don't get me wrong. The Germans carried out terrible acts of inhumanity during the two world wars. History will surely remember those as bad guys. But, as history remembers, in the Second World War the weapon of mass destruction deployed to kill and destroy the lives of more than half a million innocent, unassuming civilians was the nuclear bomb. I don't know about you, but in my book that too counts as bad. In war, there are horrible acts of inhumanity on all sides, everyone is a bad guy and no movie or history teller should ever make any of us believe a different reality. If we come to accept that killing civilians is OK in a movie, we lose sight of the truth. Since when was it OK to kill anyone? Anyone at all? Since when has the value of a life been reduced to nothing? Since we hypernormalized killing on the screen as our new accepted reality. This needs to change.

More than twelve years ago I stopped watching violent movies. The only time I allow moderate violence on my TV screen is when a movie is highly recommended to me by five – yes, five – trusted friends as a movie that will inspire my thinking and teach me something or will help me become a better person.

Very Important! →

I choose to stop the violence.

I choose to purge it out of my life even as its harm continues to extend beyond my single insignificant self. I take responsibility for the only part of the world that I am fully accountable for, my own little world, starting and often ending, with this one being – me. But don't ever underestimate the impact of changing just yourself. Believe it. Changing one person can change the whole world.

Stop the Violence

Help make others happy by alerting them to the concepts of hypernormalization of reality and the hidden triggers. Form groups to support each other and stay away from the mainstream media that propagates violence, horror, fake news and all the poisons that have been hypernormalizing our reality and driving our whole planet further and further away from what it feels like to be human.

Maybe if you and everyone reading this join me in avoiding violent movies unless they're useful, the box office revenues of violent movies will drop and Hollywood will decide it's time to create more comedies.

If we all stop listening to the lyrics that reduce women to sexual objects, maybe music will evolve. If we all stop watching the rendering of sexuality as it appears in porn, if we stop listening to and propagating fake news, maybe then our world will start to shift and, in the process, our own heads will be cleared of all the garbage that's been filling them.

Over the years, I've stopped all of the above and it has helped me find joy in life. **Will you?**

I have been seriously limiting my time spent watching the news for over a decade. I search for the headlines that interest me online just to stay updated and often I totally skip the news for months at a time. I never feel that I'm missing out on anything. I rarely ever browse social media. I spend less than a few hours a week on all social media combined, and that's only because my responsibility as an author requires me to respond to my readers. Most of the time I spend is taken up with responding to others, in voice notes not text, to connect to my followers in a way that is as human as Social Media allows. I rarely swipe mindlessly on content recommended to me by the recommendation engine and I only follow uplifting accounts that create posts that enrich my life. I choose to cleanse my life of all that poison. It's the wise thing to do.

Don't be naive. Don't get carried away by the lies that the modern world wants you to believe. Don't buy in. If you want to find happiness, make deliberate choices, and when a hidden trigger does not serve you . . .

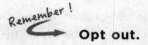

Remember! → **Opt out.**

I'm not saying leave the world behind and go live in the wilderness. What I'm saying is make choices. Be smart in terms of defining what works for you and what works against you. Don't follow the false promise that being up to date is more likely to make you change the world, or your own life, for the better. When was the last time you acted upon something you saw in the news and actually made a difference? How often does watching all the negativity add to your burdens and lead to no impact at all? Make a choice and know that opting out of a bad thing is not abstinence. It is wisdom.

Bust the Illusions

News networks broadcast content to serve an ideology or for commercial gain. Violence and fear keep us stuck to the screen. It's not their aim to inform you. Their aim is to benefit from your sticking around to watch. You're not the customer, you're the product.

Have you ever wondered what would happen if you had no access to the news for a few days? Would your life change in any meaningful way, other than perhaps feeling a lot better? Would the world cease to function because your commentary from your sofa stopped? Have you ever wondered why you keep watching when often there is nothing you can do? If a child fell in a well somewhere, would your act of watching save him? Or would it drown you in pain? What can I say? It's the Stockholm syndrome. Some of us just can't seem to get enough of what tortures us. Some even fall in love with their torturers! I hope you're not one of those. **Opt Out.**

Celebrities are just humans like you and me. (If someone looks like a human and poops like the rest of us, they are just a human.) Rationally, we all know this, and yet we turn them into gods. We listen to their opinions on the world as if to prophecies. We wear what they wear and speak like they do. Are they really trying to make your world better? Some do. Or are they just furthering their stardom? **Opt Out.**

And then we follow slogans. Words that fill our heads with noise and yet leave us empty. The more complex it sounds, the less we understand it and the more profound that makes us believe it must be. Once I heard a meditation teacher tell a student to 'find a connection with all being in isolation away from all the distractions of the self and connect with your inner energy in a peaceful blend of the divine feminine with mother nature through the heart chakra'. What he was asking her to do was simply to sit in nature for fifteen minutes a day. She then repeated his words, verbatim, as if they actually meant something.

Jargon, mysticism and name-dropping make everything sound grander that it really is and fill our world with lots of worthless inputs and very little truth. The truth does not need to be inflated. If something is complex, it's not the truth. **Opt out.**

No product that you see in an ad will ever change your life. My wonderful ex, Nibal, always used to say, 'If it was good enough and I actually needed it, they wouldn't have had to advertise it.' There's no significant improvement your current phone gives you that your old phone didn't. There won't be a significant addition that the next one will give you either. **Opt out.** Leave it all behind.

Before we close on this point, let me make it clear that I realize it is impossible to fully opt out of so much that has become the norm of our modern life. There is an upside to being on social media and sometimes it is important to watch the news. I am urging you, though, to use your best judgement to make what you let into your life work in your favour. Capture the benefit and stay away from the harm.

Very Important !

Invest in your happiness, not in the lies of the modern world.

There's a whole pile of junk that we let into our brains. It creeps in hidden and stays in us for years. Perhaps it's time to clean it up a bit.

It is worth your time to reflect on how these hidden triggers have been affecting your thoughts. This will be done in two steps. First, write down the impact the hidden triggers have on your mood and clarity of thought. Then write down an action plan to purge these negative thoughts from your life, one by one.

Practice Exercise
Banishing the Hidden Triggers

Target	A life free of contaminated sources of information
Duration	30 minutes at a time
Repeat	Repeat at least once a week as needed
You'll need	A quiet place where you will not be interrupted A notepad and a pen. This is much better done with a trusted friend

Set a timer for thirty minutes – feel free to reset the timer when it goes off if you need more time. Find a quiet place where you won't be interrupted. Take a piece of paper and a pen, stop checking the time and start reflecting.

Examine how what you saw in the media, on the internet, or what you heard in conversations with friends last week affected your thoughts, mood and actions. Write down what you find.

Examples may include: *The debates about political leaders on TV got me worried about the future of our country* or *A chat with a friend about dating apps and hook-ups got me wondering if I should remain in a committed relationship.*

Ask yourself some of the following questions to prompt your brain to admit the inputs it's been consuming:

Does the behaviour of a certain celebrity influence my choices?

Do the articles on the web sway my opinion?

Is there an ideology, political party, teacher or thought leader that I follow blindly?

Did a comment or a social media post alter my mood in the last few days?

Do I have residual negativity or fear as a result of what I hear in the news?

Is the presence of a certain friend in my life dragging me into thoughts I don't need?

Are all the notifications on my phone giving me joy or adding stress to my life?

Keep going. Find every external source of information you interacted with recently and ask yourself if it is working for you or against you, or affecting your happiness and clarity of thought.

This exercise is much better done with a trusted friend. When you have your list of hidden triggers written down, take the time to chat with a friend and exchange notes.

Now, bearing in mind that happiness is your top priority, take another fifteen minutes and ask yourself a crucial question: *Which, of all those hidden triggers, do I need to remove so that I become happier?*

Write down a clear action plan for how you will eliminate the influence of the hidden triggers affecting you and how you will purge the bad ones from your life. In my own experience, examples of actions you could consider taking include:

- I will switch off the notifications on my phone. (Trust me, this is a much more complicated process than you think. The options to switch off notifications will be hidden deep in the menus, clearly because those app providers want you to stay hooked.)
- I will stop watching violent, horror or gory movies of any sort.
- I will only read the news headlines once every three days (they tend to cling on to catchy negative stories and repeat messages that serve their agendas for days at a time).
- I will spend the next two weeks of my life strictly off the news to see if I actually miss out on anything. If it turns out that there was nothing important (and actionable) that I missed, and if it turns out that my mood has improved drastically, then I will extend my poisonous news detox by another month (or perhaps a year or endlessly).
- I will ask this friend, lovingly, to get out of my life unless they change the way they attempt to influence me, and I will ask that friend to please stop gossiping.

The actions I choose go firmly on my list of things to do, alongside writing, working out and meeting people. Limiting the use of WhatsApp to less than thirty minutes a day is currently on that list. But that's my list. **You need to come up with yours.**

When your list is ready, mark your commitments and targets with clear target dates. This is a marathon, not a sprint. It may take you months to fully detox and change the habits you've had for years. Start with one or two of the most urgent and most intense hidden triggers. Then keep turning additional targets into actions on a weekly basis.

If you can find a trusted friend to help you on this path, that would help tremendously. Set exact dates to report back to your friend on your progress, for example, in a short message at the end of every evening. This will make you stick to your commitments better. Remember to frequently reflect on how the more you purge your hidden triggers, the better you feel. This reflection will fuel you to continue making positive change.

Opt Out

Help make others happy by sharing with other readers and happiness seekers your experience with opting out. Share ideas of what you removed from your life and how it made things better.

Chapter Three

Under Attack

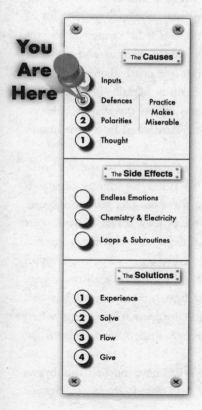

You Are Here

The Causes

Inputs

Defences

2 Polarities

1 Thought

Practice
Makes
Miserable

The Side Effects

Endless Emotions

Chemistry & Electricity

Loops & Subroutines

The Solutions

1 Experience

2 Solve

3 Flow

4 Give

The computers we create are made up of several components, each highly specialized in the task it is intended to perform. A graphics processor focuses on rendering graphics while the central processing unit focuses on crunching the rest of the maths. The memory storage keeps the information you need promptly while extended hard drives specialize in keeping large files as a backup.

This is very similar to how the different regions of your brain and nervous system work. Each component is highly geared for the role it was designed for. And just as with computers, once you know what the brain and each different part of it is supposed to be used for, you immediately understand why it operates the way it does.

Why We Think

Understanding the *why* – the reason behind someone's behaviour – is the easiest way to understand the *what* and the *how*. Because Jake had a crush on Sally back in high school, he behaved differently around her than the other boys did. He seemed to be overprotective, and he sometimes withdrew into sadness when she was friendly with others. His actions may not have made a lot of sense if you didn't know his feelings, but if he confessed to you that he really liked her, everything would start to add up. Your brain too has a big crush on someone – a crush that causes most of its actions and behaviours. Your brain is, literally, obsessed with you. This makes it overprotective and affects the way it behaves. This obsession is not just a crush. It is hardwired into your brain's architecture.

To understand how this obsession manifests in every choice your brain makes, a comparison to other biological organs is helpful. The muscles in your legs, for example, have only one primary function: flight. If a predator poses a threat to you, your legs are there so that you can take flight and run for your life. We humans push that basic functionality to its extreme. We run marathons, dance, play football and seduce mates with those legs. But make no mistake, regardless of how attractive your legs are, at their very essence they are made for you to flee, and when the need for that primary function arises, all other functions are ignored.

The same is true for your brain. We have pushed our brains beyond their primary function and used them to invent smartphones and build civilization as we know it. Yet, their primary function is entirely focused on our **survival**. The main difference between your brain and your legs, however, is that to your brain everything appears to be a threat. While you can't really use your legs to escape from a nasty comment on your social media post, you can exert a lot of brain power to deal with that worthless comment, which your brain perceives as an imminent threat analogous to the predator your legs would run away from.

If the analogy holds true, your brain is overprotective because . . .

your brain has a massive crush on you . . .

. . . and just like Jake back in school, your brain's behaviour, which otherwise may appear erratic, is fully explainable by that obsessive crush.

One look at the very basic structural wiring of your brain reveals how dedicated it is to the task of keeping you safe. For that purpose, the design of the human brain leaves nothing to chance. It includes not only safety mechanisms that are exclusively available in human brains, but it also includes earlier versions of brain designs that worked well for other species. Together, your brain operates a sophisticated system that brings together . . .

Three Defences

If you study your brain from a survival point of view, you will find three distinct subsystems. At its very core, our brainstem is responsible for the survival functions reptiles use to **avoid danger**. This is often referred to as the Reptilian Brain. Our limbic system replicates the survival functions found in other mammals, which mainly depend on **avoiding pain and seeking reward** as their simplistic, yet effective, mechanisms of survival. That brain sub-system is referred to as the Mammalian Brain. Then finally there are the parts of the brain that make us humans different from all other species – the neocortex – which are responsible for **logic, planning and self-concept**. These parts, working together, are referred to as the Rational Brain.

This concept of layered brain defence systems – known as the triune brain – is a model of evolution that was originally proposed by the American physician and neuroscientist Paul D. MacLean in the 1960s and summarized in his book *The Triune Brain in Evolution* in 1990. It's important to note that I don't view it here as a model of evolution, but rather a useful model to understand human behaviour.

The Reptilian Brain

This part of your brain is responsible for the crudest forms of survival – typically found in reptiles. Unlike a friendly puppy, a lizard will flee if you try to approach it. Even if you're holding a plate of delicious leafy greens topped with crickets, a lizard won't give that a second's thought. As a matter of fact, the reptilian brain doesn't do much thought at all. It's mostly responsible for mechanical functions – the beating of your heart must go on for you to live and so a control system for that is found in the brain-stem, which is the part that connects the brain to the nervous system. Those instructions are sent mechanically for the heart to beat without you needing to think about it. The functioning of the glands, the regulation of hormones, breathing, digesting your food or pumping blood around your body are all autonomous. This is why neuroscience often calls the system regulating them the autonomous nervous system. This system is also responsible for fear-induced danger avoidance. Your amygdala, hypothalamus and adrenal gland will engage in a fraction of a second to trigger a fight or flight response so that you escape from the approaching threat. Decisions regarding the redistribution of your limited physical resources happen at the nervous system level. Your heart rate speeds up, your digestive system shuts down and your vision is sharpened without even consulting with your logical brain. A reptile's default response to most things is fear. It will always run away from the slightest possibility of a threat.

The Mammalian Brain

The mammalian brain, your limbic system, is all about emotions – about pleasure-seeking and pain avoidance. The functions of our mammalian brain are there to ensure we survive when it comes to things that don't constitute an immediate threat to our survival. Reproduction, for example, is not a prerequisite for you to live another year but without it the species would be extinct. That's why we enjoy sex. Storing fat for a possible future famine is not something you think about when there is an abundance of food around you. You would not die without cookies. The pleasure associated with eating is needed for you to consume more than you need and keep it safely stored as fat (I really need to find a way to reverse this stupid primal instinct). Emotions and hormones support the mammalian brain functionalities. Protecting our children, for example, was counter-intuitive for personal survival in the harshness of the cavemen years. Yet, parental emotions, reflected in the limbic system, made sure that we did protect them in order for our species to propagate. Craving a sense of belonging as adults creates closer bonds among our tribe, which makes it stronger, as a unit, in the face of danger. When it comes to things that don't constitute an immediate threat to our existence, our mammalian brain subsystem is what keeps us alive.

The Rational Brain

The third, and perhaps most sophisticated brain subsystem, is the rational brain. It's the part that makes us human. This is the part of the brain responsible for planning and logic. It gives us the ability to solve problems and think analytically. It is also the part, most importantly, that brings about the concept of the self. Your rational brain is what makes you aware that you are a separate entity from the rest of living beings. This distinction establishes the boundaries that separate you from others, makes you an individual and prioritizes you, for you, over everyone else. This all happens in your rational brain (which I find funny because, as a concept, this view of separation is not very rational).

Thinking rationally is what propelled our species forward. Survival is not always about running away from a tiger. More often it is about learning where tigers tend to hide and planning a course for the journey that avoids their hiding places. It is about storing food for the winter and planting some staple grains, instead of being exposed to the possibility of a famine that may leave nothing to gather or hunt. Other animals do a bit of planning too, but we take it to a whole new level when we plan for retirement, children's tuition and life insurance. We don't just use our brains for our immediate survival. We use them to stay alive until we are old and frail.

It's not my intention here to give you a biology lesson about which parts of the brain perform which functions. That wouldn't really help you advance towards the targets of this book – happiness, success and compassion. The main reason I'm bringing the brain's three distinct defence systems to your attention is because those brain subsystems are perfectly aligned with the *only* three reasons for suffering humans experience beyond physical pain. I call these reasons that make us suffer . . .

AAA

Some of us may feel that every living moment brings endless reasons for unhappiness their way.

But this is not even remotely true. Life, with its ever-changing moods, presents us with endless varieties of conditions to react to. Our state of happiness is not a result of those conditions, it is the direct result of how we choose to react to them. Those who become unhappy are those who choose to react to life in one (or several) of three ways – **aversion, attachment or an all-pervasive dissatisfaction – the AAA**.

If your basic needs are met, you are not in any physical pain, and you manage to feel unhappy, the reason for your unhappiness is mostly inside your head. Your unhappiness, then, is the result of your brain being preoccupied with thoughts about something it is fearful of (**aversion**), or something it desires to acquire or keep (**attachment**), or it is preoccupied with an unexplained sense of 'nothing is good enough' – **an all-pervasive dissatisfaction**.

Aversion

Aversion is the result of your reptilian brain. The fear it produces to keep you safe is manifested in a sense of avoidance: *I won't be single or start dating again even though my boyfriend is abusing me; I don't think I can start a new job even though I can't stand going to my current workplace; I don't want to live elsewhere, although I don't really like it here.* Those fearful thoughts are not driven by a desire for anything specifically, just a fear of anything that you don't want in your life.

Back in 2013, I was a vice president of Google. I started and then ran the company's business in a large part of the world across many emerging markets. Over the previous seven years, I had expanded Google's business to almost half of its operations worldwide but by 2013 the expansion had slowed down and my job had turned into a large operation that needed to comply with the corporate politics (yes, there were lots of politics at Google too). My then-manager pretended to be my friend but was constantly making my life difficult, and so I was no longer enjoying my job and it was clearly time for me to move on. With so many companies trying to hire talent from Google then, and so many opportunities in Google itself it would have been reasonable to assume that if I had searched for a new job, I would find one in a reasonable amount of time. Yet, at the very moment I decided to leave, my reptilian brain started to kick in and went out of its way to frighten me. I remember thinking, *Well, this is not about you and your lifestyle, we all know that the world is becoming more and more unstable. What if a war took place and Iran launched a nuclear attack on Dubai where you have most of your assets, while climate change worsened to the point where Aya [my daughter] needed to live somewhere safer? Without the steady income from Google, you would have failed Aya.*

Yep. That's how committed my reptilian brain was to scaring me. When it comes to making up worst-case, unrealistic scenarios, our brains will never stop. *What if my husband met Beyoncé and she fell in love with him? What if the train went off the tracks on the same day that a war ignited between Uber drivers and taxi drivers? How would I get to my meeting on time? What if the economy collapsed, my company went bankrupt and the price of my favourite face cream quadrupled?* Yeah, what if?

Well, what if you slipped and broke your neck before any of that happened? It is probably a more likely scenario statistically than any of the horror stories our brains create – surely more likely than Beyoncé falling in love with your husband. Isn't it? Truth is, some aversion is OK. Saving a bit of money for a rainy day, living in a safe neighbourhood and looking left and right before you cross the street are all good ideas. But Beyoncé? Come on. Get real.

It took me one moment of reflecting on reality and one simple spreadsheet to deal with my bogeyman of a brain back then. I listed down my resources, my realistic financial needs – adding a bit of a safety buffer – and within minutes I realized that unless the world really went out of whack, I would be OK. With that realization, I went on to look for another thing to do at work and I ended up becoming the Chief Business Officer of Google X, which must have been the best job on our planet back then. That was the upside of not submitting to my fears.

Being able to spot the exact thoughts that scare you, and to question them, requires a high level of awareness. We will discuss this in depth when we talk about emotions later in the book, but it helps to understand the big picture and question if there really is a need for the kind of aversion you may experience in your life today. Your brain's primary obsession is to keep you safe. So, to keep that obsession in check, let's ask the question head on … Are you safe?

When it comes to topics that require decisive, critical interventions to keep me on a clear path to happiness, I tend to cut to the chase. If my brain's top intention is to keep me safe, and if in doing so it keeps me trapped in aversion, then perhaps the shortest cut to clean up the mess is to question the issue of my safety at its very core.

Awareness Exercise
Are You Safe?

Homework

Target	A conviction that safety may not be as big of an issue as your brain attempts to make it
Duration	30 minutes
Repeat	Repeat at least once for every reason that's causing you to feel concerned
You'll need	A quiet place where you will not be interrupted A notepad and a pen. Consider doing this with a trusted friend (optimistic friends will help you more)

I know that almost every day you hear some kind of horror story. They show up in the news, friends talk about them or they pop up on your social media feed. Those stories make us believe that life is full of disasters – a constant tale of suffering and hardship.

My mathematical brain, however, tells me that the odds of bad things happening, when compared to the good things we experience, are minute. Even when they do happen, they are, most often, much more tolerable than we fear them to be. We are almost always safe. You don't believe me? Let me ask you to do the maths yourself then. It's not hard to calculate if you reflect on your very own experience.

Find a quiet place where you will not be interrupted and set a timer for about thirty minutes. You may feel the need to repeat this awareness exercise many times till you get to the essence of it.

Don't be alarmed. Give it time. It will pay off in a big way when you see the truth. Spend as much time as you need on each of the following questions. While each will take just a few seconds to read, it will need minutes or sometimes even days of reflection for you to uncover the naked truth. You can do this with a trusted friend or a group. A diverse set of perspectives is best to dislodge our brains from the spot in which they have been stuck for years.

- I'm not being sarcastic here, though it may sound like it. I'm asking the questions rarely asked. Let's start with physical threats. Are there any tigers around? Any other predators (the kind that wants to eat you)? If you are careful crossing the street, avoid the dangerous parts of town and drive responsibly, are there other deadly threats present in your daily life? When it comes to health, how many days a year do you or anyone you know fall sick as opposed to how many days you and everyone you know feel OK?

    (I need to add a note here. Sadly, in the civilized world we live in today, the predators that we still face are other humans that prey on women or use their power against people of colour – myself included. We should remain vigilant, take the precautionary measures to ensure our safety and the safety of those we love and raise our voices to demand safer communities. Yet, we should not live in fear, but rather caution. We should recognize and celebrate that, through the right measures, our life today offers us the opportunity to feel safe through most of our days.)
- Beyond physical safety, how lethal are the other threats that concern you? A bad relationship, losing a job, life without the latest phone, nasty comments on your social media posts. Should any of those be considered a threat to your safety or just another event to learn from – part of the fun and challenge of being alive?

- If you could see through the negativity bias of the mainstream media, see through their tendency to blow things out of proportion, how likely is it that you will end up in a violent accident, a tsunami or a school shooting? The statistics are infinitesimal. How tiny is the actual ratio of someone shooting someone else as compared to the staggering number of people who kissed someone yesterday?

- Even on the rare occasions when things do go wrong, how often have you seen someone affected by one of the things that you fear who survived or even thrived? How often has a friend of yours been made fun of and not died as a result? How often did you see those moments of apparent threat prove to be turning points that catapulted someone onto a path of success? Does the worst-case scenario ever happen? Or is life just made up of a series of challenges designed to makes us better, stronger and more resilient?

- Can you remember a time when your fear of something specific persisted for a while though that thing never happened? Isn't the number of days or years of anticipation enough proof that this thing is very unlikely to happen?

- Now look at a specific fear and ask yourself if you developed it during a different phase of your life, in a different context, which has now changed. While you may have had a genuine reason to fear being bullied as a child in school by others who were several years older and physically bigger, is that still a valid concern today?

- Do you know of others, your friends or family members, who live in similar conditions to you but don't seem to be concerned and don't suffer your fear? What do they know that you don't? Why do they feel safe?

- When focusing on what you worry about, do you tend to ignore the positive aspects of your life which can help keep you safe if what you fear happened? If you're afraid to lose your job, have you considered that you may have savings that can sustain you for a few months?

If you are honest in answering the questions above, you will recognize that your fear is often a highly exaggerated emotion. It's blown way out of proportion. If we avoid recklessness, we truly are much safer than our brains would have us believe. Even in cases of unresolved trauma or PTSD (where I recommend professional help), the patient is, at the moment of suffering, safe. You see . . .

Very Important !

The very fact that you can dedicate brain cycles to think about something that scares you is, in itself, evidence that you are safe right here and now.

If there was a tiger attacking you at this moment, you would not have the luxury of time or the brain cycles you need to think about whatever it is that scares you.

Even at the level of humanity at large, the work of Steven Pinker — Canadian-American cognitive psychologist, psycholinguist, popular science author — shows that the world today is much safer than it used to be in the past. In his analysis of recent data on homicide, war, poverty, pollution and more, Pinker finds that **the world is safer now in every aspect** than when compared with thirty years ago.[1] The only reason we sometimes feel more threatened than we should be is that we can see what's happening halfway around the globe on news media and on the internet, which makes us feel there is so much wrong when, in reality, there's less but you are more informed. Remember the hidden triggers?

The world is safer. Our biggest fears very rarely play out in the way that our brains portray them. If they ever did, you would not be here. Other than some hardship, which is just a part of life that should be expected, tell your lizard brain that . . .

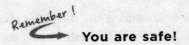

You are safe!

Attachment

Attachment, on the other hand, is developed by our emotional, mammalian brain. A focus on reward and pleasure and the avoidance of discomfort or pain keeps us attached to what we are familiar with, regardless of how valuable it actually is or how little it contributes to our happiness. Closets of clothes we never wear, boxes of junk we collect over the years, and relationships that don't enrich our lives. We remain stuck just because they've become our comfort zone. When led by your mammalian brain, you are not really worried about a possible threat in the future, just unwilling to let go of the comforts and pleasures of the past.

When my wonderful son, Ali, left our world, holding on to the things he left behind seemed like the natural thing to do. We wanted to cherish every memory we had and everything he ever touched. But his heroic, wise mother, Nibal, quickly formed a different view. At his memorial, we insisted that his dearest friends take some of the things that connected him to them the most. We gave his gaming computer to his geeky friend, his bass guitar to a member of his band. We gave each of his T-shirts away to a person that meant something to him, his video games and consoles to the friends he played those games with. Of course, I kept a few T-shirts and one of his earrings – which I wear as a necklace and consider my most beloved physical possession on the planet. Nibal kept the other earring and a handful of other items related to special memories. Aya did the same. We each have maybe seven or eight of his things, and whatever was left we gave away to people who needed them, enjoyed them or cherished them. The furniture in his room, the curtains, the endless books he consumed like a bookworm. Over time, his room was empty. We wanted to replace the things with the good karma of helping others out or making others happy. Nibal and I moved from wanting to preserve his room as a museum of love for him to an empty space full of light. Her wisdom helped us to let go. 'Ali is not his things,' she said. 'He lives in my heart without the need for things to remind me.' When I looked at his room and saw his things not being used, I felt that I wanted to give them life by giving them to those who would use them. I felt that this way, Ali lived on through the things he gave away when he left. He had some money saved in his bank account – the insurance value that was paid to him when his car was totalled while parked on the street one night. He said he did not need a car and instead kept the money. We gave it all to charity in his name. It made me feel good to give everything away and know that it was helping other people. What felt even better, however, was our freedom from attachment to these physical items. This, somehow, symbolized our freedom from attachment to his handsome physical form that left us and, instead, connected us to his beautiful pure essence that remains. By detaching from things, we were free to cherish what really matters – our love for him. I will never forget how we gave some of his clothes to a Kenyan friend of Nibal's to take back to her hometown. When she returned, she said that she gave his boots to a young man who really needed them. She met him a few days later and he told her that those boots made him feel like he could fly. In my heart, every day, I wish that he will fly, reach the highest honours in life and change our world.

This is the upside of dropping our attachments. The things that we don't really need, weigh us down. They lock us in. Without them we can fly and we give them away, others who need them can fly too.

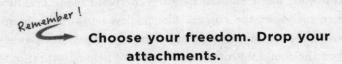

Remember!

Choose your freedom. Drop your attachments.

You know the saying: **The more things you own, the more things own you.** Let's get rid of the clutter.

One of my daughter's favourite shows on Netflix is *Tidying Up with Marie Kondo*. Often, when I visit her, we watch an episode together. The show is supposed to be about helping you tidy up your place and get rid of clutter. But if you ask me, at its core, the show is all about letting go of attachment. At least, that's what I feel when I watch it.

Practice Exercise
Cleaning Out Your Closet

Homework

Target	Learn to drop your attachment to things
Duration	An hour at a time (or as long as it takes)
Repeat	Repeat at least once a week as needed
You'll need	To be at your home and have the courage to let go
Resources	Watch *Tidying Up with Marie Kondo*

Marie's method is to first take out all your clutter, your clothes for example, and put them in one big pile in the centre of the room. That way you will recognize how much you have been hoarding over the years. Your task then is to look at everything in that pile one by one and ask yourself, when was the last time you used it, if you expect to use it in the next couple of weeks and (listen to this, this is gold) **if it gives you joy.**

If something is not giving you joy, Marie says, and you've not been using it, you will never use it. Give it away. Give it life. Let others use it and only keep in your life what gives you joy.

Let's apply this same method to every aspect of your life. Start with things that weigh on you, then move on to people who lock you in relationships that don't give you joy. If a friend is constantly adding negativity to your life, ask them to change or ask them to leave. When done with that, find your freedom from concepts and ideologies that trap you into suffering.

Every Saturday, I spend an hour looking around in my little home to find ten things to give away. An old T-shirt, a book that I finished, a box of chocolate that was gifted to me but could make someone else happier (and make me thinner), a coffee mug that does not make me smile. I don't always make it to ten, but I always try. Once a month, I take account of every single person that I met once a week or more and ask myself, assertively, if that relationship is draining me or preventing me being my best self. If it is, out of a commitment to self-love, I have a conversation with that person to discuss how we can make our relationship better for both of us. We then work on it together for another month, if they still drain me, I make it a point to meet that person less, or not meet them at all. I tell them, lovingly, that we tried and it didn't work. Those mini breakups may feel a little brutal but they, like with any dysfunctional relationship, are the best path for both sides. Every Christmas, I spend the last week of the passing year and the first week of the new year in contemplation. I take account of my thoughts and beliefs. I question what affected me positively or negatively. I clearly define what I need to remove from my life, and I define the one thing that, I believe, would give me the most joy in the coming year. I declare that to be the theme for my new year.

Transcending attachment and overcoming the fear of missing out are superpowers that contradict the nature of your mammalian brain. Make them part of your deliberate self-development.

Make them a lifetime exercise. One that only allows joy into your life and eliminates your need to associate with all else. Welcome to the land of the free.

All-Pervasive Dissatisfaction

Finally, even after we get over the fear and clinging, there is that all-pervasive dissatisfaction – something that seems to keep nagging that life is not good enough. It doesn't really matter if now is OK because, well, it can be better, bigger or more. And if there is better to be had, then perhaps now is not good enough after all. *I should be prettier. Look at the girls on Instagram. I need a bigger house. Look at my neighbour's house. My title is not as fancy as the title of my boss. I need one more pair of shoes. I want that picture-perfect vacation. My boyfriend should be taller. My girlfriend should be smaller . . .* The list goes on and on. This endless loop of disgruntlement is not driven by any real issue in your life, or any real need that is not fulfilled – just a sense of 'meh' – a dissatisfaction with what is and a belief that things should be better. Even when life occasionally fulfils those unjustified needs by granting us more, bigger and better, we feel a tiny jolt of happiness that lasts only momentarily and then we move the goalposts, turn our attention to what we don't have and feel disgruntled again as we realize we still want more.

I remember vividly my first fancy car. It was a blue BMW 5 Series, with all the luxury options of the time. I bought it from a friend, and it was a real bargain. It was practically in brand-new condition, and I paid a fraction of the price of a new car. The day I registered it, I took it to the dealership to perform whatever services were needed. I felt that this was my new treasure, it made me very happy and I wanted to treat it right. It made me happy, that is, until I sat in the BMW showroom waiting for the service to be finished. There I saw a used sand-gold BMW 7 Series for sale. I found myself thinking, *I wish I had that car instead. It's so much more than mine.* My car was still beautiful, but the happiness I'd previously felt vanished and was replaced with dissatisfaction over not having the other. Now I look back at that version of me with astonishment. But I can't blame young Mo. This dissatisfaction is part of the design of our logical brain. It is one of the core characteristics of intelligent beings. Our dedicated brains are never at ease that now is OK because what about tomorrow? They are never content that now is good enough because there seems to be more to attain. With an insatiable appetite for more, we always feel that we have less than we deserve. As the Arabic proverb goes:

Remember !

→ **Nothing will ever fill a human's desiring eye but sand – the sand of the grave.**

Well, there is something other than sand that can do the trick much earlier than resting in our graves. It is called gratitude.

Gratitude is not the practice of getting what you want. It is the practice of loving what you have. Let's spend a bit of time to try and figure out what it is that you have and to see if you can feel grateful for it.

Every spiritual teaching that I have ever studied contains a practice dedicated to gratitude. This practice is central to happiness because it dampens the all-pervasive dissatisfaction and the illusion that 'nothing is good enough.'

Awareness Exercise
Count Your Blessings

Target	See the beauty in life. Stop the unwarranted dissatisfaction
Duration	10 minutes every night
Repeat	Repeat forever. This is one of the best habits you can ever develop
You'll need	A quiet moment of reflection before you close your eyes at night
	A notepad to keep track of your blessings would be a fabulous resource indeed

If I was asked to recommend only one practice that encompasses all that I teach about happiness, gratitude would be a strong candidate. Counting our blessings is the best way to remind us that life is not that bad after all — which for most of us, by the way, is the truth. When we remember what we should be grateful for, we recognize the truth that our hypercautious rational brains constantly attempt to hide — that almost every one of us has more reason to be happy than to be sad. Gratitude, by definition, reminds us that many events in our life are not only meeting our expectations, but exceeding them by so much that we should feel grateful. When events meet or exceed expectations, your happiness equation is solved correctly and you feel happy.

All it takes is ten minutes every night before you sleep. Force your brain to find just three things (or more) that you are grateful for about your day. Think of things that you want to have in your life for another day. Start with the basics – a friend that you appreciate, the roof over your head, the food that you eat. Then move to the blessings that keep you away from harm or hardship (which many on our planet suffer every day): if you are not a refugee running away from a war zone, if you are not suffering from a chronic pain, not homeless during the harsh winter on the streets of New York, those alone can give you an endless supply of things you should be grateful for – things that you have been given through the sheer luck of being born where you have been and not, for example, in Syria or North Korea.

If you are, please know that my heart is with you. I hope that things will become easier and I hope you still manage to find gratitude for what you still have, despite the pain of some of life's toughest challenges.

Then, in those last few moments before you fall asleep, think of the things that have been generous blessings for you alone – the presence of a certain loved one in your life, a hobby that you're good at and thoroughly enjoy, or perhaps your intelligence and self-knowledge, which enables you to perform this simple exercise religiously every night.

When I count my blessings, I don't just list them down. I say them out loud. I fully visualize them and see them in my heart as if I'm living them again. I am grateful for all the love I have been given, all the love I am able to give and every experience that has helped me become a better person. I am grateful that my daughter, Aya, is healthy and close to me. I'm grateful that Nibal is still my best friend, and I am grateful for my journey through life; every bit of it, with its harshness, its blessings and its pain. If you want to be happy, ignore your brain's all-pervasive dissatisfaction. Instead,

Very Important!

**Just open your heart and see
that life is beautiful.**

A Healthy Dose of AAAs

Our three defences, when pushed to excess and out of control, cause a ton of unhappiness — needlessly. Their excessive presence in our life does not make us safer, it just makes us miserable. There's no denying, however, that aversion to genuine threats, attachment to what's vital and life-sustaining, and a proper dose of dissatisfaction with what is going wrong are needed to bring safety and predictability to your life.

Finding that delicate balance that keeps you safe but doesn't make you miserable requires you to become an observer of your mind so that you recognize how those exaggerated responses are there, not because your brain dislikes you, but because it is obsessive about your safety, and because it believes that you can never be too safe.

Remember!

**Your brain finds it wiser to mark
something as a threat when it isn't than
to mark it as safe when it stands the tiniest
chance of being a threat.**

It finds it wiser to attach to things than be open to an uncertain, though possibly exciting, adventure. It finds it wiser to want more because, after all, having more enhances your chances of confronting whatever uncertainty life may ever throw your way.

The fact is, however, that for the most part we're surviving just fine. There is very little reason for our brains to cause such a fuss. We need to take charge and teach them to see and acknowledge things differently, and when we do, we live with a healthy dose of AAAs. Train your brain to behave like it's supposed to. Which takes me to our next topic ... training your brain.

The first thing you should do before you teach a student anything is to understand how the student learns. So let me ask you to perform a quick awareness exercise that will help shed some light on your own brain's learning habits. I call this exercise the Biased Brain Test.

I learned this quick but effective exercise from a TEDx Talk by Willoughby Britton, a neuroscientist at Brown University.

It will help you measure what your brain has been learning effectively in the last few years.

Awareness Exercise
The Biased Brain Test

Homework

Target	Discovering which parts of your brain have been developing and growing
Duration	3 minutes
Repeat	Once is enough for awareness
You'll need	A quiet place where you will not be interrupted A stopwatch

Please find the stopwatch app on your mobile phone. When you are ready, start reading the three questions below, one by one. Start your stopwatch once you have read the question and measure how many seconds it takes you until the answer pops up in your head.

Question 1: What did you have for lunch yesterday?

Question 2: What's one thing you don't like about yourself?

Question 3: What's one thing you really like about yourself?

Great. Thanks for participating. It doesn't really matter exactly how long answering each of these questions took. What matters is which you answered the fastest, and which the slowest.

I have asked hundreds of participants to perform this test and most take the longest to answer Question 1. They answer Question 3 faster and Question 2 significantly faster still. What was the ranking of your own responses? Write your rank below; we will return to it later when we discuss the next concept.

Fastest response   Q (_____)

Second fastest   Q (_____)

Slowest response   Q (_____)

When you're done, don't wait. Move to the next chapter and meet me at the elementary school of your brain.

Chapter Four

Practice Makes Miserable

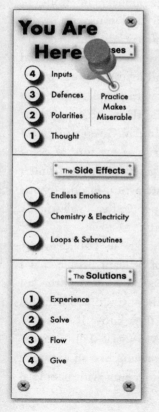

You Are Here

4 Inputs
3 Defences
2 Polarities
1 Thought

Practice Makes Miserable

The Side Effects

Endless Emotions
Chemistry & Electricity
Loops & Subroutines

The Solutions

1 Experience
2 Solve
3 Flow
4 Give

I'm sure a coach or a parent once told you that practice makes perfect. They would be right to make that claim, but they would also be wrong. Depending on the practice, it can also make you weak, or confused, or violent, and if you practise unhappiness often enough, your practice makes you miserable.

There is an old story, attributed to the Cherokee people, of a grandfather sitting by a campfire with his grandson. The grandson asks: 'Are people good by nature?'

The old man replies: 'Within every one of us, a fight is raging between two wolves. One is bad. It harbours anger, jealousy, resentment, greed, vanity, self-pity, inferiority, lies, pride, narcissism and ego. The other is good. It stands for joy, satisfaction, love, hope, calmness, humility, kindness, sympathy, generosity, truth and compassion.'

After a moment of silence, the grandson asks: 'Which wolf wins the fight?'

The old man smiles and answers: **'The wolf that you feed.'**

Shy Me

We've All Been There!

I'm the ultimate introvert. This fact may elude you as you watch my videos on YouTube, speaking publicly in front of thousands of people and interacting with hundreds of them afterwards. But make no mistake, as a child I was incredibly quiet and even shy. I was a nerd. I preferred to spend my time alone with a book or in front of my computer. Being with people, other than very close friends or loved ones, drained me, then, and being alone energized me. I am still exactly the same today. Given a choice, I would hide away from the world and write as my way of communicating with it. In my free time, I am rarely at a group dinner or a party. I spend most of my human interaction in one-to-one intimate conversations with the very few people that I call friends. I still am a nerd and the ultimate introvert.

Nevertheless, I spend hours of every day in public events. Over time, there have been thousands of brilliant people that I can recall by name and remember the detailed context of the last time we met. If you asked any of them, they would confirm that Mo is one of the most social extroverts they know. Remember, I'm not, but I'm not pretending either. My social skills over the years have evolved to the point where behaving like an extrovert comes almost naturally to me. I even enjoy being with people as much as I enjoy my solo recharge time.

How did I move from being awkwardly shy and introverted to someone who can so comfortably alternate between being painfully introverted and loudly extroverted? **Practice!**

I can vividly pinpoint the moment I decided to flip that switch. It was in 1995, when I first started to manage a team. Up until that moment, all of my success in life could be attributed to my contributions as an individual. I locked myself up and read a physics textbook from cover to cover in one night or spent three days at home finishing a complex piece of code. I didn't need people to make progress. As a matter of fact, I viewed them as a hindrance. But then things changed. As a manager, I quickly realized that humans were a lot more complex than objects. They are moody. They need to be convinced and they support you better when they like you. Please don't judge me, but that was a revelation to me and a bit annoying, if I'm honest. What was the drama all about, why did they not respond like my computer did? Why couldn't they just compile my requests as a manager and run them like simple code?

Quickly, however, I realized that this new dilemma I was facing — dealing with humans — was not going away any time soon. If anything, it was just going to get more intense. My success was going to depend on my ability to connect with people more than it depended on anything else. Darn!

As with everything I did then, I resorted to what I knew best: I read every book that I could find on people management, how to talk to strangers, how to make friends and influence others, and even the forty-eight laws of power, all in an attempt to understand why humans behave the way they do. I attended any kind of training my corporate job could offer me on the topic of 'dealing' with people. And, as with everything else I did then, the knowledge I acquired helped me grasp the concepts intellectually. However, they did not impact my behaviour, make me more socially outgoing or reduce the bitter shyness I had by then become adequate at hiding, while it ate me up from the inside.

It wasn't until I began putting what I had read into practice that my life started to change. Based on the advice I had read, I took a small slice of my social inadequacy – feeling uncomfortable talking to strangers and holding a conversation – and started to practise changing that by talking to what one book called 'low-risk individuals' first. In a way my analytical brain understood, the book said that we are not equally shy with all people. A young man like me would feel much more awkward approaching a beautiful supermodel than talking to the barista at Starbucks or the wonderful old lady in the supermarket queue. So, I gave myself a simple challenge. I would talk to at least one person in any cafe, elevator (that was a tough one) or shop I walked into. At first, I started by asking them a simple question and then, when my shy brain realized that most people don't bite when you speak to them, I became courageous enough to make a light comment or even a joke. The numbers quickly added up. In no time at all I was triggering four or five unsolicited conversations a day. Like with going to the gym, my social muscles started to grow and today I can (and do) speak to anyone, anywhere, at any time – even though deep inside, if I was left in my comfort zone, I would much rather not talk to anyone at all.

Anything that you practise repeatedly, in bite-size tasks over an extended period of time, improves. It's just the way our brains operate.

How We Learn

As I've mentioned a couple of times before, your highly sophisticated brain is nothing more than a piece of meat. This makes your brain comparable to your muscles, at least with regards to one important rule . . .

What you use tends to grow and what you don't shrinks.

For most of the twentieth century, this was believed to be true only until a certain age. It was believed that your brain developed only until your early twenties and then you were stuck with what you had, with very little possible future development and mostly decay, until your old age. Recent studies, however, prove that this is not true – that our brains constantly change and develop through two processes known as neuroplasticity and neurogenesis. Bear with me, please, as I explain some simplified technicalities, before we dive into the practical tools you can use.

Neurogenesis is the process by which the cells of our nervous system, known as neurons, are produced from stem cells. The development of new neurons continues during adulthood in some regions of the brain.[1] This process helps us repair damaged parts of our brains in the case of an accident and continue to develop even as we age. We can continue to create more 'brain'. This is good news.

What is even better news is the idea of neuroplasticity. Plasticity, in physics, is defined as the quality of being easily shaped or moulded. Neuroplasticity is the brain's ability to reorganize itself by forming new neural connections to better perform its tasks.

The day I first read about neuroplasticity was a happy day for me. As a self-development junky, it felt good to know that I can continue to invest in myself, learn, develop and improve, regardless of the age of my brain. I believe that it is my life's purpose to become the best possible version of myself. I am nowhere near there yet, so I need lots of neuroplasticity to keep moving forward.

When it comes to happiness, for example, if I am to inspire others I need to keep developing until I become the Olympic champion of happiness. Practice and neuroplasticity are the only methods I have to tread on this track. This is the same approach used to master the technique to swim like Michael Phelps, play the guitar like Jimi Hendrix or understand physics like Albert Einstein. For all of these, we need to exercise the brain in ways that enhance three processes: chemical signalling, structural changes and functional changes. Let me show you how each of these reshape your brain.

The Making of Memories

A few months ago, I found myself feeling so burdened by the work I do to spread happiness that I contemplated giving up. Between the foundation, podcasting, writing, posting on social media, the occasional negative comments, interviews and public speaking, some days had become seriously overwhelming.

When I really struggle, I have learned to listen to the advice I get from my son, Ali. I believe we found a way to communicate, after he left our world, through music (ignore this bit if you don't believe in the metaphysical). When he wants to say something, I find the weirdest song, usually one I dislike, humming in my head. On my music player, I play music radio on random and wait for the fourth song (that's the code I have observed for how Ali communicates). That day the fourth song was a song I'd never heard before – the acoustic version of 'Life is Beautiful' by Sixx:A.M. I snapped into attention once I heard the first two sentences of the lyrics and then played it on repeat at least twenty times in a row, sitting in a slightly uncomfortable blue dining chair with my back to the window, my feet on another chair. There was a strong smell of coffee brewing. I wept like a baby every time a certain verse played. That verse clearly sounded like an instruction from Ali to not give up. It was asking me to swear on my life that his death will bring happiness to the world, that no one will cry at Ali's funeral. In my heart, I understood this sentence to mean don't let my death be a reason for sadness and because of my love for him, his remembrance, his funeral, will be till the day I leave.

There I was with neurons in my brain firing as they sensed the uncomfortable pressure of the two chairs on my body, other neurons firing at the sight of the room from this unfamiliar angle, and yet more neurons firing as I heard certain words, certain guitar riffs, and smelled that dark smoky coffee scent. Other neurons in my brain fired to remind me of a very specific memory borrowed from his funeral, and a bunch of other neurons fired to facilitate the weeping, which was special because it combined feelings of missing him with the feeling of empowerment I needed to deliver on his request, as well as the feeling of relief that he was still by my side – an unusual mix of emotions indeed.

Every time the song played, I built a stronger memory of the whole experience. Over the next few days, sitting in my same chair, I must have played that song more than a hundred times, and until this day I play it at least a few times every week.

'Life is Beautiful'

Listen to the acoustic version from the album Seven by Sixx:A.M.

Well, do it just for fun to see how, I believe, my son has managed to stay in touch from another dimension.

My brain is now a master of this memory. As a result, every time I hear this song, I remember the chairs and the coffee. Every time I smell the same coffee, the song pops up in my mind. Every time I remember the lyrics, I weep in exactly the same way and every time I weep for remembering that he set me on my current path when he left us, this song starts to play in my head to comfort me. A hardwired network centred around this memory is engraved into my brain.

The process that creates our memories applies the exact same way when it comes to developing our skills. Take video-gaming. When Ali was around seven, he started to play video games and we would often play against each other in a fighting game called *Tekken*. Usually, I had no fatherly manners. I just wanted to win. When it was time to play, I would ask Ali, 'Would you like me to kick your a[censored]?' Ali, being so chill even at that age, would say, 'Papa, can we just play and have fun?' We would play, we would have fun, but make no mistake, I would win (sorry, Ali, I can't believe I was that way). One time, however, I was away on a long business trip during the summer vacation. On my return, even though it was late at night, Ali met me at the door, hugged me and said, 'Papa, would you like me to kick your a[censored]?' My gamer's pride was provoked. I immediately said, 'Let's do it. One more game you will lose' (horrible father). Well, he won that night and every other night for the rest of his life. He became a true video-game legend and I never won against him ever again.

I asked him, 'What did you do?' He replied, 'I played four hours a day, every day.' He could have simply answered with one word: neuroplasticity. Every single skill you have ever developed is the result of your brain using neuroplasticity. Here is how it works.

The Switchboard

The easiest way to picture how neuroplasticity works is to think of early telephone switchboard systems. Till the early 1900s, phone calls were made by picking up the headset to inform an operator who you wanted to speak to, and she would physically patch the wire coming from your telephone to the one connecting to the telephone of the person you were calling.

Your brain behaves in a very similar way. When you are practising a skill or logging a memory that requires two or more parts of your brain to work together, your brain starts with signalling. In the switchboard days, the operator used a patch wire to connect the call. Your brain uses chemicals called neurotransmitters instead.

Imagine a long, fibre-like wire, called an axon, connecting to the junction of a nerve cell, known as a synapse. This is like the wire between a phone and the switch. When you picked up the phone, that wire could get you to the operator but not the other phone. When a neuron fires (becomes active), an electric impulse moves down that wire. But it doesn't get to other neurons until it triggers the release of a chemical, known as a neurotransmitter, which closes the small gap between the nerve cells just like the operator's patch wire connects two phones.

Some of the well-known neurotransmitters include serotonin, an inhibitor involved in the regulation of sleep, mood and eating; dopamine, an excitatory involved in regulating movement and experiencing pleasure; and endorphin, which moderates pain.

Once the connection is completed, the neurotransmitters are degraded, a bit like hanging up a call, which 'resets' the system. That way, the synapse is once again prepared to respond to the next signal.[2]

Now picture this. If you kept calling the operator and asking to connect to the same person over and over, the operator would become very good at patching that call. She might even keep the patch wire in place and just push it to establish the connection when you call. This too happens inside your head. When you try to learn a few sequences of notes on the guitar or choreograph your actions to shoot a few aliens in a specific order while playing a video game, you will notice that every time you repeat the sequence, it feels just a tiny bit easier than the time before. This is because the repetitive production of chemical signals prepares the relevant neurons to fire more in sync.

This chemical signalling effect, however, may not last to the next day. For that to take place, you need structural changes. This is where the real magic starts to happen. Let's see how this works.

Imagine if you happened to be Theodore Roosevelt and, at the early time of tech development, there were a few people that you spoke to many times every single day. To make that happen promptly, the phone company would have kept your phones hardwired to the phones of those you need to speak to. That too is what your brain does. If two neurons repeatedly fire together, structural changes take place to establish a more permanent connection between them. This process of hardwiring separate parts of the brain changes its very design, almost as if you are upgrading a computer system while in the middle of a complex calculation to build something that is better suited to solve the present problem. As neuroscientist Donald Hebb puts it . . .

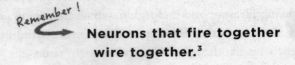

Remember!

Neurons that fire together wire together.[3]

We create new thinking patterns every time we think. Those patterns are strengthened in the very wiring of our brains. As a result, future thinking using this new wiring becomes easier and more effective to use.

This structural redesign not only strengthens certain connections, it also prunes the unused ones. Each neuron, at birth, has the potential to connect through synapses to 5,000 other neurons. When some of those connections are often used, other connections fade and disappear. It's like the work Google did when they built their early data centres using their own stripped-down versions of servers. By removing the parts of the computer that were not really needed for the functions Google intended them to be used for, those computers became more efficient at the tasks they needed to focus on.

Over time, the structural changes taking place in our brains accumulate. As a result, parts of our brain become much stronger and other parts completely disappear. As I mentioned before – what we use tends to grow and what we don't shrinks.

First chemical signalling makes us better at a task, then structural changes make those improvements permanent. Then our brilliant brain takes one further step to optimize the functions it is expected to perform. The next layer of learning is known as functional change.

Neurons constantly get repurposed to perform functions other than those they were originally intended to perform – functions that the brain deems a higher priority, and hence allocates more resources to. This is easily observable during the process of recovery after an accident. Damage to certain parts of the brain may lead to loss of certain motor control functions, for example. Over time, as the patient recovers, different regions of the brain start to assume the original responsibilities of the damaged part, thus gradually regaining movement without recovering any of the lost cells. This is also true for the way our cells are repurposed as we need more cells to focus on certain functions. Braille readers, for example, have larger hand motor control areas on the right side of their brain, and London cab drivers have larger areas of their brain dedicated to spatial memory. Their brains need to dedicate more resources to those functions that they perform thousands of times every day for years.

Put it all together and you find that your brain, right now, is different from the one you started reading this book with. It will be different again by the end of this page. It will have a different wiring between its different cells and it may even have reassigned some of its cells to new functions. Fascinating!

Learning on the Inside

Now, here's something crucial that I need to bring to your attention. For your muscles to grow, you need to keep going back to the gym over and over to put in more sets of exercises. You may need to use external stimuli – say dumbbells – to get your muscles to perform the task that leads them to grow. This is not the case for your brain. Recall is as effective as new practice when it comes to developing your brain. You know this to be true. If you read a headline while passing a magazine kiosk, and you want to remember it, you don't need to go back to the kiosk and read it over and over again. All you need to do is to recall it several times – inside your head. Professional dancers and athletes benefit tremendously from visualizing their moves while sitting down without making a single move. When we say that practice makes perfect, that practice can be nothing more than a thought played over and over inside your own head.

Recall is a powerful practice but its power can work against you if you add tiny variations to the memory or skill that you recall. Have you ever recounted a shared experience with a friend, only to find that the way they remembered it was different from the way you did? Of course, you have. That difference between your stories, naturally, could have resulted from a different vantage point. But even if what you both saw was identical, time and repetitive recall can cause both stories to vary drastically. Imagine for example that the story you shared involved the presence of a third party that stood in a bit of a dark place and so was not visually recognizable. If the first time you recalled that memory, your brain generated long hair for that individual as part of what you remembered, consecutive recalls might generate further fictional details such as a dress or high heels. If your friend's first recall, however, started with a bald head, the final character in her story might look more like me. The same is true when it comes to skills. I am a self-taught guitar player. When I learned as a young teen, I developed a few technical mistakes which, with repeated practice, became so ingrained in the way my brain instructs my hands to play that unlearning them is proving to be much more difficult than learning new techniques.

Repeat After Me

Another important thing to observe is that real learning does not happen as a result of performing a certain function intensively, but rather from doing that function repeatedly, over and over and over again. This is easy to observe in fitness. In order to achieve your desired level of fitness, going to the gym once a month to lift incredibly heavy weights won't work. What you need is to develop the habit of going to the gym several times a week. Every time you exercise a muscle, it becomes a little stronger, and as you keep exercising it over an extended period of time you get closer and closer to your goal. The same is true for the way your brain learns.

You may recall from those dreadful school years that memorizing something once rarely made it stick. Reciting it many times was what worked. While every single use of your brain shapes it slightly differently, time and repeated use are like drops of water wearing down stone. Every drop matters, but no single drop can result in any noticeable change.

Remember !

Time and repeated use are the only way to reshape our brains.

Learning Against Yourself

This – our ability to change over time – is perhaps the most incredible quality we possess as humans. It is, however, a double-edged sword. It can work for or against you.

Repetition of habits that lead to happiness – a mindful way of living in the present moment, for example – can turn an angry wreck into a peaceful calm monk over the years, while years of selfish focus on one's own ego can turn a normal child into ... well, Donald Trump. You see? Our brains, and the rest of our biology, are not selective when it comes to what we choose to develop. They simply respond to the environment we subject them to and grow the parts relevant for optimum performance in those circumstances.

If you go to the gym four times a week to exercise your upper body, the results will show. You'll become physically fitter and stronger but you will look like a triangle. If, however, you choose to only squat with heavy weights every time you go, well ... you'll just turn into one big pear. Your body will not stop and correct you or alert you to other exercises that you should do. It will follow, regardless of how odd your choices may be. Some people choose to exercise their ears to carry heavy weights and spin. Yes, this is a real sport. The world champion of hanging heavy weights from his ear lobes and spinning is Erik Sprague, better known as Lizardman, who can lift 16 kilograms with his pierced ears and spin. Don't believe me? Go check it out. He even has a Wikipedia page.

Erik's body did not stage a riot and scream: *This is mad. I'm not doing it.* It responded and actually made his ears and the back of his neck stronger. What makes someone dedicate their life to such an unusual ambition, I will never know. But then I don't understand those who dedicate their lives to complaining about things that happened years ago, or those who spend a lifetime looking for everything that is wrong with a perfectly good life, either. I'm not judging Erik here. If I had lived his life, I would probably have his exact tattoos and I would be spinning as we speak. I'm just trying to make a point:

Your brain will learn whatever you spend your time practising.

Our brains are not choosy about which parts of them grow. You choose, you practise, and over time you see the fruits of the brain that you choose to nurture. You end up with the wolf that you feed. It grows and grows, even though, sometimes, you don't even know that you're feeding it.

Habituation

Our brains, capable as they are, only have limited resources at their disposal. They can't think about everything at the same time. Usually, we don't want to have to wait for answers but our brains are not supercomputers, and that's why they tend to be picky about what they choose to dedicate their thinking powers to. In doing so, they don't focus the same amount of attention on all the other tasks which need to be performed. How do they do that? Habituation.

If you have purchased some apples from a supermarket recently, each individual apple would probably have had a little label stuck on it. That annoying little sticker did not grow on the tree. It was the innovation of someone, some time ago, to brand their own apples and attract your attention, or perhaps to make the work of sorting apples easier. It does not serve you, the consumer, in any way. Quite the opposite, in fact. It just annoys you every time you pick up an apple to eat. You have to get your fingernail under the label to try and take it off, then find a way to unstick that stubborn thing from your finger to throw it away.

Despite all this, none of us pays any attention to that annoying additional sticker removal that's been added to every apple eater's life.

But have you ever considered that hundreds of billions of apples are consumed every year, and if we did pay attention we would recognize the significant impact one little sticker can have? Can you see it? Hundreds of billions of pieces of paper that go to waste every year, adding up to a little forest that we could have preserved to keep our planet alive – and that's in addition to all the wasted time humanity spends removing them. I mean, think about it. Around 90 million tons of apples are produced every year. If each one had a sticker and every sticker took five seconds, just five seconds, to remove, then humanity combined would be wasting 200,000 human years removing stickers. All of this waste goes unnoticed because we've become habituated to the apple sticker. When something becomes a part of our habitual life, our brains ignore it. This applies to stickers, as much as it applies to the noise and pollution in the cities we live in as well as every tiny habit, including those that lead you to unhappiness, that we get used to. Every time you repeat your habit, it seems unworthy of your attention. But give it time and repetition along with neuroplasticity and it adds up to a massive difference to the way you are.

I very much doubt that while purchasing your apples you give any thought to the sticker phenomenon. I doubt that you search for stickerless apples or that you even recall removing the last sticker. Well, now you will. I'm sure you will. Why? Because by bringing it to your attention, I have removed it from the mechanical habituated practices of your brain and placed it into your area of awareness. We need to do this with all the other habits that blend into the background of our cognitive processing, especially the ones that make us unhappy.

When it comes to the way our brains learn, a habit that is not noticed, like that apple sticker, does not just get discarded in the garbage bin. It leaves a trace on your brain through neuroplasticity, and you become a slightly different you as a result. Let me give you a few examples.

Every time our brains find something that upsets them, they are habituated to spend cycles analysing it silently in the back of our heads. Every time they do this, they become just a tiny bit better at finding things to get upset about. Over time, they end up being really good at being upset. It all happens unnoticed, day after day, as your life slips away. Every time our brain clings to a negative thought and obsesses over it, it becomes a tiny bit better at holding on to negative thoughts, until it develops the ability to spend days or years focusing on them. Every time we let our fears linger, our brain learns to be more afraid, and every time we get carried away with the political debates on TV, it learns to debate from our own living room, ending up as a disgruntled passive activist.

Those little habits add up to a noticeable negative impact over time. Over the years, I've come to give them a name. I call them stickers (yes, they do stick and they're annoying) – and I've learned to search for them and remove them.

It is crucial to recognize which part of your own brain has been growing. If it's a part that you don't want to grow then you might as well be informed so that you have the awareness needed to reverse course. But finding out which parts of your brain have been growing is hard. Because brains are hidden inside our skulls, we don't see them growing in the way that we see our muscles grow when we go to the gym. There are no physical symptoms that indicate the difference between a brain that's been trained for happiness and another that's becoming a misery machine. And while other people may easily be able to spot which side of the fence you're on, that discovery is not easy for you to make. Over the years we become accustomed to our own habitual behaviours – too accustomed to notice or criticize them.

So how can we tell which parts of our brain have been growing because of what we may have been unconsciously practising? It's simple. The parts of our brain that have been receiving frequent workouts operate better. They normally work faster and, as a result, they become the parts that we rely on most and use more frequently. This means that we could – and many of us often do – consistently practise being our very own worst enemies. We become so good at it that it becomes the thing we do best and most frequently. **Our best and worst habits, over time, shape our most prominent actions and behaviours.**

Remember !

Practice does make you miserable if what you repeatedly practise is your own unhappiness.

When written so clearly, this sounds obvious ... Yet in the context of neuroplasticity, this is the bottom line. You are in full control. You can shape your own happiness or unhappiness through repetitive training and good habits.

With that in mind, allow me to join you in a tour of your very own brain. You need to start noticing your apple stickers. Let's discover together what it is you have been investing your brain resources in learning.

What Have You Been Learning?

Do you remember the Biased Brain Test (the awareness exercise we did at the end of the last chapter)? I asked you to answer three questions and measure the time it took you to find each answer. Look back at your results now. The speed at which you answered each of the questions corresponds to the fittest parts of your brain – the parts that you have been exercising more throughout your life.

If you managed to find one thing you dislike about yourself quicker than one thing you really like about yourself, it means that you have been practising self-criticism more than self-love (Question 1 about yesterday's lunch was just intended to distract you). I find that most of us are incredibly good at being unkind to ourselves. Looking for what is not so good about oneself seems to be praised as a positive thing in our highly competitive modern world because we believe that this makes us work harder on becoming 'better'. I strongly disagree with this premise. As young children we are taught to be motivated by the negative side of things. We study hard in school not always to learn (a positive outcome), but to avoid bad grades or to brag about our success (negatively motivated outcomes). I was like that too, until I realized that I don't need a negative to act. I can act just as well, even better, when I motivate myself with a positive outcome. I don't need to believe that something is wrong with me in order to become better. I can strive to be better while still believing that I'm a good person exactly as I am. Teaching our children to be self-critical as a motivation for change and improvement is wrong. It leads to diminished self-esteem and to more of the third A – a lifetime of all-pervasive dissatisfaction. Yet we spend hours and hours every day practising self-criticism. *I wish my butt was bigger, I wish it was rounder, I wish it was more toned, tanned, harder, softer. I wish my butt was not my butt. I am bald, fat, ugly, stupid, reckless, unfocused, rigid* . . . The list goes on and on. Every time you exercise the brain muscle responsible for self-criticism, you become better at criticizing yourself, and it becomes easier. Easier makes you do more of it, which makes you even better at it as you slide down in an endless spiral, **becoming really, really good at doing something that is really, really bad for you**. Furthermore, there's a side effect that comes with practising a habit that's bad for you. If you actively spend your waking moments exercising the self-criticism neurons, you stop exercising the self-love ones. As a result, they diminish. Which leads you down a parallel downward spiral of **becoming really bad at something that's really good for you.**

Without noticing it, we are slowly but surely learning what works against us.

Now, if you don't mind me asking, what else have you been unconsciously learning?

When you're watching the late-night comedy shows where the host so casually ridicules others, what are you learning? When you respond aggressively to a post online, what are you learning? When you watch a violent movie where lives are carelessly wasted and humans are tortured or beaten on the screen, what are you learning? When you celebrate the death of a human without the fair course of justice, even if the media told you he was an enemy, what are you learning? When you're watching porn where a woman is reduced to nothing more than her body, what are you learning? When you walk by a homeless person and dampen your empathy by ignoring his/her presence, what are you learning? When you post a picture on social media that you know will cause negative feelings for your friends, what are you learning?

More importantly, when you are dedicating so much of your time and brain resources to those learnings, what are you *not* learning?

Our modern world is constantly focusing our brains on violence, greed, fear, ego, hate, envy, sarcasm, disrespect, narcissism and negativity. We call them different names. We convince ourselves that what we practise is patriotism, freedom, humour and ambition. Day after day, we become negativity itself and, in the process, we become more and more unhappy. We lose our own beautiful nature as individuals and then things become even worse.

The same reinforcing vicious cycle affects our society, even humanity, at large. If you picture yourself as one more neuron in the cumulative brain of humanity, what is the collective brain of humanity learning? How is what we are learning manifesting? Depression rates are sky-high. Teen suicide is at an all-time high and rising. Female suicide is at an all-time high. Our climate is changing. Some of the planet's most valuable resources are depleted, and ecologists agree we are in the midst of a mass extinction.[4]

Just lean back for a minute and observe our collective brain. It seems to me that the joint psyche of our planet is in a very bad mood.

None of this mounting negativity is forced upon us. It is the result of our own choices, of what we keep learning. For that, reversing the trend cannot be the work of one leader. It can't be assigned to a few of us to resolve. It must be a combined effort involving each of us. Just like 100 billion neurons constantly being reconfigured inside your brain, changing our world begins with you. For your own individual happiness and for everyone around you, you need to look at yourself and . . .

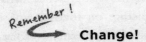

Remember !

Change!

Minor actions repeated over a long time are more lethal than any one action. Small actions are harder to spot and assessing their long-term impact on you and others is even harder. A group of smart, positive-minded individuals can truly help you find and purge bad habits from your life.

Practice Exercise
The Mirror

Group Discussion

Target	Clarity on the actions we take repeatedly that teach us unwanted skills
	A joint effort for your group to rid yourselves of bad habits and influence others to do the same
Duration	60 minutes
Repeat	Repeat at least once a week as needed
You'll need	A quiet place where you will not be interrupted
	Note: If you prefer to work through this alone, that's fine too – just adjust the exercises accordingly

Attempt to collect a group of positive thinkers – two or three good friends will suffice. Like-mindedness and a willingness to change is the most important thing.

Think of one kind of activity that you or your friends tend to do several times a week. Examples could include: *I watch the news on a daily basis. I swipe through Instagram on my commute to work. I argue with my spouse several times a week. I think about what would happen if I lost my job almost all the time.* There are no correct actions to bring up. The idea is to bring up all your different examples before you start to address the important ones.

As your flow of ideas slows down, we can move on to the next step, which is understanding the long-term impact of repeating these actions as they become habits and attitudes. Think about or discuss it for ten minutes. If the conversation is good and it takes longer, let it flow.

When you feel that a topic is covered adequately, move on to the next topic. Here are some questions to use:

- What good lessons will repetition of this habit be likely to develop within an individual?
- What drawbacks is it likely to bring?
- Can you think of examples of individuals (other friends, celebrities, politicians, etc.) who display the kinds of characteristics we learn from such habits? For example, say the habit is posting pictures on social media exaggerating your looks or masking your life to make it look amazing. Does this remind you of a specific celebrity who takes this to the extreme? All the fancy clothing, expensive material possessions and plastic surgery – is that person really how you want to be in life?
- What alternative activities might be better to adopt which would still deliver the same results? (For example, is searching for news headlines on Google better than receiving notifications or watching the news?)

- Can you think of examples of individuals who might act as positive role models, displaying the characteristics that such alternative habits tend to develop? For example, say the alternative habit is to only share useful, inspiring content online. Can you think of a friend who often does that? A public figure, say Oprah, who only shares good vibes and spreads positivity? What do you admire about that person? Are those traits you would be proud to have as part of who you are?

Write down measurable actions that you are willing to commit to in order to reverse the direction of your learning. For example: *I will not use face filters when I post my pictures on social media. I will share positive inspirational messages. I will respond positively to others' posts even when I disagree with them. I will only use kind and respectful words.*

Set achievable targets. It's hard to eliminate a bad habit overnight; it takes repetitive practice for neuroplasticity to reverse course. Commit to a target and start right away. Don't wait for your commitment to fade as you get carried away with the mundane tasks of life. When you achieve your target, celebrate, then increase it gradually until you fully purge that bad habit from your life.

If you do this with friends, you'll find that peer support will open your mind and empower you to change and develop positively. Hold each other accountable and celebrate progress together. If it's working, that means you chose the right group of friends. Keep evolving together. As an old Islamic saying goes:

Remember!

One is of the religion (ideology) of one's friends. Fiercely seek out who to let into your life and who to purge.

Chapter Five

Both of You

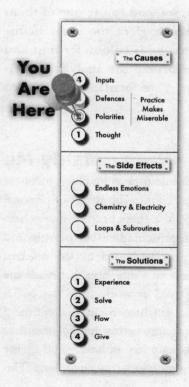

You Are Here

The Causes

4 Inputs

Defences

3 Polarities

Practice Makes Miserable

1 Thought

The Side Effects

Endless Emotions

Chemistry & Electricity

Loops & Subroutines

The Solutions

1 Experience

2 Solve

3 Flow

4 Give

When it comes to personal computers, one of the biggest innovations is the invention of the graphics processor. This processor is responsible for rendering incredible quality images on your screen. It understands images very well and is designed to produce them much quicker than the central processing unit (CPU) of a PC. The CPU, on the other hand, is better at crunching numbers and performing tasks. Together they make the personal computer the platform of choice for serious gamers around the world — two different processors performing very different functions, each doing its task very well. If you removed the graphics processor from a computer, the machine would become sluggish and probably wouldn't perform at all.

This, surprisingly, is not at all different from the way our brains work. If you hold a human brain in your hand, you will notice that what we actually have inside our skull is not one but two brains, two hemispheres connected by a very thin fibre, the corpus callosum. Your brain's left hemisphere and right hemisphere are designed to perform totally different functions. They are each really good at what they do but terrible at what the other is capable of doing.

Sadly, in the modern world, we tend to use one of them more than the other. We often neglect the right hemisphere, the side of the brain that adds colour, feelings and creativity to our life, as we prioritize the analytical, controlling, number-crunching and performance-orientated left hemisphere.

Manly Me

We've All Been There!

Around the same time as graphic processors were introduced into the world of personal computers to help them become more complete, I was approaching my late twenties and was being relentlessly led by the modern world to move in a direction that made me incomplete. Every message I received at work, from the MBA degree I had just finished to the self-help business literature I was consuming in abundance, was instructing me to prioritize my analytical processor – my left-brain hemisphere – and ignore my intuitive, creative and sensing processor – my right brain. This aligned well with my Middle Eastern upbringing where boys are raised to be competitive, driven, stubborn and often dismissive of the value of anything but 'manly' traits.

The results? I progressed impressively in my work, career and ability to make money. And I was miserable. I often suffered long, deep patches of depression. I was harsh and way too strict with my beloved family, and in my attempt to escape my depression, I stubbornly continued even more in my left-brain-driven behaviour. I pushed myself harder. I became opinionated and refused lots of the sensible advice that was generously offered to me by my wonderful then-wife. I completely lacked self-love and constantly ordered myself to 'man up' and 'do' more. The more I revved my analytical engines, the more I believed that I just needed to try harder and, with time, I would emerge triumphant (as in happy). But I was wrong. I dug myself deeper and deeper into unhappiness, stubbornness and confusion. I removed myself further and further from my loving family. I was such a dreadful, aggressive personality that you would not have wanted to spend a single minute with me. I was alone – sad and alone.

Little did I know then that the lie bestowed on me by our hypermasculine, left-brained society and magnified by our selfish, capitalist work culture – the lie that I believed so blindly – was depriving me of the human equivalent of a separate processor. One that is capable of much more than just analysis and discipline. My conditioning had completely deprived me of my right-hemisphere qualities, and that was blinding me to endless alternative possibilities of being. I lacked awareness, feelings, emotions and the intuition needed to dig myself out of my hole.

It took me years of research using my functioning left-brain hemisphere to find my path to happiness through an engineering approach – the topic of my first book. Occasionally, after many months or sometimes years of research, I would discover something profound. Once I did, I always ran to my mentor, my wonderful son, Ali, to tell him what I had found.

Ali never lacked the balance that I so desperately needed. Even as a young child, he had a need to see the truth, the heart to feel and sense with empathy, and the wisdom to summarize it all in just a few words. When I described my findings about happiness to him, in my highly logical and methodical engineer's style, he would respond by asking me a few questions, which he clearly did not need to ask, just to make me feel that what I was saying was catching his interest.

He would listen attentively to my answers and then he would smile at me and say: 'Wow, I'm so proud of you, Papa.' Like a child, my heart would dance with joy when he did this. All I wanted was his admiration. He was my self-assigned mentor and his endorsement of my work reassured me that I was on the right track.

Then the magic would happen. He would recite back to me what I said using my left brain as it would be felt by the heart and expressed by the right. The picture would suddenly be clear. I would finally get it.

For years, until I learned to develop my own, Ali was my heart. He was my right brain, my graphics processor. He made me complete.

The kind of struggle I faced in my late twenties is not unusual in the workplace or in most societies. Certain contributions to society – especially those associated with traditional 'male' behaviour – have often been over-glorified. So many of us, men and women, rely on only half of our processing power. So many glorify the left side of our brains, and as a result focus on doing, doing, doing. We ignore the powers of the right-brain hemisphere and thus deprive ourselves and our world of a desperately needed balance and an opportunity to just 'be'.

I believe our modern world puts far too much emphasis on

the left-brain hemisphere. Three in every four people you meet in the workplace today will prioritize logic – IQ – over emotional intelligence – EQ. This is a natural response to the demands of work where analytical thinking, results orientation, planning, competitiveness and other capabilities of the left brain are highly valued. Emotions, meanwhile, are supposed to be kept under wraps, and intuition, without solid proof, kept to oneself. But is one side of our brain, one half of what makes us human, really more useful than the other?

Our understanding of the difference between the capabilities of the two brain hemispheres originated in the work of Roger W. Sperry, who became a Nobel Prize winner in 1981 for his work on epilepsy. Sperry discovered that cutting the corpus callosum – the fibre that connects the two hemispheres – could reduce or eliminate seizures. In the process, his work also shed light on our understanding of how each side of the brain works at a fundamental level when isolated from the other.

Besides a reduction in epileptic attacks, his recovering patients experienced other symptoms. Cutting the communication pathway between the two sides of the brain made patients unable to name objects that were observed by the left eye, and accordingly processed by the right side of the brain, while they continued to be able to name objects that were processed by the left side – observed by the right eye. Based on this information, Sperry suggested that language was controlled by the left side of the brain.[1] Many others followed the work of this discovery, which led us to understand both sides of the brain in great detail. Let me spare you the technical detail and introduce you to both sides of your brain in a more colloquial, story-based way.

Imagine your two brains as two humans. For the sake of argument, let's call them Lefty and Righty. They would be very different people. Lefty will tend to be analytical; Righty will tend

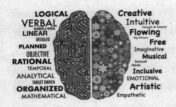

to be intuitive. Lefty will want to talk – in words – about the details, while Righty will describe a more poetic picture of the whole. After a rational analysis of the situation, Lefty will recommend a cautious plan while Righty might take a more adventurous approach and act on impulse. As Lefty will attempt to invoke some discipline using short, logical statements, Righty will paint a vision using imagination and creativity, which will not mean much to Lefty who will just turn around and start to **do** things while Righty will lean back to just **be** and stay true to what they feel. Sounds familiar? Can you recognize either of these in yourself?

Before we go any further, I need to make one thing clear. I am talking about left brain attributes as archetypally masculine (as opposed to male!) and right brain attributes as archetypally feminine (not female). This is a convenient way to explore them and does not equate to gender. Modern neuroscience clearly states that the left and right brains are not directly aligned to the male and female biology of humans. Obviously, each and every one of us has both brains. My attempt here is to show that different parts of our brains are responsible for certain characteristics that we associate with feminine or masculine traits and behaviours. Understanding the wider spectrum of qualities our brains are capable of will enable us to utilize more of them. The use of those archetypes is intended to indicate femininity and masculinity that are present in all of us.

A Stroke of Insight

I have never found a clearer explanation of the distinction between our two brain hemispheres than in the work of neuroscientist Jill Bolte Taylor – her book *A Stroke of Insight* and her TED Talk back in 2008 – which describe her experience of suffering a stroke that disabled her left-brain hemisphere. Without the restrictions that her left-brain functionalities imposed on the way she could see the world, she could experience life as viewed solely by the right brain.

Here's what she said:

> For a moment my left-hemisphere brain chatter went totally silent just like someone took a remote control and pushed the mute button . . . Imagine what it would be like to be totally disconnected from your brain chatter . . . So here I am in this space and my job, and any stress related to my job – it was gone. And I felt lighter in my body . . . And I felt this sense of peacefulness. Imagine what it would feel like to lose thirty-seven years of emotional baggage. Euphoria! It was beautiful.[2]

We know from neuroscience that our brain chatter, inner and outer, and the use of words in general is a function of the left brain. Extremes of this quality, such as excessive debate or being a brainiac, are associated with our archetypally masculine side. Disabling that part of us gives us inner silence and enables our right brain to engage.

Here is how Jill described what her right brain experienced:

> I looked down at my arm and I realized that I can no longer define the boundaries of my body. I couldn't define where I begin or where I am because the atoms and the molecules of my arm blended with the atoms and molecules of the wall and everything around me. I felt

enormous and expansive like a genie just liberated from her bottle, one with all the energy that was. I had found Nirvana.

This sense of oneness with everything that Jill described is surely a function of the right brain hemisphere. It, also, is highly associated with the feminine. I urge you to visit Jill's work to better understand the differences between our two brain hemispheres. For now, however, it's enough to say that we truly have . . .

Two Different Brains

If Lefty was a human, I imagine them as a maths geek who works as a factory supervisor. If asked about their values and attitudes they would say: *I am an individual first, then a member of society. I am responsible for my own success. I think systematically, solve problems, learn from the past and plan for the future. I am interested in detail. I am good with words and when I put my mind to something I will not deviate until it gets done.*

Righty, on the other hand, would be young, free spirited, someone who spends time in nature. Asked about themselves, they would say: *I am one with all there is. All living beings talk to me. I holistically let in the big picture of all there is, all that's to be sensed and all that's to be felt. I allow myself to fully be and flow where life wants to go. I am creative and adventurous. I feel and imagine. I embrace paradoxes, nurture life, appreciate beauty and inspire.*

Two totally different characters. Which is 'better'? Well, interestingly, that kind of question would only be asked by Lefty (who wants everything to be labelled and categorized). The answer is: neither one is better than the other.

What we often forget is that the difference between our left- and right-brain hemispheres represents one of the biggest gifts humanity has ever been given. How can we even conceive of one side being better than the other? Their polarity is what gives us a diversity of perspective and grants us access to a wide spectrum of cognitive processing and intelligence tools. It's what leads to variety and human ingenuity. Our left-brain functionalities bring order to our lives. They help us solve maths problems and plan strategically. They help us set targets, see them through and make rational decisions. They helped our ancestors hunt and are helping us build incredible technologies today. Make no mistake, without our left brain, humanity would have vanished a long, long time ago.

But if we only had left brains, life would be colourless, bland and boring. We would not have art or music, we would lack empathy for one another and fail to form societies. We would just think and not feel. We would not love, laugh, or venture beyond our strict order to explore and enjoy what life has to offer. We would fail to see the bigger picture or dream about the things that our left brain helps us build. Without our right brain, we'd be more like gears in a machine. We would still be hunting because we would never have imagined any other way. Without our right brain, humanity would have vanished from lack of creativity and advancement. And if that did not get us, we would have surely all died of boredom.

Remember!

It's not one hemisphere or the other that makes us thrive as humans. It's the balance and interaction between them that does.

Yet, our hypermasculine modern societies encourage us to think, do, analyse, criticize, find what's wrong, and plan for the future – all left-brain functionalities. This has been true through-out long periods of history but never more so than today. We're encouraged to suppress the invaluable life-nourishing presence of archetypally feminine qualities. We're told that we should be in a constant state of doing, we should not trust our intuition and we should not show emotions. By not empowering our right hemispheres, we're losing out on a big part of what makes us human just as we lose out on a big part of what makes us happy. What's even worse is that we are proud of it because, sadly, we (men and women, especially in the workplace) are often taught to think that embracing our feminine side is wrong.

Wrong and Right

Sometimes as I walk through the charming old streets of my birth town, Cairo, in Egypt, I imagine what it must have been like in the old days. The way Arabia is portrayed in the movies is the way it's always been – a bit like what you see in Disney's *Aladdin* (2019). (By the way, well done, Will Smith. You aced it.) I wish I was Aladdin. I wish, more than anything, that I had that lamp. My first wish is obvious. That all-powerful blue genie would be my cheat to achieve my OneBillionHappy mission. I would rub that lamp the second I laid my hands on it without hesitation and wish for happiness for billions, and still be left with two more wishes to spare. I'd probably never ask for the third wish. I'd keep the genie stuck with me because that guy's funny as hell and I think we'd really get along. Which leaves me with one more wish. One wish that gives me the power to change the world – to fix it. Now that's an interesting puzzle. What would you choose if you were allowed one, and only one, thing to change?

I would choose to empower the right (sometimes known as the correct) side of humanity's brain. I believe that this one strategic move would completely change the state of our planet and fix most of our world's current problems.

Think about it. Each problem that humanity is facing requires a different skill set if it were to be resolved in isolation. To reverse the current environmental risks of climate change, you need a very different skill set than the skill set you need to reduce our economic dependency on the war machine. Then you need yet another very different skill set to end hunger or protect humanity against potential future pandemics. When seemingly unrelated problems keep popping up in any functional system, an engineering approach to problem-solving recommends looking for the underlying root cause.

Remember !

The underlying cause for many challenges facing humanity today is our hyper left-brain centricity.

Collectively, it seems, we have not fully utilized our right-brain-hemisphere power. We need the qualities of the feminine to become fully present in humanity. In fact, for our world to become better, we need the feminine to lead.

In his book *The Master and His Emissary*, Iain McGilchrist advocates that to restore the balance in each of us and for humanity at large, we need to empower our right brain and give it the leadership position. We need to use our empathy and intuition first, to define what matters, then we need to use our creativity to devise different solutions – all 'feminine' qualities. Then, and only then, should we hand over to our left-brain side to get things done. Doing, without being informed by the feminine as to what should be done, is leading us astray.

In the conclusion to his book, McGilchrist describes a world where the left brain is so dominant that it completely suppresses the qualities of the right (I love that chapter). He writes:

The left hemisphere prefers the impersonal to the personal and that tendency would in any case be instantiated in the fabric of a technologically driven and bureaucratically administered society. The impersonal would come to replace the personal. There would be a focus on material things at the expense of the living. Social cohesion and the bonds between person and person and just as importantly between person and place, the context in which each person belongs, would be neglected perhaps actively disrupted as both inconvenient and incomprehensible to the left hemisphere acting on its own . . . Exploitation rather than cooperation would be the default relationship between human beings and between humanity and the rest of the world.[3]

Please read this again. Isn't this the world we live in today? And you know what? None of it is even making us happy. We build, do, think and acquire more, while what we truly seek, our happiness, gets harder and harder to find. We're not so smart after all, Lefty, are we?

Being Human

There are hundreds of qualities that make us human. They define our attitudes and the way we behave. They include empathy, inclusion, focus, discipline, strength, imagination; and the list goes on. Humans have sometimes designated each of these as 'male' or 'female' qualities. This is an assumption I wish to challenge at its core.

In my initial research, I looked at close to a hundred human qualities and attempted to categorize them based on majority viewpoint — as seen by sociology, spirituality and common beliefs — into archetypally 'feminine' (right brain) and 'masculine' (left brain) qualities. For the purposes of this book, I have narrowed these down to only seventeen traits.

Which seventeen and why is irrelevant. This is not an exact science, as you are about to see. What we seek is an understanding of a complex topic – what is the feminine archetype and what is the masculine – in a simplified way that we all can agree on.

The seventeen I picked are: intuition, resilience, inclusion, creativity, empathy, awareness, passion, communication, compassion, discipline, responsibility, action orientation, courage, focus, strength, linear thinking and assertiveness.

None of those qualities in itself can ever be bad. A quality is a quality. As with everything, however, too much of anything is bad. Overdoing any of those qualities turns it from a positive for the individual showing it to a negative. Linear thinking, for example, is a good way to organize our approach to problem-solving. Do too much of it and you may miss important information, or creative solutions that may enable you to better solve the problem. Intuition, at the other extreme, is also a positive quality. It allows us to consult our gut feelings when too much or too little information about a specific problem is presented. Rely on intuition too much, however, and you may become irrational and miss out on important facts.

Now, I associate linear thinking with the masculine archetype and intuition with the feminine archetype simply because statistical correlation will show that those of us who are perceived to be feminine are more likely to be intuitive while those who we perceive as masculine will more likely be linear thinkers. By observing how prevalent (commonly present and intense) a certain quality happens to be in those we identify as masculine makes it a masculine quality, and a measure of how prevalent another is in those we identify as feminine makes it commonly agreed by society as a feminine quality.

Another important point to highlight here is that the feminine and masculine are not directly associated with a certain biology or gender identity. The recent global awakening surrounding gender fluidity proves beyond the shadow of a doubt that our choice to live within the framework of femininity or masculinity should not be dictated by society or biology.

Qualities, whether feminine or masculine, are present, to varying degrees, in each of us. No quality is ever exclusive to a few. But here's the catch. When a quality is strongly represented in the left brain it is often weakly represented in the right brain, and vice versa. Also, when a quality is strongly present in the feminine archetype, its opposite, almost, is represented in the masculine. As a result, if we take a large enough statistical sample, we will find that the intensity of each of those qualities within us tends to follow a distribution curve that looks very similar to the Chinese symbol of balance between the feminine and the masculine – the Yin-Yang.

This chart is a visual representation of how much each of the seventeen qualities I chose is attributed to the right brain – the black bars of the yang – and how much each is attributed to the left brain – the white bars of the yin.

Those qualities are each driven by different parts of our brains. They get their distinctive characters from the way our brains engage them and not from our biology.

This means they follow the same rules of neuroplasticity that every other part of your brain development follows. Embracing any one of our human qualities makes you better at that quality. Suppressing a quality makes it diminish.

When we become adults, society or the workplace often forces us to suppress our 'feminine' qualities by making us feel that some aspects of those attributes are not welcomed. This, obviously, leads to unhappiness as we attempt to navigate life without being true to our nature. Without our feminine qualities, much of what we need in order to find balance in life is taken away.

You see, the truth that is seldom discussed is that all of us are starved of the 'feminine' qualities because our society is structured that way. In this new light, I'd like us to take some time to reflect on our own qualities, to connect with our hidden feminine. This will be a crucial first step in the direction of becoming free.

Which qualities do you lead with? Do you know?

This short exercise will offer you some time and space to reflect on your own qualities and get to meet both of your sides.

Awareness Exercise Both of You

Target	Discovering which qualities (left or right brain, 'masculine' or 'feminine') define you
Duration	15 minutes
Repeat	Once is enough for awareness
You'll need	A quiet place where you will not be interrupted

Before you read further, please take a few minutes to investigate which of the qualities mentioned below are present in you intensely enough to inform your behaviour and identify you as an individual.

'Feminine' Qualities	'Masculine' Qualities
Intuition	
Resilience	
Inclusion	
Creativity	
Empathy	
Awareness	
Passion	
Communication	
Compassion	
	Discipline
	Responsibility
	Action Orientation
	Courage
	Focus
	Strength
	Linear thinking
	Assertiveness

Please don't skip this exercise. It's an important, overdue introduction to your real self.

Being Me

So far, I hope you agree with the logic that left and right brain qualities are part of each and every one of us. That the qualities that make us archetypally feminine or masculine are truly nothing more than brain functions and, accordingly, they can be allowed to develop, and they can be suppressed. In our modern world, we have more often than not suppressed the feminine, and our world greatly needs more of the feminine to function well.

Let's go back to intuition – which many cultures view as a traditionally 'feminine' quality. For you as an individual, the question to which you need to know the answer is how intense your intuition is and how much you allow it to drive your choices and behaviours. Say, for example, that you use your intuition most of the time and that you are really comfortable with it. Would that categorize you as 'feminine'? Well, it does not even categorize you as intuitive. You see, you could be more or less intuitive than someone who relies on her intuition less or more often than you. This is a complex statement, because how intuitive you are is measured not only by how frequently you rely on your intuition, but also by it's intensity, as in, how good you are at being intuitive. Intuition is not just an on-off switch. On top of how frequently you use it, you could have a certain amount of it on a varying scale from zero to 100 per cent.

Remember !

The qualities that define each of us are not binary in nature, they are a sliding scale.

Attempting to fit each of us into a discrete category is an attempt to approximate the truth. To assume that there is a fixed number of discrete categories between the colour black and the colour white limits our understanding of the true nature of grey. This chart on the left, deceivingly, makes it seem that there are only fourteen shades of grey between black and white. This is only true if we create the chart that way and force the other countless shades to fit into the nearest one of the fourteen categories. There must be at least fifty shades — if we are to believe Hollywood! Or are there more?

The true nature of grey is better represented by this chart on the right. Can 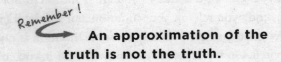 you tell me which of the points on the scale here is grey? Almost every point, to a varying degree, is grey. It's wrong to assign that quality — greyness — to one specific point because that denies millions of other, equally grey, points the recognition they deserve for their true nature.

Discrete categories are a human attempt to simplify the complexity of our rich universe. It is just way too difficult for our left brains to make sense of anything when there are so many variations of everything. The act of categorization is an approximation of the truth for our limited brains to cope with. But . . .

Remember !

An approximation of the truth is not the truth.

Which means it's false. It misleads us.

If you, say, had the ability to utilize the 'feminine' quality of intuition at the extreme of its scale, if you were the most intuitive person on the planet, does that make you feminine? Not necessarily. You could be super intuitive and yet also very disciplined, courageous, strong and assertive — all prominent qualities of the 'masculine'. What would that make you? Allow me to answer this using the categories we've become accustomed to when it comes to dietary preferences.

From the day I turned twenty-five, I stopped eating meat, which, by common standards, made me a vegetarian. But I didn't eat eggs or drink milk either, which would have made me vegan had it not been for a small glitch – I continued to eat cheese and yoghurt. I would often have that conversation over dinner. I would be asked what I am. None of the categories fit me, so what choice did I have? Well, the choice is simple.

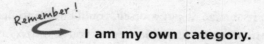

Remember!

I am my own category.

When asked about my diet, I would say: I am a Mo-tarian – I eat what Mo likes to eat. I owe it to no one to fit within a category to simplify their cognitive processes while complicating my own life. I am me and that is that.

The same applies to my relationship with the categories of 'feminine' and 'masculine'. I do not feel masculine – which is a big statement for a man of Middle Eastern origin to make. If I want to be true to myself, **I feel I'm 58 per cent feminine**.

When I think of myself with my 58 per cent feminine side, I recognize the extent of my true qualities. (This calculation is accurate, by the way. I developed a tool that measures the presence of each of our qualities in each of us – a more comprehensive version of the 'Both of You' exercise above – but that's a topic for another book.) With an understanding of the very specific blend of qualities that define me, I am, in fact, the only one of me that exists. Which means that the only category I accept to belong to is not man, woman, gay, straight, feminine or masculine. The only category I truly belong to is one that's called *the Mo*. It's the only point on the endless scale of human variety that fits me. Similarly, the only category you fit perfectly into is you. You can call it by your name, just as scientists name each of the billions of stars they discover in the vast universe. Your category, to which you're the only one that belongs, is a very unique blend of traits felt at varying intensities and expressed in an infinite variety of behaviours.

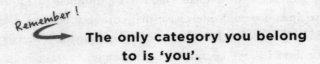

Remember!

The only category you belong to is 'you'.

Once you recognize this in yourself, you'll be able to flex as much of your masculine or feminine side as you want to on demand, to freely express who you truly are. By being, and behaving, in a manner that's true to your nature, you'll be able to achieve the success that you deserve in life and, perhaps more importantly, demystify and erase one of the deepest neural reasons for suffering, trying to fit in.

I know it's taken us lots of pages, and a few untraditional concepts, to get to the topic of happiness in this chapter but it gets easier from here. So please feel free to get up and have a stretch before you continue to read.

Left, Right and Happy

Finally, I feel, we are ready to discuss how the imbalance we suffer between left and right, first and foremost, is a major reason for unhappiness.

Life is bound to throw a few tough events along the path of each and every one of us. Those, if we let them linger, surely make us unhappy. When faced with a challenge, it's wise to throw everything you've got back at life. Dealing with a challenge with a subset of your capabilities makes it harder to succeed. How do you gather all of you to face a challenge?

Masterful happiness practitioners, I notice, tend to follow a systematic approach that helps them move back to their state of happiness swiftly and predictably. Those steps are so effective and repeatable that they deserve to be summarized in what I call the happiness flow chart, which I will share in detail in Chapter Eleven, but let's discuss the big picture here first.

The first half of our path to succeed at anything, including happiness, is all about awareness. Awareness is not something you can do. It is a state that you attain when you pay deliberate attention to what's inside you and surrounding you. In order to exert that level of attention, you need to stop doing. You need to just ... **Be**. The second half of the path is all about taking action to make a difference to the world. Awareness in itself is passive. For the world around to change, there will always be things to ... **Do**. This is where we face a challenge. Most of us, regardless of our biology, are better at one, being or doing, than the other. Some of us just run around doing things all the time. Often without stopping to figure out why we're doing what we're doing. The rest of us are in touch with our feelings and emotions but tend to do nothing about them. We just sit there waiting for things to change. Neither can tread a full path to happiness. Some are right-brainers who are good at being. They start on the path to happiness but stop halfway. The others are left-brainers who are good at doing. They attempt to finish what has not been started and waste cycles doing what does not need to be done.

It goes without saying that our left-brain-led world favours the doing part. Every article about happiness in every magazine tells you what you need to 'do' so that you find that elusive joyful feeling. Most of our actions follow those recommendations. We book vacations, go to parties and buy things. We repeat mantras and

affirmations. And we 'do' what we're told but rarely reach a state of lasting happiness. Why? Because . . .

Remember!

> **The full path to happiness requires you to 'be' before you 'do'.**

Learning to Be

Our inability to access the full spectrum of our qualities is nothing more than heavy conditioning by our modern world of egos. Perhaps a parent who forced us into one side of our polarity or peer pressure at a young age. Those qualities, however, are still within us even if dormant. With practice, everyone, including you, can make the shift between being and doing on demand. The good news is that once you learn to make that shift repeatedly, it will set you miles ahead of the rest of us, not only in terms of your happiness, but in every aspect of your life. When you find the balance between your different sides, you will feel complete as never before. Reaching that state may take time, but it surely is worth investing your time and effort to reach it.

Those who understand the true nature of awareness understand that this approach comes with a bigger challenge. Being requires you to stop doing, and once you start doing you are no longer able to be. To master this approach to happiness, you don't only need to use both sides of your brain equally competently, you need to learn to isolate them too – in a deliberate fashion – so that you can fully be with no left-brain interruptions, then fully do with no right-brain distractions. And that, I will tell you, is some hard, Jedi Master-level skill. We will get there together. But there's still more to learn before we put it all into practice because . . . what good is doing anything if you don't have the knowledge and training to do it right?

When you are fully aware of where you are and what you need to do, it pays to put in the time to learn how to best do what needs to be done. You may have already noticed that this has been the backbone of my approach in this book: a model that we will call Be–Learn–Do.

Awareness exercises and group discussions are designed to help you be – to connect with your ability to become aware of what's going on inside you in terms of thoughts, feelings and beliefs. Practice exercises, on the other hand, are designed to help you take the actions you need to take in order to make things better and make yourself happier. The rest of the book really is about learning.

Flowing through this rhythm – to be, learn, then do – requires you to master the use of what we have learned about the brain so far – the right hemisphere for being, neuroplasticity for learning, and the left hemisphere for doing.

We will put this model into practice shortly, but first, I'd like to share a very personal story to convey my admiration for the gift of living on the right side of the brain.

I or Us

I never could really guess, during his life, what made my wonderful son, Ali, the person that he was. He had a magnetism to him. If you were near him you felt love – an all-encompassing, immersive love that drew you closer. Without a single word, in Ali's arms you felt safe. He had an ability to make you feel that everything was OK. Looking back now, I'm starting to recognize that in the last few years of his life, Ali, despite his Middle Eastern, masculine upbringing, managed to fully integrate the feminine. Nibal, his mother, is the epitome of pure love and, from her, Ali too became pure love.

Three years before he died, his band – Fox Hill V – got an invitation to tour the US to open for a famous rock band. After three of the band members arrived in the US, the fourth, due to unforeseen circumstances, had to cancel. Due to the short notice, and being in a foreign country, the band could not replace him and, instead of touring, the three of them ended up spending three weeks in a small town in the USA. When Ali returned to Dubai, he was nothing more than skin on a skeleton. My heart sank; I asked him what was wrong. He said: 'Papa, America is not what I thought. There is so much pain, so much poverty. People in the place we stayed had no money, no food, they escaped to drugs.' He said: 'I felt the pain of each and every one of them. I couldn't eat and couldn't sleep.'

This trip, I believe, changed the remainder of Ali's life. He could no longer separate himself from the rest of being. The veil was removed, and he became one with all. For the rest of his life, he felt the happiness and the pain of everyone. The more he connected, the more he demanded change from everyone he could reach. I could see him becoming expansive, bigger than himself, and despite his dissatisfaction with the state of our world, every passing day he was more and more at peace. His words changed. The topics he championed and the way he discussed them became different. He wanted nothing more than a world without suffering. The years to come were the years when his wisdom reached its peak. He had died before he died. It was as if he had already died, while he was fully alive. As shown in the teachings of Sufism, he died before he died.

He attempted to teach me to open up, to connect my emotional side to my hyperanalytical left brain. I was stubborn. I told him that these left-brain qualities were what had helped me achieve and make a difference. That we lived in a world that was all about doing and that nothing would change if we didn't do. He failed to change me, because I was stupid, but he kept trying until two days before he left our world. That day he told me point-blank: 'Papa, I never want you to stop working but there's one thing I want you to change. **Count on your heart a bit more often.**' It was as if a dying sage was dictating his will. He knew, without a shadow of a doubt, that the one thing that would change my life, and the lives of those around me, would be for me to balance my masculine – never stop working – with my feminine – count on my heart. He was right.

Here I am, years later, having made a bigger difference to our world with my mission – OneBillionHappy – than I ever did with my long career in the leading tech companies of the world. With glimpses of what it is like to live fully on the right side of my brain, to let my heart lead, I – like Ali – have learned to find total peace. I would even dare say that I'm on my path to finding the Nirvana that he lived in. Thank you, Ali.

In the closing part of Jill Bolte Taylor's TED talk I mentioned above, she said:

> *Right here right now I can choose to step into the consciousness of my left hemisphere where I become a single individual separate from the flow of life. Or, I can step into the consciousness of my right hemisphere where we are – I am – the life force, the power of the universe where I am one with everything. I think our first job as humans is to love one another and I think that is our primary way of being. It is the essence of our right brain.*

I have practised happiness for the majority of my adult life but have never really felt complete until this other side of me came out, and, boy, am I glad to meet her at last.

Very Important !

Learn to Be. Switch on that right brain.

In the previous awareness exercise – 'Both of You' – I wanted you to experience first-hand that we all have both left-brain and right-brain qualities. Every one of us, however, tends to use one side of our brain more than the other. It's good to know which side you use more.

Awareness Exercise Which Side are You On?

Homework

Target	Discovering which side of your brain you tend to rely on most
Duration	15 minutes
Repeat	Once is enough for awareness
You'll need	A quiet place where you will not be interrupted

Some live more on the being side while others are more on the doing side. It's important to be aware of which side you personally rely on. Each side of your brain produces different habits. By observing those habits you can discover your left brain–right brain bias.

Now, please take a minute to reflect on your own tendencies.

Do you tend to feel and share or reflect, deeply associating with your fluctuating emotions wherever they take you? If so, you're living more in your feminine. You'll find it easier to be but prepare for some challenges when it is time to do.

Or do you tend to set targets and work relentlessly to achieve them regardless of how you feel inside? Do you rarely stop to consider how those targets affect you emotionally or fit within the bigger world around you (the targets of your family members and loved ones, for example)? Do you tend to prefer actions and solutions over 'sharing and chit-chat'? If so, then you're living more in your 'masculine' half. Just being feels alien to you, though you ace the doing side of life.

In a quiet place, reflect on something that made you unhappy recently and how you reacted to it. Did you sit alone to think about what was going wrong, maybe complain about it, repetitively analyse it, talk to others but feel uncomfortable if they offered solutions? Did you end up awake at night ruminating about it? If yes, you tend to defer to your archetypally feminine side when confronted with a challenge.

If, on the other hand, you reacted by jumping out of your seat and immediately taking action, submerging yourself in work, parties or distractions to forget about the problem, if most of your thinking was focused on solutions and actions, not feelings, if you even dismissed the issue, telling yourself that you're strong enough to handle it without any need for reflection – then, like the old me, you naturally default to the left side of you when there is a reason to feel unhappy.

This is an awareness exercise. You don't need to do or to change anything about what you discover. I don't want you to criticize yourself for being on one side or the other. Neither side is good or bad, Just different. The sole purpose of this exercise is to recognize that one side of you is lived less than the other. This is all you need to define the areas you need to work on, to find your happiness more often in the future.

Now, based on what you have discovered, please tell yourself, out loud, either:

I need to *be* a little more often.
OR
I need to *do* a little more.

This next exercise will help you experience what it is like to think on each side of the brain. By recognizing the side engaged when certain observations are triggered, perhaps you will be able to invite that part of your brain in on demand, or at least recognize when you're stuck on one side or the other.

Awareness Exercise
Experiencing Left and Right?

Target	Experience how each side of the brain views the world
Duration	15 minutes
Repeat	Repeat as a fun game using other images whenever you have the time
You'll need	A quiet place where you will not be interrupted

Look at the image opposite and write down what you see. Take your time — at least a minute or two — before you continue to read.

Did you see a busy street – the big picture – first? Or did you focus first on some of the details? Did you notice that the picture is curved around the edges and not just a rectangle? Seeing the big picture is a right-brain capability. Focusing on the details is a characteristic of the left brain.

Did you see the stylish women in the centre and on the right side of the image quickly? This would be your right brain in action. Appreciation of art and beauty happens there. Did you see that most people are walking to the right? Finding those who are walking to the left requires attention to detail and for that you need to use your left brain. Do it now. One of them is carrying a mobile phone. Where is the other? Ask your left brain. That kind of skill also helps you detect things like the kinds of bags and backpacks that those pedestrians are carrying, as well as the letter **e** that is hidden at the back on the right. Noticing the traffic light in the middle on the top is also a left-brain capability as the left brain tends to pay more attention to possible threats and any information needed for planning purposes.

If you've noticed the poor guy that slipped and fell, that was with your left brain, but if you related to how that might have felt, it was the empathy of your right brain. Reading the sign that says 'caution, wet floor' uses your left brain, which processes words, and if the number 11 came to your mind – the answer to the maths equation – it was calculated on that side too. The time on the street clock – 5.05 – is recognized there too – in the left, temporal, side of the brain. If your right brain is really active, you may have started to hear the sounds and noises of this busy road crossing and perhaps feel the summer temperature that enables everyone to dress as they are. If you appreciate the drawing and the patterns in general, that was your right brain too. The right brain would also observe any relativity between the positions and interactions of the different characters in that picture. This is where all forms of art are recognized. Finally, for those with an active right brain, you are probably now thinking, *Ah, I get what Mo is trying to do. I think he should have added this, this and that to make things clearer* – that kind of active imagination and creativity would be the representation of your right brain at its very finest. I hope this exercise was fun for you. Playfulness and flow are part of what we do on the right. Now that you know the differences, here's another crucial exercise.

We often fail to find deep, genuine respect for each other's qualities and contributions – because it is hard to understand how those different to us think and behave. It's just human nature to believe that your way of doing things is the better way. Let's attempt to change that.

Practice Exercise
Establishing Respect

Group Discussion

Target	Establish respect for the diverse qualities the feminine and the masculine bring to our perspective and abilities

Duration	60 minutes
Repeat	Repeat as a fun game as often as you can
You'll need	A well-balanced, respectful and positive group of friends or co-workers

Find a balanced group of friends or co-workers that represents a wide spectrum of femininity and masculinity. Pick a challenge to discuss and ask the group to work through it together. The group should assign a moderator whose task is to make sure everyone in the group gets to speak. Make sure no one is interrupted and that all are primed to listen attentively.

Your focus as a group is not necessarily to overcome the challenge but, perhaps more importantly, to observe the diverse perspectives each member brings.

Notice that the masculine will tend to side more with Doing and the feminine with Being. Try to observe those differences and, at the end, ask the group to share those observations. Ask them if or how they would change their approach now that they are informed by the diverse views of the other members to arrive at a better solution.

Learning to recognize, even praise, the value that difference brings will teach you to establish respect for the other side. But *nothing* will help you value the other side more than to step in the other side's shoes. Even if just for a day.

This is what we will do in the next exercise, it is much easier read than done. In it we will attempt to kickstart your weaker side on your path to balance. Now that you have observed how others think, it's time to think like they do.

Practice Exercise
Trading Places

Group
Discussion

Target	Learn to cultivate your weaker side
Duration	60 minutes
Repeat	Repeat as a fun game using other images whenever you have the time
You'll need	A well-balanced, respectful and positive group of friends or co-workers

Get together with the same group you did the 'Establishing Respect' exercise with. Repeat the same activity of discussing a challenge, only this time, play the role that you learned to respect. It might seem simplistic, but consider taking the seat of the other and start your answer with, 'If I were to get out of my comfort zone I would address the challenge this way.'

If you tend to often Do, try to focus on observations, emotions and empathy. Try to feel and connect. Resist the urge to directly jump into action. If, on the other hand, you tend to Be, try to focus on what can be done about the situation. Plan the steps needed to get things done.

At the end of this exercise, encourage every member of the group to express how they experienced using the opposite qualities and what they struggled with.

Now that you've got a glimpse of both sides, let's practise the full process.

Both sides of our brain deserve our respect and attention. With this in mind and a bit of neuroplasticity (i.e. practice), you are now ready to access the full spectrum of your qualities.

Practice Exercise
Be–Learn–Do

Target	Follow a systematic approach to success
Duration	30 minutes (or maybe days)
Repeat	Repeat whenever you want to address a challenge
You'll need	A quiet place where you will not be interrupted, paper and a pen

Find a quiet place, set a timer and write down a particular personal challenge you'd like to address. Split the time you dedicate to the task accurately: a third for being, a third for learning and a third for doing.

When in the 'being' time, seek a comprehensive awareness of the challenge at hand. Think about it from all angles – its nature, its causes, how it affects you, how its presence shapes your behaviour and affects others, how present it is in others that you know, and so on. It is key at this stage to note your observations in the form of facts and feelings, without attempting to offer solutions or take actions. If your awareness is flowing, allocate more time to being and keep going. Let your awareness lead you. Flow.

When done, shift to 'learning', which comes in many forms. It could be learning by asking a friend to shed more light on some of your observations. Or by searching the internet for general information about your observations or the nature of your challenge. Or you can learn by reading or watching a video where others suggest steps and things to do.

Once again, stick with learning for as long as the learning flows. Don't deprive yourself of the privilege to discover and explore. Keep going for days if you need to. As a lifelong learner myself, I often do. For as long as you're still in the learning phase, resist the urge to act. Only when you feel that you are fully informed and educated should you move on to the next phase and start to 'do'.

Doing comes in many forms – from taking a small action, planning and scheduling, to having a difficult conversation, all the way to quitting your job, leaving your partner, giving up smoking or selling your home. What matters when you start to 'do' is that you commit to what you need to do. Be systematic and disciplined until the desired impact is achieved. If you notice that your actions, however, are not yielding the results you expected, then don't just change them. Go back to being. Observe why your actions did not deliver and what might have changed. Then learn whatever you need based on your new awareness before you go back to doing.

Whatever you do, remember there is one golden rule that will change your life and has the potential to change our whole world.

Very Important ! →

Be before you learn and learn before you do.

Chapter Six

Talk Talk Talk

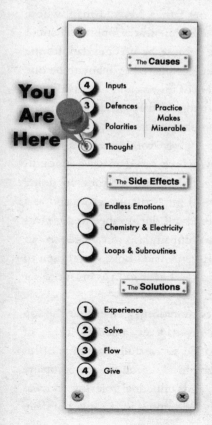

You Are Here

The Causes
4 Inputs
3 Defences — Practice Makes Miserable
Polarities
Thought

The Side Effects
Endless Emotions
Chemistry & Electricity
Loops & Subroutines

The Solutions
1 Experience
2 Solve
3 Flow
4 Give

What's 3+7? Does finding the answer to a simple maths or logic question invoke any emotion in you? Do you get emotional when cleaning the dishes?

Problem-solving and motor control skills are some of the functions your brain performs on a regular basis. As you focus on finding an answer, those thoughts don't really trigger emotions. The kinds of thoughts that most often do, however, are the ones we have when we're not paying attention, thoughts that go astray, that are not useful. Thinking: *I suck at maths* or *I will spend the rest of my life washing dishes* repeatedly inside your head are the kinds of thoughts that don't help solve problems or make any difference to the world, other than perhaps making us unhappy. This type of thought is commonly known as incessant thinking.

A Thought that Kills

We've All Been There!

All of my love for science, maths, logic and engineering, all my tendency to work hard, I got from my father. My old man, whose name was also Ali, was simply brilliant. I say that not because he was my dad. It's the truth. He was considered by many to be one of the most distinguished engineers of his era, and he contributed greatly to Egypt by starting the Bridge and Road division in the largest Egyptian construction company of its time. This division brought the business and expertise away from expensive foreign consultants and into the country, which saved massive amounts of fiscal spend and created tens of thousands of jobs. In doing so, Egypt's appetite to invest in road infrastructure grew, and as a result many roads and bridges were built during the twenty years he spent leading this division. The company was so valuable to our economy that its founder and CEO, my dad's boss, was chosen to become the minister of public works – but as soon as his successor took over, things changed for my dad.

As is often the case with big corporations, a change at the top led to a change of policy. Soon my dad was asked to let go of the division he had founded and led successfully for most of his career, to move on to run a geographical region for the company. While it was still a very strategic and influential role, my dad was so disappointed that he eventually led himself into a spiral of deep depression that lasted several years. His vitality dwindled rapidly. Signs of ageing showed on him with almost every passing week and, eventually, this depression took his life when he had a sudden heart attack at the age of fifty-eight.

This original Ali, my beloved dad, has had as much of an impact on who I am today as my son Ali. He loved me abundantly and taught me generously. When he went into depression, most people seemed to blame him for it. They knew he was smart and rational so they expected him to pull himself out of it. But that's not how depression works. Instead of pushing him, I just became a good son. I spent hours next to him, brought him what he needed and listened to him whenever he allowed himself to share. When I asked why he was sad, the same answer always came back: 'They never appreciated my work!'

As I think back on this now, I realize that this thought was wrong. It grew and grew in my father's brilliant mind, but it wasn't true. They did appreciate his work, tremendously, for more than twenty years, but somehow his brain found a way to ignore that fact. One thought that repeated itself incessantly, over and over inside his head, took my father away from me.

The night he died, I spent the whole night next to him, crying that he had left me, praying that he was safe in his new journey, apologizing for the moments when I wasn't fully there and, most of all, raging in anger at the beast that took him away — sadness. As I grew older, however, I realized that his sadness was just the symptom, that what truly took him away from me was that one thought. Looking back now, I believe it was then that my obsession with happiness started. I vowed, even though I have failed repeatedly along the path, to never let such a thought take me or a loved one ever again. It was that moment which started it all and got me here today, vowing to help a billion people abolish one of the most dangerous diseases threating humanity . . .

Incessant Thinking

Incessant thinking is defined as a loop of obsessive rumination in which you replay the same thought again and again and again. It's called rumination because the act of repetitive thinking is similar to the regurgitation of cud by 'ruminant' animals such as goats, sheep and cows. It's the act of bringing back an old thought to chew on it one more time ... Yuck.

When engaged in incessant thinking, the part of our brain that is active is known as the Default Mode Network (DMN).[1] This is a wide network of brain regions that light up when our minds wander and we find ourselves reminiscing or lost in self-referential thoughts. The DMN generally becomes active when we're thinking while not paying deliberate attention. Often those kinds of thoughts are all over the place, as if they are reaching out to explore the furthest — sometimes irrational — corners of our brains.

Watch *Inception*, my favourite movie of all time.

Some Pop to Remember

One of the most intriguing insights in Inception is how Cobb (Leonardo DiCaprio) attempts to bring his wife, Mal (Marion Cotillard), back from a long mission in the dream world by planting in her head the seed of the idea that her world is not real. By the time they went back to the real world, the idea had grown so deeply in Mal's mind that even after she woke up, she was still convinced that her world wasn't real, that they had to kill themselves in order to wake up. It was this one incessant thought, this splinter in her mind, that led to her tragic suicide.

She left me because I ate the last yoghurt in the fridge. What else could it be? She left right after she opened the fridge and I know she loves her yoghurt. Why did I do that? I could have had a bagel instead. I miss her. I will never eat yoghurt again.

Incessant thinking has a very particular character. These thoughts are self-generated and directed at ourselves or our loved ones. In the absence of deliberate attention, our thoughts look only within us to find fuel to think only about us. This gives us a clue as to the reasons why we ruminate.

When our brains are given some space and some free processing cycles, they wander to explore possible threats and opportunities that may not be found via deliberate focused thinking. It's a bit like looking for something you lost. If you can accurately remember the last time you used it, you will probably head to that specific place to look for it there. That process is analogous to deliberate thinking – the kind you have when you are actively addressing a well-defined problem. If you don't remember, however, you may start looking everywhere and just move from one place to the next, from a pocket to a shelf, exploring every possible corner to find it. This is very much like incessant thinking, only incessant thinking does not even really know what it's looking for – just that something must be missing.

Allowing yourself to roam the far corners of your thoughts freely can sometimes be incredibly valuable. It's the process by which all 'Aha' moments are found. Prime your brain with a problem and let it roam free – the results may surprise you. *How do I end this relationship without having to confront her? I know, I'll eat her yoghurt. It's her favourite thing! If I eat enough of it, she will not want to be with me any more.* Devious? Yes! But creative nonetheless, thanks to your incessant thinking. Jokes aside, some of history's greatest discoveries happened in the background of the minds of geniuses. Archimedes' eureka moment did not happen while he was deliberately addressing the problem of how to measure the volume of the irregular shapes of the king's gold. The overflowing water of the bathtub as he submerged his irregular body shape in it offered that moment of insight. Yes, sometimes flowing and overflowing thoughts help us, but thinking without regulated attention, however, most often makes us unhappy.

Matt Killingsworth, a researcher at Harvard University, conducted an interesting study using an app that asked participants to record, several times a day, what they were doing at a specific moment and how they felt. The app primarily attempted to measure if they were focused on what they were doing or if their minds were wandering and how that made them feel. The results of the study were undeniable . . .

Very Important !

A wandering mind is an unhappy mind.

Participants reported that they were significantly happier when they were focused on what they were doing. Even if they did not like what they did, focusing fully on it made the average participant happier. If the participant's mind was elsewhere, however, they tended to feel less happy, even if they actually enjoyed what they were doing.

This discovery is far more prevalent than we realize. Multiple clinical studies have identified that people experiencing depression are more prone to rumination and repetitive thoughts of shame, anger, regret and sorrow. The prefrontal cortex – which is the part of your brain that regulates attention – tends to be underactive in many clinical conditions. Attention deficit hyperactivity disorder (ADHD) is the clinical definition of that state, but unregulated attention seems to trigger other unhappy conditions such as depression, substance abuse, and anxiety.

There is undeniable evidence that patients suffering from extreme cases of unhappiness tend to ruminate more often and find it difficult to regulate their attention. They find it hard to move to the deliberate thoughts that would help improve their life situation or alleviate their state of unhappiness.

In a study led by Dr Paul Hamilton of Stanford University in July 2015, it was shown that beyond a certain point, when we fail to regulate our attention, part of our thinking starts to work against us and focus our thoughts on negativity.[2] This means that the more our mind wanders, the more negative our thoughts become. This swiftly filters into our emotions.

Our prefrontal cortex modulates or inhibits the limbic system, which is our emotional system. A weak attention regulation system makes one's emotions more reactive and out of control. In neuroscience this is known as hypofrontality and a really good example of it happens during adolescence. As our limbic systems start to kick into gear during our early teenage years, we get a lot of passion and a lot of emotion without enough prefrontal cortex functionality to moderate it, because our prefrontal cortex only develops in our late teens and early twenties.[3] The next time you witness rage or emotional rollercoasters in teens, be grateful for your ability to exert deliberate attention. Soon they will have that ability too.

While the correlation between unregulated attention and unhappiness is clear, the cause isn't. There is a debate about which leads to which. Do those of us who lack the skill of regulating our attention become sad? Or do those who practise sadness, through neuroplasticity, become less capable of deliberate attention, leading them to feel sadder?

To me, it doesn't really matter. What matters is that what we use grows, and so to reverse the trend and stop our incessant thinking from gripping us, we need to focus more on exercising deliberate attention and less on ruminating. With neuroplasticity, the more attention we exercise, the more active the right parts of the brain become. It's clear that with time and repetitive practice . . .

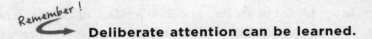

Remember!

Deliberate attention can be learned.

As a matter of fact, it's the mind wandering that can be unlearned. In the infant brain, there is limited evidence of the default network. The DMN only becomes more consistent in children aged between nine and twelve, suggesting that the DMN undergoes developmental changes that lead to unhappiness. It seems that we start life with a calmer mind and then learn to be distracted.

In that sense, our brains are like a little beast in the making – a Pitbull puppy, if you like. Train them well and they become loyal and wonderful pets that protect you and make you happy. Let them go astray and they may bite you and everyone in your path.

If I asked you to tame a beast, the first step you would take would be to observe the beast and be fully informed about its behavioural patterns. Correct?

Let me share with you some exercises to help you be aware of your brain's beastly patterns. The first thing you need to do is listen. You need to attentively observe the dialogue taking place inside your head.

I call my brain Becky (or sometimes Brian). Yes. It's the easiest way I have found to remind myself that my brain is not me, and that it's up to me if I actually want to listen to its incessant thoughts, obey or tell it to shut up. Becky speaks a lot, especially when ignored.

Awareness Exercise Meet Becky

Homework

Target	Observe how your brain talks
Duration	25 minutes
Repeat	I do this at least three to four times a week
You'll need	A quiet place, a timer, a pencil and a notepad

The best way, I have found, to calm my brain is to spend time listening to it – to meet Becky. When it feels heard, it surprisingly loses the urge to speak incessantly.

Find a quiet place where you will not be interrupted. Set your phone timer to twenty-five minutes, then place your phone face down in front of you.

This is not a mind-training meditation, so let your brain go wild. Let it come up with as many thoughts as it pleases. There are only two rules to observe:

1. Listen attentively to every thought that comes up, acknowledge it and repeat it out loud, then let it go. Don't hang on to any thought. Don't analyse it, or offer solutions. When you've acknowledged it, ask your brain for the next thought.
2. Your brain is allowed to go wherever it wants but it's not allowed to repeat any one thought twice. If it does, point it out and ask for the next thought.

This practice contradicts our natural behaviour. Normally, thoughts rush through our heads. A few of them stick like Velcro and so we let them linger. We repeat them and reinforce them with other thoughts from the same, usually negative, fabric until we build a dark cloak that covers up our clarity and insight. As for all the other thoughts, we tend to completely ignore those, so they turn into white noise in the background of our consciousness. It will take a bit of practice to learn this new skill. Observe every thought attentively, then let it go to allow another one to take its place. When you get the hang of it, your thoughts will flow in a pattern that looks something like this:

The Thought	Your Response
Oh, I did not notice the noise of the fridge before. It's annoying.	OK, the noise of the fridge is annoying us. Anything else?
My teacher hates me.	Roger that. Teacher hates us. What else?
I should remember to call Aya.	Yes. I'll take a note of that. Call Aya. Next thought?
I like football.	Cool, I like football too. Any other thoughts?
My teacher hates me.	You said that before. What else?
[Censored] you.	Don't be rude, brain. Anything else?

Don't stop until the alarm goes off. Normally you will notice two distinctive waves. First, you will notice that as soon as you listen attentively to your thoughts, what may have been a random storm of thoughts will turn into a stream. It's almost as if your brain becomes a little surprised to realize that you are listening and so adjusts its behaviour accordingly. It will parse every thought and present them to you one after the other, instead of randomly popping them up all over the place. The more you acknowledge the thoughts, the more your brain will start to think, *Whoops, (s)he's actually listening. I might as well say something intelligent.* As a result, you will notice the stream slowing down to a trickle.

By making it a point not to accept repeated thoughts, the trickle will slow down even more until it becomes a few distant drops, before it completely stops. You'll find yourself asking for the next thought and then you will observe a noticeable pause before your brain says: *Ummmm ... that's it really, I have nothing more to say!*

A long stretch of silence and pure joy will set in. This moment will be up there among the most memorable moments in your life. It will feel a lot better than your first kiss. You will remember that moment as your first bliss.

During those moments of bliss, incredible insights set in. You will observe your brain interrupt periods of long silence with fully formed insights of genius. Eureka! And if you're like me, you will find yourself extending your timer by another twenty-five minutes and then another, just to prolong the joy.

By listening attentively, you have now observed the beast. Congratulations. You have not fully tamed it yet, but I hope you have experienced what life feels like when it is tamed.

If you feel distracted or find it hard to concentrate, this exercise may become your favourite in the book. I call this exercise 'Wish You Were Here' after one of my favourite songs of all time (by Pink Floyd, of course).

Practice Exercise
Wish You Were Here

Homework

Target	Use neuroplasticity to develop the brain circuitry needed for deliberate attention
Duration	5 minutes several times a day
Repeat	Repeat for 21 days
You'll need	A quiet corner

Over the years, I have advised many of my loved ones and good friends to stick to it for twenty-one days. Independently of each other, they came back and said it changed their lives.

Deliberate attention is the backbone of happiness, and focus is the backbone of achievement and success in life. In this exercise, you will develop the skills needed for both.

Several times a day, find five minutes and start to observe the physical world around you. Play a simple game with your brain. Give it a clear instruction to seek and point out certain things or to perform a task in a way that is different from how you usually perform it. Here is a reasonably long list to keep you occupied for a few practice runs. Give your brain any of the following instructions and don't stop until the task is completed.

Hey brain, wish you were here. Find me every white (red, black, blue) thing in this room.

Hey brain, wish you were here. Tell me who the last ten people I met were.

Hey brain, wish you were here. Count downwards from 163.

Hey brain, wish you were here. Tap my index finger rhythmically for two minutes.

Hey brain, wish you were here. Read this sentence backwards, letter by letter.

Hey brain, wish you were here. How many days will it be till my mother's birthday?

Hey brain, wish you were here. Count the flowers on this bush.

Hey brain, wish you were here. Keep your eye on this fly. Don't let it escape your attention.

Hey brain, wish you were here. Tell me the lyrics of 'Wish You Were Here'. Say it, don't sing it.

Hey brain, wish you were here. Point out the number nine whenever it shows up during our commute.

Those are just a few ideas. You can create your own games. Remember that neuroplasticity is better reinforced with repetition. To develop those prefrontal cortex attention resources, you need to do a few minutes of this a few times a day (not a single long twenty-minute session once a day). Do this for twenty-one days and you will see the miracle. Thanks for being here. It's lovely to have you with us.

The true miracle of your brain shines when your attention is regulated. Find a way to be in the here and now by focusing your attention on the reality of your life, instead of the unregulated thoughts inside your head, and you will experience a world of happiness.

If asked for the top skill that enables us to find happiness, my answer always is . . . deliberate attention. Make it your reality. Stop wishing . . .

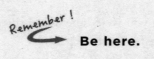

Remember!

Be here.

Summary of Part One

4-3-2-1, those are the reasons our brains make us unhappy.

4 (wrong) **Inputs** *distort our perception of the truth. Three come
from within us. Those are conditioning, recycled thoughts and trapped
emotions. But the biggest one is all-pervasive around us. It is the
hidden triggers, from the news media to the entertainment industry,
all the way to the advice of a friend that does not apply to your life
context. Don't let your thoughts be influenced by your inner inputs.
See them for what they are and weed them out. Then, whatever you
do, stop injecting your life with hidden triggers. You are what you
think. Stop letting the thoughts of others make you who you are.*

3 (exaggerated) **Defences** *keep us safe but make us suffer. Our
brains have built within them every defence mechanism that's helped
other species. A reptilian brain that lives for avoiding danger, a
mammalian brain that exists to seek rewards and avoid pain, and
a rational brain that is constantly planning and analysing. Those
defences keep us stuck in Aversion, Attachment and an All-Pervasive
Dissatisfaction. Learn to make your reptile feel safe, make your*

mammal enjoy what is and remind your rational human to see that all is OK.

2 (opposite) **Polarities** are part of every one of us. The feminine and the masculine. Those polarities are not determined by biology, gender or sexual preference. They are a way of life. One is about *being* and the other about *doing*. Our modern world, and each of us, are submerged in doing. We need more of our feminine qualities. We need to learn to be.

1 (harmful) **Thought** – the incessant type of thinking – is the result of letting our thoughts repeat, unchecked by our deliberate attention. Many clinical conditions that are associated with unhappiness are the result of scattered thoughts and mind-wandering. Learning to pay deliberate attention has always been my top advice for anyone who seeks to be happy. Be here.

Repeat a bad habit often enough, and you become really good at it because, through neuroplasticity, **Practice Makes Miserable**. Stop practising your own unhappiness. Turn the process the opposite way. Learn to go to the happiness gym and work on the habits that reverse the 4-3-2-1 model.

Practise limiting your information diet only to what's good for you. Remember to practise your gratitude muscle. Live more in the feminine and pay deliberate attention. One small step after another and your brain will be rewired for happiness to be its default state.

Part Two

The Side Effects of Thought

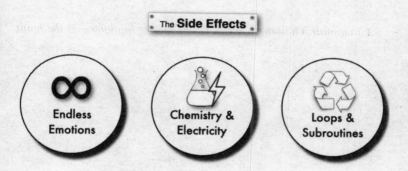

The **Side Effects**

Endless Emotions

Chemistry & Electricity

Loops & Subroutines

*Our brain doesn't seem to want to stay confined within our skull.
It ventures out, affecting our emotions and physical sensations. It
even affects its own self as it repeats thoughts of its choice over
and over again.*

Chapter Seven

Can You Feel It?

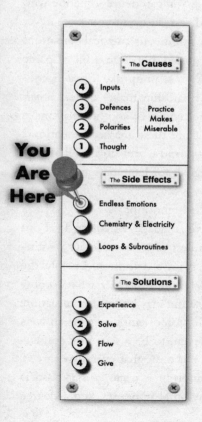

The Causes

4 Inputs
3 Defences | Practice
2 Polarities | Makes
1 Thought | Miserable

You Are Here

The Side Effects

Endless Emotions

Chemistry & Electricity

Loops & Subroutines

The Solutions

1 Experience
2 Solve
3 Flow
4 Give

As we established earlier, the primary purpose of thinking is to keep us safe. The authority of our brain, however, is not limited to the thoughts it produces. Our brains control our emotions and physical sensations too. They choose to make us feel a certain way. Your brain chooses when a certain thought starts and when it gets repeated. Like a true dictator, it controls everything within your physical form and as a result **it fully controls you**. The tools it uses include emotions, chemicals (hormones) and electrical signals, and repetitive thoughts – which we will call loops – and groups of thought that cluster together, which we will call subroutines.

The Making of Emotions

We feel so much emotion every minute of every day – anger, happiness, excitement, anxiety, lust – the list goes on and on, and when there are no emotions, we feel boredom. Those sensations are not necessarily associated with a physical trigger. Nothing needs to touch your physical form or interact with it in any way for you to feel empathy, for example. You can desire someone who you have never met in person and fear an event you have never experienced. Emotions may even numb our physical sensations or mimic them. You may feel exhausted, but then a bit of panic would mask your fatigue and make you jump like a flea. Sometimes desperation due to repeated hardship makes us feel *numb*, and disapproval of the unethical behaviour of another may make us feel *sick* to our stomachs. What are these magical sensations? How do they arise? What is their purpose and how well are we engaging with them to reach our goals for happiness and success? The answers are fascinating.

Let's start at the basics. What is an emotion?

Because English is not my native language, whenever I set out to write about any concept, regardless of its complexity or simplicity, I start with a Google search for a definition. Luckily, the language barrier humbles me and reminds me that what I know may not be accurate – the true meaning may be lost in translation.

Have you ever looked for a definition of emotion? The answers will surprise you. There does not seem to be a scientific consensus. I could find many definitions but none that everyone agreed.

Wikipedia started with: 'An emotion is *a mental state* associated with thoughts, feelings, behavioural responses, and a degree of pleasure or displeasure.' A Google search returned: 'Emotion (noun) is *a strong feeling* deriving from one's circumstances, mood, or relationships with others.' The Encyclopaedia Britannica defined it as: 'Emotion, a complex *experience* of consciousness, bodily sensation, and behaviour that reflects the personal significance of a thing, an event.'

Is it a feeling? A mental state? Or an experience? What is it?

How can something as pervasive and impactful as our emotions have no agreed definition, and how can I work on anything as an engineer if I don't even know what it is? Even more interestingly, as an engineer, my definition of this emotion thing happens to be different from all of these. We'll come to that in a minute. But first, let's investigate further and see how emotions are expressed across the world.

Comfortably Numb

Perhaps the reason why we don't have a definition is because the modern world looks down on emotions. In the Western world, specifically, showing your emotions or your vulnerabilities is considered weak. We hide behind our workplace culture: fake it till you make it (the worst advice in the history of humanity), peer pressure and the need to show your best in order to be accepted. We choose to show the mask of a happy, well-functioning, successful individual to the world when, in reality, we're more like a mushy, sensitive softy on the inside. We take the stance of superheroes when, in reality, we need to be rescued.

We are told to hide our emotions, so we choose to hide them from ourselves too. Then we choose not to feel them. They're easier to hide when we, ourselves, are unaware they exist. When asked how we feel, we answer, we're just fine! Without even consulting with our true emotions.

We do it day after day until we become comfortable with our own lie. We become comfortably numb.

'Comfortably Numb'

Pink Floyd's legend.
What can I say? Just listen.

When it comes to hiding our emotions, men, generally, have it worse than women. Across cultures globally, boys are told they're not supposed to cry. They're expected to 'man up' and suppress their emotions.

This separation from how we feel is deeply ingrained in us; it makes us grit our teeth in the face of adversity and say: *It doesn't hurt.* Even when we're in agony. The only way to deal with the pain over the years is to pretend it does not exist. So many men become numb and oblivious to how they feel. Then we blame them for not being emotionally available. For not opening their hearts. But I can assure you, boys do cry.

Often I meet men who seem to be keeping it all together until they connect with their true emotions, and then they start to cry and cry for their lost years of emotional self-oppression. I almost fell into that trap myself.

In the beginning, I copied the actions of those around me. When asked how I was, I would mechanically answer: 'I'm doing great.' But then I stopped. I realized that I was lying. Sometimes I was having a tough day, and sometimes things were outright painful, and so I changed. For years, as I walked the corridors of our offices, when someone asked, 'How are you doing, Mo?' I would stop, look the person in the eyes, pause and think a little.

Then I would say something like, 'I feel physically energetic today, but I am a bit stressed because of such and such project ... How about you? How do you feel today?' At first, people would be a bit thrown. This was not the scenario they expected. They would freeze for a few seconds, then snap back into robot mode and say ... 'I'm just fine.' Later, so many people came to me and complimented me for being authentic and for showing my vulnerabilities. I could feel many of them trying to get closer to me, trying to get to know me better.

When I later asked them why they wanted to be friends, they often said, 'Because you're real. It's refreshing.'

This phenomenon of suppressing our emotions in the modern world does not end as we punch out of work. I have so many friends who come and cry in front of me, complaining about how their romantic relationship is driving them crazy. They recite long lists of things they need and deserve that their partner is not providing and when I ask them, 'Have you expressed those needs and emotions openly?' they look at me strangely and say, 'Of course not. It would scare him /her away.' They keep it bottled up inside until the mounting emotions finally explode and scare their partner away.

One day I asked a friend – who was a senior HR executive (at a different company) – why emotions have been banished from the workplace and why they are often even suppressed within work and personal relationships. She said, 'Well, emotions are too diverse. They seem to be irrational and unpredictable. They pop up unexpectedly and then they can become too intense. It's too confusing. We don't think people should bring their emotions to work. We don't have the infrastructure to handle such uncertainty and, in any case, work is about delivering results. Predictability is what we need. It's just easier this way.'

I completely disagree! Who are we fooling? Don't we all know that those who don't show emotions are just pretending? In recent years, with the rise of awareness around mental health and its impact on the wellbeing and productivity of everyone around us, we are starting to realize that this kind of challenge can no longer be ignored. Emotion left unexpressed is a disaster waiting to happen and the results are showing up more and more in the cost that mental health issues, in terms of burnout, lower engagement and medical bills, are adding to the balance sheet.

Besides, contrary to common belief, emotions are surely predictable. When someone pisses me off, I get pissed off. That seems predictable enough to me. After that conversation with my friend, I found myself trying to bust the myth that emotions are irrational. I felt a need to reverse this left-brained bullying – we should be allowed to live like complete humans who not only think but also feel. I told myself that perhaps, if I could succeed in the impossible target of proving the rationality of emotions, people would grant themselves the licence to feel again. Perhaps then they would open up and express how they feel and we humans would find a way to connect again.

Where do I start to work on this problem? Well, for me, there's only one path. When confused, I resort to maths.

Hyperpredictable

Before our technology could identify the existence of germs, what did people think? Back then it all seemed like the roll of a massive dice. People fell sick and no one knew why. Then, as the village prepared to dig their graves, people sometimes recovered and no one had a clue what had saved them.

Now, due to the advancements in modern science, disease seems to follow a predictable process. Think about it: today we know that when you catch the flu, this is the result of a microscopic germ – the flu virus that enters your body and finds a favourable environment to spread and infect your health. We know that the virus causes the flu but the fever is the result of your immune system fighting it, and the inflammation is the result of different germs – bacteria that capitalize on your weakened immunity. There's no voodoo involved. It's all predictable!

It all must have seemed very irrational until we understood the science behind it – the little germs that the eye can't see. The same is true with emotions!

Germs trigger illness and . . .

Remember!

Our thoughts trigger our emotions.

This is true for every emotion you have ever felt (other than unconditional love, but that's a topic for another book).

Although it feels otherwise – because when we are emotional, thoughts rush frantically through our heads – the truth is that the emotion is first triggered by a very specific thought. Then, when we are in the rush of emotions, a flood of thoughts takes over as our brain attempts to analyse what's happening. There's no chicken-and-egg confusion here. The chicken (a thought in your head) lays the eggs (the emotions), which then hatch into more thoughts, leading to more emotions.

If a woman, for example, feels anxious and irritable because her boyfriend didn't call or text her for a while, she might have a flood of thoughts such as: *Should I call him or will that be too clingy? But if I don't, it would mean I don't care. I need to lose weight to stay attractive for him. I shouldn't let him spend so much time with his friends. No, no, I should embrace his freedom.*

Every thought triggers a slightly different emotion but, at the core of it all, a very specific thought triggered the avalanche.

Perhaps the thought *Has he lost interest in me?* or *Does he not love me?*

Personally, I find this to be true every single time. Some thought seeps into our heads and then the emotion erupts. And here's where the maths comes in.

I dare to say that the path a thought follows to trigger your emotions is as predictable as Newton's laws of motion. And if anything follows a predictable repeatable pattern, then it can be described with maths. Emotions are that predictable. They are so predictable, as a matter of fact, that they can each be summarized, for the maths geeks reading, in a simple mathematical equation.

Envy, for example, is an emotion that is triggered by the thought *I wish I had what another person has, but I don't.* It is a comparison between what you wish you could have (which another has) and what you actually have. This makes . . .

$$\text{Envy} = \text{What another has (which I wish I had)} - \text{What I have}$$

Regret always has one thought at the heart of it: *I wish I had done things differently.* Which makes . . .

$$\text{Regret} = \text{What I wish I had done} - \text{What I actually did}$$

The same is true, of course, for happiness and unhappiness. Every single time you have ever felt unhappy, it was because of the thought: *An event in my life has missed my expectations (hopes, wishes and beliefs) for how life should be.*

$$\text{Happiness} \geq \text{The events of your life} - \text{Your expectations of how life should be}$$

You get the idea. Fear is when my perception of safety at a moment in the future (T_1) is less than my perception of safety now (T_0).

$$\text{Fear} \geq \text{Perception of safety @ } T_0 - \\ \text{Perception of safety @ } T_1$$

Anxiety is a thought that says: *I am not capable of handling the expected threat.*

$$\text{Anxiety} \geq \text{What I need to feel safe } - \\ \text{What I think I am capable of}$$

Panic happens when the threat triggering our fear is imminent.

$$\text{Panic} \geq 1 \, / \, \text{The perceived time before} \\ \text{an imminent danger}$$

I could go on and on and on. I love simplified mathematics. But I will leave that up to you. Take a few minutes now, perhaps, to think about the logic, not necessarily the maths, that drives other prominent emotions. What thought triggers pride? Optimism? Trust? Lust? When you know the trigger, you will become much more capable of dealing with your emotions when they arise because . . .

Very Important !

Emotions are as predictable as Newton's laws of motion.

The Elephant in the Room

Emotions are also predictable in that they don't just fade away. An emotion that's not allowed to be felt, expressed and shared tends to reside inside us and grow into a little monster.

We hurt ourselves and others when we prevent ourselves from expressing how we feel fully. Obviously, I'd understand if you decided to withdraw your emotions from someone who was harsh or disrespectful — it is good to be selective when it comes to sharing our vulnerable side. But to shut off completely is a disaster. It's an explosion waiting to happen.

You witness those explosions yourself over and over. They manifest as the burnout of a colleague at work under stress or the emotional outburst of a loved one. When pent-up emotions are finally released, they do so with so much energy that they can be destructive. If they were released as they were felt, their energy would have been gentler.

The reasons we don't open up to others are plenty, including fear of being hurt, judged or taken advantage of. But most importantly, we don't open up to others because we close down to our own selves. Our modern-world programming is so ingrained in us that we stop expressing our emotions even to ourselves. We deny their existence and let our numbness take us through a cold and unfulfilled life without the joy of fully feeling. When we don't acknowledge how we feel and fully embrace it, we don't share it with others. Sharing emotions is the only way we, as humans, can truly connect. If we share a space, a meal or an intellectual conversation with someone without showing our emotions fully, we become robots. We say words we don't mean, often words we learn at work, or from the simulated characters on TV and social media, and the conversation becomes intellectual-cerebral. Brains

talking to brains. Without emotional connectio
even when surrounded by millions of other peopl
tions, so much seems to be missing because . . .

Remember !

→ **We only feel alive when we feel.**

A Butterfly in the Palm of Your Hand

Our emotions are fragile. They are delicate. They need to be held tenderly, with love and acceptance, and allowed the space they need to become strong enough to reveal themselves. Hold your heart kindly like a delicate butterfly in the palm of your hand. Don't blame it for feeling what it feels.

When you deal with your heart, and its gushing emotions, picture a cute six-year-old girl that fell and hurt her knee. How would you treat her if she cried, if she screamed? Would you discipline her and tell her that what she feels is unwarranted? Or would you hold her, even as she screams, understand her feelings and tell her that all will be OK?

Treat your heart with kindness until it is ready to feel and then take it further: help others feel. Please remember that your approach to others can help them open up and get in touch with their deepest emotions too. **Hold space** – allow those who interact with you to feel safe enough to show you how they feel. **Don't judge** – if you had walked in their shoes you might have felt the same way. **Empathize** – treat others as you would wish to be treated if you felt as vulnerable as they do. One day, regardless of how tough you think you are, you will be there too.

Try this, even if for a day. Feel freely and let others feel in your presence, and your whole world will change. People will start to flock to you, seeing you as a sanctuary, a rare safe zone, someone to whom they can show who they really are. When the masks drop and the emotions flow, you will find true joy – the joy of connecting with other humans, as humans rather than robots shaped by the iron fist of society. If you don't mind me saying, it's a joy that's as good as the best sex you ever had, only without the physical touch. It's what true intimacy is all about – connecting to someone's essence.

Perhaps when we stop judging those who embrace and express their emotions, perhaps when we allow ourselves to feel and show our emotions freely, we will remember the core of what makes us human and that emotions are the spice of life; without them our life would be bland and tasteless. Love, laughter, excitement – even a bit of insecurity, shyness and regret – are the moments when we actually learn, love and live.

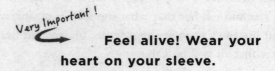

Very Important !

Feel alive! Wear your heart on your sleeve.

When you feel, you start to 'be'. As your emotions become part of your awareness, you will see your truth. **Feeling is the only way to 'be'! It's the first step on your path to happiness.**

Feel and fully embrace how you feel. And though it may seem hard at first, all you need is to stay true to your intention. With time, neuroplasticity will work in your favour. Feeling after feeling will rewire your brain, and that will make the act of feeling itself easier.

Learning to Feel

Did you first resist when I said emotions were predictable? Did you gasp a little when you read further? Did you think to yourself: *Damn, he's right. They are predictable (as in, they are generated as a result of a path we can logically define and trace). They can be described with equations. Sooooo cool!*

I hope you did because to fully grasp this concept marks a pivotal turning point in becoming the caring custodian of your emotions – to set them free but still direct them to where they should be.

You know what else is hyperpredictable? Neuroplasticity. As discussed above, it's common to say that people never change, but that's not true. I was a depressed, angry control freak when I was in my late twenties. Look at me now: I am as calm and chilled as a turtle. Neuroplasticity, over time, always works. Even when it comes to our emotional habits, with practice and determination we can change.

Neuroplasticity applies to every process that is initiated in the brain. The parts of your brain that you use more often become stronger. This means that, just as with memories and skills . . .

Very Important !

The emotions you practise, over time, become easier to feel.

You may have noticed this in a friend or yourself before. Those who have a temper seem to find it easier to develop a temper, and those who seem mostly calm become calmer and calmer over time. We find it easier to feel what we frequently feel. We love our drama. *She said this, he did that.* It breaks your heart but still you keep repeating the same story over and over. Every time you tell it you strengthen your neural networks; not only the ones related to the memory but also the ones related to the emotion. In doing so, you learn to break your heart again and again. You become a little bit better at breaking it with every passing cycle, until you become the best at breaking your own heart. We value our fear, we think it keeps us safe, so we seek more of it. We watch more news, more opinions and more conspiracy theorists. We look for what scares us, and we find it, so it scares us into searching for more until we become the best at being scared.

It's natural for your emotional skills to develop like any other skill. To engage a certain emotion, you need to engage specific parts of the brain as you develop a type of thought or recall a particular memory. As you do this, the neurons you use establish a stronger network, corresponding to the way that emotion is gen- erated, between them. Conversely, the ones you don't use — the ones you need to engage a different emotion — become weaker until the networks between them fade.

Believe it or not, to become angry, fragile or upset is a skill, like any other skill. The more you practise it, the more it becomes you.

So ... which are your skills?

Which of your brain muscles have been working out to take over your emotional landscape? And, more importantly, what are you going to do about it?

Just like practising anger, over time, makes it easier for you to get angry, so too you can practise feeling grateful and exercise that muscle. You can practise contentment. You can practise desire for the one you love. You can practise amusement and awe for all the beauty life has to offer. You can practise liking, even admiring, the good in all that surrounds you (and stop practising criticism and negativity). Most importantly, you can practise love, self-love and compassion.

The first step you need to take in order to change what you

practise is to become aware. The model is clear: Be before you learn and learn before you do. We need to start with being and there is nowhere better to start the practice than to become fully convinced of how emotions work. Here's a little exercise for that. I call it Observe the Drama.

The purpose of this exercise is to help you observe, in action, the process of turning thoughts into emotions. By observing how changing the thought changes your emotion, you will be convinced without a doubt that emotions are a product of the brain. They do get triggered by your thoughts.

Awareness Exercise
Observe the Drama

Target	Observe how your brain turns thoughts into emotions
Duration	15 minutes
Repeat	Repeat till the concept is firmly integrated
You'll need	A quiet place where you will not be interrupted

Find a quiet place and allow yourself ample time.

Recall two emotional memories – one happy and one sad. Reflect deeply on how each memory makes you feel.

Try to name the feeling in one word.

Write down the series of events that led to that feeling. Then write down a specific dominant thought that those events triggered which you can associate most closely with the emotion e.g. *I felt humiliated* or *Everyone admired my achievement*.

Now, take a few seconds to clear your mind, then start to alternate between the two thoughts. Invite the happy thought, *Everyone admired my achievement*, into your mind along with the memories in context and see if you can regenerate the emotion. Then close your eyes, think of ice cream for a few seconds, or sing out loud as a form of distraction. When the happy thought is no longer in your mind, think the second thought, *I felt humiliated*, and see how that makes you feel.

Observe how the emotion is regenerated when you rethink the thought, how that emotion was not there before the thought was triggered, and how it disappears when you stop thinking it.

Without that thought, there's no emotion. The thoughts are the trigger.

This is not an easy exercise. You don't have to get it right the first time. Keep trying till you do.

We have been conditioned to believe that emotions are just things we randomly feel – that they arise without a cause. Success here is when you learn to pay attention to this important link between thoughts and emotions. Keep practising until you see how each different thought triggers a different story, a different drama and a different emotion.

The purpose of this exercise is to give you a priceless opportunity to stay connected to your emotions. By using the frequent triggers that society throws at us, we can find our own precious awareness.

Awareness Exercise
Don't Say: I'm Fine

Homework

Target   Frequently get in touch with your emotions

Duration	2 minutes – several times a day
Repeat	Repeat for the rest of your life
You'll need	To stay alert and do the right thing

Do you notice how you respond when someone asks how you are? Do you notice yourself mechanically responding, 'I'm OK!' when sometimes you actually are not?

How often do you robotically respond to someone by saying, 'I'm doing just fine'? They're not listening and you're actually not communicating. There are words being exchanged between you but no real human connection. It's time to end this.

In this simple practice, please take a moment of reflection before you answer whenever someone asks you how you are.

Don't say, 'I'm fine.' Instead, try to use the opportunity to find out how you actually feel. 'I feel energetic, with a bit of pain in my thumb because of typing too much on my phone.' Or, 'I feel a bit irritated after having spent an hour in traffic, but I am glad I could still make it here on time.' Or, 'I feel anxious about the report I need to submit tomorrow, but I'm excited about how my date went last night! I'm also a bit constipated.'

The next time someone asks, 'What's wrong?' don't just say, 'Nothing!'

Instead, ask in return, 'Why do you ask? Does it look like there is something wrong? Give me a minute. Let me check what's inside.'

Learn to be curious about how you feel. Make responding to this kind of micro-awareness trigger your habit. It will boost your ability to frequently get in touch with yourself.

Remember !

Find out how you actually feel.

To help you keep track of how you feel, download the free version of Appii from the App Store or Google Play store. Appii, like a fitness app, will track your mood and customize your happiness journey to fit your exact needs.

Use the promo code ThatLittleVoice to get a three-month premium subscription for free.

As part of your mission to spread happiness, help others to get in touch with their emotions. When someone mechanically answers your question about how they are, stop them and say: 'Tell me more. What has been going on?' Be curious and listen attentively. Show empathy. You'll be surprised how much people will open up and connect. It's a true win-win for both you and them.

Now may be a very good time to take a little break and check in with yourself to see how you feel right now. How have things been recently? Have you been fully experiencing your emotions?

Emotions are important and should not be ignored, censored or suppressed. Take a bit of time to reflect on the place they occupy in your life and what we've discussed about them so far. When you feel relaxed and fresh, please continue to read. There are a few more crucial emotional skills we still need to learn and practise.

The biggest skill to learn here is how to bring any change in your mood instantly to your attention.

This will feel very alien at first. Countless emotions will slip by unnoticed but, with practice, you'll get the hang of it and capture critical emotions the minute they pop up.

Awareness Exercise
On Alert

Homework

Target	Notice when your emotions change
Duration	An interrupt level, once set, remains to be always on
Repeat	Make this a lifestyle. Repeat for as long as is needed
You'll need	A lot of practice

Take any negative emotion that you often show — say anger, shyness or boredom — and start monitoring it for the next few days. Stay alert and pinpoint with high accuracy when that emotion surfaces. Keep a record in a journal if you like. Every time you spot that emotion, add a tick to your record.

As the emotion you are monitoring comes up, I ask you to become 'fully embodied', i.e. completely in touch with how you physically feel in response. Start with noticing how you feel when no negative emotions are affecting you. This peaceful calmness is felt in your body as a sense of relaxation and ease. When a negative emotion takes over, this state changes. For example, when you are anxious you will physically feel abdominal discomfort. We will discuss this in detail shortly. I call it the physical signature of an emotion, and it pays to master that link between our emotional and our physical states. For now, however, just notice the change – the shift away from your calm peacefulness into any other state. This allows you to recognize the change in your emotional state just as you recognize pain, pleasure and fatigue.

This is an awareness exercise, so there's no action required. Don't attempt to fix anything about the way you feel. Just learn to notice the change every time it shows. Becoming aware of those physical changes will count as your interrupt level – the awareness you need to recognize that your routine needs to change.

At the end of every day, take stock of your emotions. Spend a few minutes in bed before you fall asleep acknowledging how the day went and the emotion that you felt. Take note of the physical signature, the sensation in your body that is associated with each emotion.

When you've got the hang of that emotion, add another to your record, and then another and another until you have all your recurring negative emotions fully recorded.

For each of your emotions, try to reflect on the sequence of events that triggered them. Try to find some repetitive patterns – for example, *Every time someone told me I was wrong, I got angry and defensive*, or *I usually get shy when I am expected to speak in front of someone I don't know well*. Once again, don't attempt to plan corrective actions. Just observe. Just be.

This may take you weeks to master. Until you do, keep practising. While you do, read on. We are only at the start of this rabbit hole.

Experiencing the Storm

Do you know how many people ask Google questions? Billions. Sometimes, when important news breaks, billions of people search for the same information at the same time. How does Google manage to answer them all? By considering each of them to be a separate request and handling each one all the way through to its completion. While our human brain never chooses to engage in billions of transactions, it is often distracted by many requests and demands that arrive concurrently. Any parent of several kids knows how that feels. One needs a diaper change, while another is crying because the third hit him and yet another is asking for a cookie. How do they do it? By shutting off the distraction as they finish changing the diaper, before attending to the one crying and then reaching out to open the cookie jar. We learn to recognize an incoming flow of tasks, prioritize them and handle them each to completion. Many of us, however, fail to do that with our emotions. When they arise, we fail to acknowledge them, prioritize them or act upon them. Instead, we suppress them. I am no exception. As a driven, analytical-minded business executive, I ignored my emotions for years until I realized that I would never be complete until I had fully integrated them. To do that, I needed to learn to . . .

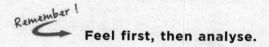

Remember! **Feel first, then analyse.**

I believe there are four distinct reasons why we have created a world that's so devoid of emotions. These are societal traditions and pressures, emotional storms, emotional camouflage, and emotional discomfort.

We've discussed how the societal traditions and pressures affect us enough in this book so far. Let's discuss the other three.

Emotional Storms

One reason many of us don't acknowledge many of our emotions is because we never really experience only one emotion at any one moment. Can you recall a moment when you felt only one crisp, clear emotion that you could parse and say, this is it, this is how I feel? I'm sure this does not happen that often. There is always a storm raging — a storm of good and bad, happy and sad, physical and emotional sensations — inside each of us.

Allow me to reflect deep inside me to find out and tell you exactly how I feel right now . . . *I'm very happy with the progress I've been making on this book. I am optimistic that it will be ready soon. Aya, my daughter, told me she's a bit down because someone she loves is not feeling well. My heart hurts for her heartache. As always, I feel intense love for her, and I miss her. I feel humbled that so many people around the world have been thanking me for my work. This makes me feel motivated to work harder, but I also feel a bit guilty that I am unable to answer all the messages I receive. My sinuses hurt a tiny bit. My left-hand thumb hurts from typing on my phone. Oh, and I'm hungry.*

All of this combined does not even begin to accurately describe how I feel — but you get the picture.

Remember!

We always experience storms of emotions and physical sensations . . .

. . . which makes it hard to parse any one specific emotion or even recognize its tones and characters, when blended with the characters of all the other emotions and sensations we feel at any point in time.

The storm is giant. Just take a look at the word collage I've included here to reflect on the breadth and variety of all the emotions that you can feel.

This image, are at least a part of it, is what is often happening inside you. Picture that.

Like with colour theory, any one colour, say beige, is made up of several elementary colours mixed in very specific ratios. A talented artist has the skill needed to deconstruct a colour into its constituents. This kind of skill is what we need when it comes to deconstructing emotional storms.

What you feel right now is not a single emotion. It's a blend of several emotions and physical sensations. You can learn to deconstruct your experience into a mix of well-defined emotions. It starts with observing the physical signature of every emotion. I will come back to this after understanding another emotional block that this can also help with . . .

Emotional Camouflage

Emotions are signposts. Your brain uses them to sum up heaps of analysis into an emotion. Feeling concerned is not a result of observing one indication of threat. It's an extended analysis, performed by your brain in the background, of many observations, memories, assessments of one's own capabilities and so on. Emotions, then, typically morph and hide among many other equally complex emotions. Sometimes, it's hard to tell if you're driven by purpose or by ego, if you are running for desire or from fear. You need to accurately understand how emotions work, so it becomes easier to spot them.

When Aya was a young child, she was full of energy and curiosity (she still is). This made her wander and explore whenever we went out. A few minutes after walking into a shopping mall, if we didn't hold young Aya's hand firmly, something would catch her attention and she would follow it and disappear somewhere, not to be found. No matter how often that happened, panic always set in (both for Aya wherever she was and her mother next to me). The panic would make Aya rush around trying to find us. This would simply take her further and further away, making it even more difficult to locate her. For months we attempted to convince her to stay alert and stick to us wherever we were. Obviously with her active, creative mind, that did not prove to be viable. Eventually, I had to deal with the reality, so I asked her to remember one thing, and one thing only: 'Whenever you look around you and can't find us, don't move. Stay exactly where you are.'

This simple request was the result of a lot of analysis on my part. I realized that for a while she was going to continue to wander and that at her young age there was no way I could change that. I realized that the panic made things much worse both for her and her mother. And, of course, I realized that in times of panic, it's difficult to make complex choices, especially for a child. Sum all of that up into one simple instruction and it becomes much easier to remember and harder to ignore. Even today, twenty years later, Aya and I still joke about it when we go out together. I say: 'Aya, if we lose each other what should you do?' She laughs, hugs me and says: 'Stay in my place.'

This kind of simplification is what our brains do to sum up a complex range of situations. Some negative behaviour from a friend combines with a comment you hear on the radio, some cold winter conditions and the absence of sunshine for a week, and your brain concludes: *Let's just switch on the feeling lonely indicator.*

Nice story, Mo, how does this help me? Well, there's a coding system that is used by our brain to make us feel emotions after it's done with its complex analysis. It's almost impossible to trace an emotion from its complex origins. It's easier to let it happen and then handle its signature – its impact on you. The way our brains make us feel emotions is actually quite physical. Every emotion, regardless of what triggers it, eventually has a very specific signature that you can feel in your body. Those sensations act as signposts for what it is that you're feeling. They help you pinpoint your emotions by examining the physical symptoms associated with them, just like a physician would when examining your physical state to check for disease. They don't always do a lab test or analyse what you did for the last few days, at least not at first. Instead, they look for the symptoms.

Butterflies in your stomach. A lump in your throat. Those are more than just clichéd expressions. Let's take a couple of extreme emotions as examples. Allow me to start with an emotion that's very physical in its expression – lust.

Lust is an easy one to physically spot. There are clear physical symptoms associated with that emotion which are almost impossible to miss. Do I need to list those down? I'm sure you get it.

For someone who is very emotionally aware, detecting the physical signature of other emotions is not much harder. Panic, for example, is an emotion the brain uses to prepare the body for a flight response in the face of an imminent threat. Even if the threat is not physical, panic is felt all over the body in the form of a surge of energy mixed with the desire to run away. Anger, on the other hand, is the emotion that prepares us for a fight response. When you're angry, your blood is boiling, your whole body feels tense and you feel a desire to attack. When you're afraid, your heart pounds, your thoughts race and you want to hide. Disgust makes you feel sick. It feels the same whether it's triggered by eating something bad or by the unethical behaviour of another. You feel it in your stomach. You recoil and try to avoid the trigger of your disgust. Sadness makes you feel empty. Your body feels weak and you feel overwhelmed with a tendency to withdraw. Excitement gets you energized. Your thoughts become optimistic and you feel an openness to engage and seek more. And so forth.

On a much deeper level, some specific emotions that result from unique personal experiences come with their very own signatures. Missing my wonderful son, Ali, has a very distinct physical signature. When the thought of missing him takes over, I feel a sharp, deep wound in the bottom right-hand corner of my heart, as if that part is missing. It feels as intense today as on the day he left. I've learned to recognize that pain because I use it as the trigger that keeps me going with my mission. As soon as I feel as if a sharp object is penetrating that part of my heart, I jump out of my seat and tell myself it's time to honour Ali and create something that will make another one thousand people happy today.

These physical symptoms are mainly the result of the chemical language the brain masterminds through the use of hormones. The surge of energy we feel during panic or anger is the result of secretion of adrenaline in the bloodstream. The energy we feel when excited is the result of dopamine. They feel different and affect us very differently. We will discuss the chemical workings of our brain in the next chapter. So, hang in there and stay focused on your emotions for now. We have one more reason for denying ourselves the openness to fully feel and embrace our emotions and that is . . .

Emotional Discomfort

You don't need an essay to help you find this in yourself. Sometimes the reason we refuse to acknowledge our emotions is simply that . . . they feel uncomfortable. We all have times when we do not want to feel the pain of the alcohol touching our wounds. We think that by ignoring the wound it will eventually go away.

In the famous analysis of the five stages of grief — the work of Elisabeth Kübler-Ross and David Kessler[1] — the first stage is denial. In the case of loss, our first reaction is to tell ourselves that nothing happened. Denial is the brain's way of attempting to avoid the pain. But the pain always catches up with us. Sooner or later, it becomes too much to ignore.

Any doctor will tell you that it's always better to attend to an infection as soon as you feel the pain. The earlier the treatment, the easier the cure.

What's funny is that even positive emotions sometimes suffer the same fate. We refuse to feel the full joy of love sometimes because the emotional storm it brings also includes fear. We fear that love won't last and so we don't fully embrace it. We'd rather stay neutral to avoid the possibility of a future heartbreak than dive in completely and feel the joy, excitement and rush of the moment. This is wrong.

Emotions are what make us human. Even the difficult ones make us feel alive. Besides . . .

Remember!

You can't improve what you can't observe.

The model is clear. Be before you learn and learn before you do. Feel first then analyse. **There is no way you can even begin to work on your own emotions and find a path to happiness if you don't acknowledge them to start with.**

We need to notice as soon as our emotions rise. We need to feel comfortable in the presence of our gushing emotions. To allow an emotion to be, first we need to learn to . . .

Sit With It

Close your eyes now. Imagine a child. She runs to you to tell you how much fun it was in the playground and that she could swing high and see the sky. What would you do?

Would you tell her you're too busy? Would you explain to her, logically, that being too excited sometimes blurs one's judgement? Would you tell her that swinging high is not a big deal and that she should set herself more ambitious targets?

Imagine a child that's crying because she's lost and can't find her mother. What would you do?

Would you tell the child to toughen up? Would you blame her for straying away? Would you use logic to explain the steps to be taken until her mother is found? Would you ask for a practical plan to make sure such mistakes never happen again? No. You would . . .

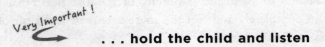

Very Important!

. . . hold the child and listen

You are that wounded, excited, anxious, shy, confused child. You are every emotional child that ever needed a hug.

We never aged a day beyond those emotional moments. We've just forced ourselves to suppress our emotions as we got older. We deprive ourselves from this highly needed hug.

The basis for processing trauma in psychology is to gradually walk towards that which one is trying to avoid, to allow the patient the space to discover, acknowledge and process the residual emotions that have not been resolved. Perhaps allowing ourselves to let the emotions surface before they remain in our psyche and wear us down is a wise approach; we should cleanse the negativity before it torments us.

Instead of avoiding our emotions, we should approach them. Let them surface just like we allow a child to express what's inside. We should learn to hold our own selves as we would hold a child – tenderly. And if at first this process makes us feel uncomfortable, we should learn to **sit with it**.

Part of sitting with an emotion is to allow for a space between the rise of the emotion and all the actions you may want to take as a result.

Very Important !

'Between stimulus and response there is a space. In that space is our power to choose our response. In our response lies our growth and our freedom.'

Fun fact: This quote is often wrongly attributed to Viktor Frankl. It was popularized by the influential motivational author Stephen Covey who could never recall who originally said it[2].

I am asking you to sit calmly in that space, even if it feels uncomfortable, and fully embrace the emotion but ignore the urge to react. Tough, I know, but totally liberating.

To hold your emotion tenderly and sit with it, you need to keep one firm belief in mind . . .

Remember !

> **No emotion can ever hurt you unless you grant it the power to do so.**

Emotions are not external events that threaten us. They are felt within us. An emotion triggered by an event in the past does not regenerate the event or recreate the pain. An emotion triggered by a thought about the future will not set the future in motion (though you do need to be careful about manifesting negativity in your life by lending it too much of your energy). **An emotion starts and ends within you**. Sit with it.

Moreover, no emotion is good or bad. An emotion is just what it is. It is what you feel and **what you feel is always true** – for you. Remember that you are always allowed to feel what you feel. Your path through life so far already has got you here where you're supposed to feel it.

Through it all, remember that regardless of how uncomfortable our emotions sometimes feel, here is the silver lining . . .

Remember !

> **We only feel when we're alive and we're only alive when we feel.**

The joy of fully feeling – anything really – is found in the joy of living. To feel what you feel is to recognize the lifeblood pumping through your veins. It reminds you that you are here to experience another day, that you're alive, and that's always a good thing, don't you agree?

There is no way I can explain any of what we've discussed here well enough using words. You need to feel it for yourself. So let's practise . . .

Every emotion is unique in its physical signature.

This exercise will bring you to the awareness of how you physically feel when an emotion takes over. Physical sensations are easier to recognize than emotions, especially when your emotion is but one small part of a storm.

Awareness Exercise
Feel the Emotion (Physically)

Group Discussion

Target	Experience the physical signature of emotions
Duration	60 minutes
Repeat	Repeat as long as you see value to the conversation
You'll need	A group of trusted, positive friends
	Note: If you prefer to work through this alone, that's fine too – just adjust the exercises accordingly. Refer to atlasofemotions.org for more insights

This exercise is good to do with a friend or group of friends.

Find a quiet place and plan a lot of free time.

Do a quick scan of your body. Sit upright, relax and take account of your current physical state. This state marks the starting point – call it the control state.

Think of an emotion to investigate. Attempt to recall an emotional memory that can trigger this specific emotion and allow yourself to feel it as intensely as you can.

Now, take a few minutes to scan your body again and check for any changes as compared to the control state. These changes might be subtle, so you need to be fully in tune with how your body feels. Obviously, the more intensely you manage to recreate the emotion, the more vividly you will be able to recognize its physical signature. Make a note of the emotion and its physical signature. Stop frequently and feel fully. Add what you feel to your notes. Discuss and exchange notes with the group. After your conversation, check the description of that emotion and its physical signature on atlasofemotions.org.

Repeat these steps for another emotion. Take a systematic approach to this and bring up a variety of emotions so you learn the full spectrum of all physical signatures. Take as long as you need to explore as many different emotions as you can.

Emotions never come solo, they come in storms.

This exercise prepares you to recognize the wide spectrum of emotions you may experience at any point in time.

Awareness Exercise Experience the Storm

Homework

Target	Experience the storm of emotions
Duration	30 minutes
Repeat	Repeat as needed
You'll need	A quiet corner, paper and a pen.

Close your eyes and take a moment to calm your mind and feel fully present. This will very much feel like a meditation exercise. Start with the easy part. Focus on your body.

In your mind, scan every inch of it, moving up from your toes to your head. Ask yourself how you feel. If there are any pains, pleasures or subtle sensations, note them down. A slight headache, sinuses inflamed, a runny nose, sore muscles, and so on. Is the light too bright? Is it hurting your eyes? Is it too dim? Take note of it all and as much time as you need.

Next, switch your attention to your emotions. Keep asking yourself how you feel. Expand your awareness to include the full spectrum of the storm. Excitement about your date tonight mixed with a bit of stress because you don't know what to wear? A smidge of guilt for how your last relationship ended?

It's harder to find all those subtleties than it is to recognize that your foot hurts (which you did not even notice till you sat down to reflect). So, remember to look for the physical signature of each emotion and give it time. Introspect. Get to know yourself at a whole new level.

Dry lips. Neck pain. A bit of indigestion. Anxious about the test. Excited about the summer vacations. Annoyed to miss the football game. A bit sleepy and ... in love.

Whatever it is, if you feel it, write it down.

This is the Jedi Master level of awareness. It won't come easy. It will take a lot of practice but with dedication you will make it. In the process you will realize that, regardless of whichever emotions and sensations you find, connecting with yourself at this level is pure joy. Finding that joy is key to helping you stick to the practice and that's when the miracle will happen. An ability to fully connect with the force of your emotions and sensations. Congratulations, Master Skywalker.

Master the way you react to your emotions so that you can feel safe to let them show.

Practice Exercise
Create a Buffer

Target	Develop the skill to refrain from responding to your emotions
Duration	The longer the better
Repeat	Repeat for the rest of your life
You'll need	A quiet corner

We tend to forget that even the most exemplary leaders in terms of wisdom and composure are not without emotions. It's not that Gandhi did not feel the urge to fight the Brits or that His Holiness the Dalai Lama did not feel the pain of his people as their homes were taken away. What set them apart from the rest of us, though, was how they chose to react to those emotions.

Once I hosted Arun Gandhi, grandson of Mahatma Gandhi, on my podcast, Slo Mo. He wrote a book called *The Gift of Anger*. I asked how anger can be a gift? And he said, 'Well, anger is energy. You can use it to punch someone in the face or you can use it to stand up, make a speech and change the world.' An emotion is never good or bad. It's just what it is. **If you feel it, it's real.** Feeling an emotion can never hurt you. Emotions only lead to actual events in the real world when you act on them.

Committed happiness practitioners learn to separate what they feel (pure being) from what they want to do.

To learn to do this, I will take you through a series of exercises that start easy and get harder as we go along.

Sit on Your Hands

That's it really. Your task, strange as it may sound, is to sit on your hands for five minutes straight. It will feel easy at first until . . . you feel that your nose, or other parts of your body, itch. Now that's a challenge! Don't touch that nose no matter how badly you want to scratch it.

Here's a tip that I hope will help ease the challenge. The best way to survive the serious irritation to scratch an itch is not to ignore it, it's to do the opposite . . . focus on it.

Direct your awareness to the part that's itching and give it your undivided attention. **Sit with it.** Remind yourself that it is just an itch. That it really has no power to harm you.

Remember that, just as with every other itch you ever had, it will go away. Lose the urge to act. When you fully accept it and learn to sit with it, the magic will happen. It will go away.

Stay Hungry

Let's take this up a notch. In this practice, we're taking away the habit of lunch.

'Stay Hungry'

Search the web for 'Stay Hungry' by Twisted Sister.

Try to see beyond the noise, the heavy metal guitar, the way the band looks and the intensity of the music. Listen to the depth of the lyrics.

Keep your target in sight. Remember what you're fighting for, remember what you seek. Stay hungry!

Yep, you read that correctly. For a week, if your constitution and working hours allow, don't just eat lunch because it's time. Wait till you actually feel hungry, then wait till you are really hungry and then stay hungry for thirty more minutes and then, only then, eat. Feel free to go out with friends for lunch but don't eat. **Sit with it!** Wait till you feel it, then wait a little more.

You know this by now. The way to survive hunger is not to ignore it and distract yourself. It's to tune into it, fully – to embrace it. Direct your full attention to your growling stomach and wait for the magic to happen and the hunger to go away!

Bite Your Tongue

Another urge that some of us find hard to resist is the urge to talk.

Blah blah blah. I honestly can't understand what a lot of the noise is all about. Everyone seems to have something to say. We talk to co-workers, fellow students, then go somewhere to talk to friends. On the way we call someone and talk into our little Bluetooth headsets as we rush through the streets of our buzzing city of talk. We write email after email throughout the day, comment on social media in our free time and when we finally get home we switch on the TV and what do we find? Talk talk talk. Stop the madness! Sssshhhhhhhhhh!

For a week, make a vow to not speak unless spoken to (or unless you really need to, of course.) Even when you are busting to say something in a meeting or are out with friends, don't say it ... zip it. Choose to shut up. This will feel difficult at first but in no time at all, you will find that silence is bliss.

If you're the A+ kind of achiever, extend this exercise for another week and practise purity of speech, a concept I learned from many spiritual teachings — Islam, Buddhism, Hinduism and others — and one of the dearest practices to my heart . . .

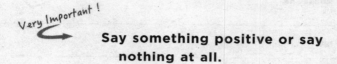

Very Important !

Say something positive or say nothing at all.

Throughout this week, when you feel the urge to speak, say what you're about to say inside your head first and ask yourself if it sounds positive — if saying it will make things better. If yes, then say it lovingly. If no, then keep it to yourself and say nothing.

If you succeed with this for a whole week, why not make it your commitment for the rest of your life? Do that and watch the love of the universe and all its living beings pour on you.

Just like with itches and hunger, the more you listen to what's being said around you and to what your brain is saying inside your head, the more you will be reminded of your need to be silent and the more your urge to speak will go away. Magic!

These exercises are not about making you stronger by subjecting you to hardship. Quite the opposite. They are about making you softer so you can embrace what you feel and sit with it, as you lose the urge to act on it.

It's not the toughest of trees that survive the hurricane. It's the ones that can sway with the wind and not resist. By learning to sit with simple urges such as an itch or hunger, you learn to sway with your emotions. The more you do it, the more ready you become to experience a storm of emotions and . . . sit with it.

This exercise will, over time, teach you how to hold space for your emotions, acknowledge them and embrace them fully.

This must be the hardest exercise in this entire book. I will take you through it step by step and I apologize in advance if it causes you hardship.

Practice Exercise
Sit With It

Target	Feel
Duration	30 minutes for each exercise
Repeat	Repeat for the rest of your life
You'll need	A quiet corner, paper and a pen

To start with, please recognize that beyond being positive or negative, emotions can also be passive or active. Passive emotions tend to hold you back or keep you still. When you feel them you have no energy and no urge to act. These include boredom, sadness and embarrassment on the negative side, and calm or tranquillity on the positive side. Active emotions, on the other hand, come with a surge of energy that drives you to do something. Anger and fear are active negative emotions. Excitement is an active positive one.

By their very nature, it's easier to sit with passive emotions. When you're bored, for example, there's not much you can do but sit there and do nothing. So, let us start there.

White Noise Detox

Find a quiet place indoors. Set your phone timer to thirty minutes, then put your phone down and do absolutely nothing. That's it. Nothing.

For the duration of this exercise, allow yourself to fully embrace your boredom. No browsing the internet, no social media, no TV, no music, no books to read, no gossip magazine to waste your life on, no meditation even, no nature to contemplate, no people-watching and no friend to chat about little nothings with. You may wonder why I'm asking for this. Isn't connecting with nature, for example, an amazing meditation exercise? Of course, but what we're aiming for here is a different skill. Connecting with the beauty of nature and all living beings is bliss. What we are doing here, however, is practising the grit of dealing with the space that boredom brings. We're learning to sit with it, and in doing so learning to eliminate the need to react to it by constantly seeking distractions. This is like building your strength in preparation for sitting with stronger emotions by first sitting with other things that itch and annoy you. This develops your ability to overcome the urge to act upon an impulse.

Can you feel it coming? *I'm booooooooooooored*. Yep, that's good. Embrace it.

When the urge to pick up your phone and check your messages becomes all too much to bear, stay a little more. Learn to sit with it. This will feel much harder than resisting the urge to scratch your nose, believe it or not, because we have all been pouring distractions into our lives as a form of escape for years.

The instructions for all our emotional practices so far apply here too. Don't try to ignore your boredom. Focus on it. Entertain yourself by tuning into that incredible feeling. Embrace it. Feel alive.

Re-live a Memory

Now, close your eyes and recall an event that engages you emotionally. Start with something happy, like a fun day you spent with a friend. When I do this exercise, I remember the first time I took the kids to Disney when they were young. If you have a photo album to help you remember, bring it out.

Remember every little detail, every smell, every experience and every vivid colour. Reflect deeply, not only on the events that you can remember but how you felt as you experienced them. See if you can regenerate those feelings. When you do, pause. Allow yourself to feel. Laugh or smile if that's how you feel. As your mind tries to stray away, to bring up other worrying thoughts from the future or bad experiences from the past, focus on the memory or the photo album. Continue to feel.

When you've got the hang of this, the real challenge begins. Do this exercise again but this time recall a tough memory. Pick one that was pivotal in your life but one when you felt a passive emotion, not charged with energy. For me, when I do this, I choose the death of Ali.

Instead of trying to escape the thoughts that trigger the emotions associated with this event, I invite you to recall them in detail. As the emotion starts to arise, allow yourself to feel. Allow yourself to let it all out. If you feel like crying, cry. If you want to scream, scream. If you want to say something, say it. Out loud. Don't look for solutions or think about actions or judge yourself. Just hold yourself like a child. Listen to what your heart feels as you would listen to child who is in pain. Don't rush yourself out of it. Hold your emotions as gently as you would hold a beautiful butterfly that's been wounded by the wind and is gathering its strength before it can fly again.

I know this is hard, but it gets easier. Like draining a bathtub, it takes a long time and at first you don't really notice anything happening. But with time, the effects become clear until there is nothing left to drain.

If you can solicit the help of a trusted friend, I'd recommend it. Ask him or her to listen and hold you, as you should hold yourself. That's all they need to do.

When you get the hang of sitting with passive negative

emotions, tread carefully and attempt to invite in some of the memories that cause you anger, fear or other active emotions. Do this exercise only in the presence of a trusted friend. Attempt to sit with the emotion by focusing your thoughts away from actions. No plans for actions, no strategies, no 'I should have said this', or 'Next time I will do that.' Focus only on how you feel. Express that to your friend. Cry if you'd like to. Shout if you feel like it. Don't hold it in. Feel it fully. Your friend is there to make sure you express what you feel but only what you feel. If you start to express what you want to do, he or she should invite you to stay with the emotion and make sure you feel safe enough to express it.

Remember !

It's not weak to express your emotions. It makes you as strong as you'll ever be.

Wait for the Storm

If you can resist scratching an itch, feeding a hunger and blabbering your thoughts out; if you can invite passive and active, positive and negative emotions from your past and sit with them, even express them without doing – you're ready.

When I was a young child, I had to wait for the school bus early in the morning when it was freezing. I'd find myself shivering, uncontrollably, until I tuned into the feeling. I don't know how I discovered that, but I'd find myself focusing on the shiver, ordering it with my thoughts to stop, then telling myself that I felt warm. When I did, I actually felt warm. You can do this with the most active of all feelings and emotions. The next time you feel angry, tune into it. Focus on your anger. Feel it. Sense your blood boiling. Notice your eyes tearing up, observe your voice rising and listen to your heart beating faster. Watch yourself losing control and then ... right before it slips out ... sit with it. Don't do anything about it. Don't even try to stop it or calm it down. Just let it be. Let it eat you. Do nothing. Absolutely nothing! By focusing on it, by letting it be, it will take its course. When the time is right, think just one thought in your head – *I am calm*. When you do, the anger will go away. When it does, you will have the clarity you need to devise a plan and, most importantly, you will have fired a few neurons in a way that will allow neuro-plasticity to kick in and make it easier for you to sit with that emotion the next time it arises.

I know this sounds like some kind of *Matrix*-like movie. But please try it. It works. Sit with the emotion. Then manifest its opposite.

The next time you feel jealous, don't tell yourself that you shouldn't. If you feel jealous, then you should.

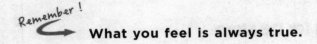

Remember!

What you feel is always true.

Remember the golden rule: embrace how you feel but don't immediately act on it. Then, when the time is right, think: *I'm open to making things better*. When that becomes your reality, only then, start to talk or do.

Do this with every other emotion you frequently experience, and remember, these practices are not designed to remove any of your emotions, just to remove their control over you.

Learn to feel comfortable with something that has always made you feel uneasy. When space is created and you stop trying to con-trol it, the difficult emotion will slowly go away. Then you can be whatever you want to be.

Learn to enjoy the discomfort. It's not unusual for us humans to love a negative feeling – a bitter taste, a sore muscle or a challenging experience – when we know that it's good for us.

But don't just practise sitting with the negative. The next time you feel joy, don't let it pass while you jump from meeting to meeting. Find a quiet place and sit with it. Let it take you over. Savour it. Feel it in every cell of your body. Notice the emotion, acknowledge it and embrace it so it becomes a frequent visitor.

Now, I have bad news and good news for you here.

Karate Kid

Watch the original movie from the 80s (the new one is not as good).

When Mr Miyagi sets out to teach young Daniel to defend himself against bullies who happen to be aggressive black-belt karate champions, he asks him to wax a car and paint a fence. Discipline and constant practice are the path to championship. Remember, as you practise – wax on, wax off. That's the path.

The bad news is that I don't know how to show you how to do this other than through commitment and hard work. When it comes to unlearning the hundreds of times you've tried to evade your emotions, the only path back is through hundreds of instances of acknowledging them. You're going to have to do the work to make this openness your new norm.

The good news, however, is that if you do the work, you will figure it out. If you find it difficult at first, go back and sit with your itches, hunger and urges to speak till you're ready.

Whatever you do, don't stop trying till your heart opens. This may be the single most important skill you will ever learn. Learn to feel.

Chapter Eight

Alchemy

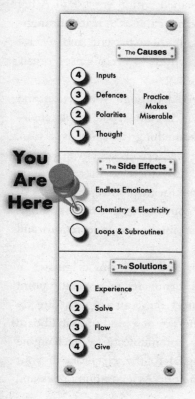

The **Causes**

4. Inputs
3. Defences
2. Polarities
1. Thought

Practice Makes Miserable

You Are Here

The **Side Effects**

Endless Emotions

Chemistry & Electricity

Loops & Subroutines

The **Solutions**

1. Experience
2. Solve
3. Flow
4. Give

Early computer systems, known as mainframes, were based on a design that kept all processing confined to the server. Wires connected remote screens to the communication subsystems. The functionality of those screens was confined to input and output – displaying information on a screen and capturing the user input from a keyboard. Those 'dumb' terminals – yep, that's what we called them – left all the thinking and control up to the centre.

Over the years, as the personal computer, smartphones and the internet emerged, intelligence is now everywhere.

From the palm of your hand to the massive systems that power the internet. Every part of the network is smart and capable of performing on its own.

A look at the anatomy of our brain and its nervous system may give us the false impression that we are similar to mainframes, in that all intelligence is kept to the brain and every other part of the body just does what it's told. Nothing could be further from the truth.

Brain Chemistry and Electricity

Your 'brain' functions are not contained within your skull. A big part of the brain – the nervous system – extends to reach throughout your entire body. This wiring is there to send and receive sensory data and your brain's instructions to every sensor, organ, muscle and gland.

Information is constantly collected through your senses and sent up the nerves so the brain can become aware of its environment. When you recognize something that needs action, commands are sent down the somatic nervous system to control your voluntary movements. And then there is the autonomic nervous system, which is responsible for involuntary functions of your physical form: the beating of your heart, your fight-or-flight response, your temperature, your varying hormone secretions, and so on.

Every single function that your body performs originates in a specific point in your brain and terminates in a specific point in your body. A few nerves connect those two points directly, while most other nerves stop on the way at a kind of switchboard known as a ganglion, where they communicate by exchanging chemicals to send an accurate signal to the receptors in your organs. That's how they get the job done. As a computer geek and a robotics fanatic, I can't help but admire the unparalleled genius of the design of this machine.

In computer systems design, this is very similar to the dominant computer architecture of the PC era known as client server computing, and of the internet, where intelligence existed both on the server side and at the end of the cable on the client side, which was at that time a personal computer but is now every device that exists.

Our brains and nervous systems go one step further. **They possess intelligence everywhere, including in the cable itself.** The autonomic nervous system – the one running all the things that you do not consciously control – is made up of three separate systems. The first of those, the human gut, is lined with more than 100 million nerve cells that operate independently of the brain. This is why your gut is often known as the second brain.

The other two autonomic systems, which deserve extensive exploration here, are the sympathetic and parasympathetic nervous systems.

These two systems are not opposites; they bicker a lot but seem to complement each other very well. They are a bit like two partners – a loving couple – who just can't agree how their home should be set up. One partner walks in and moves things around to make the place look pretty, and as soon as the other partner walks in, they move them back to make it more practical. Then, when they walk out, the first partner comes back in to change it all up again.

Similarly, back and forth, the sympathetic and parasympathetic systems keep on changing the state of your body. When the sympathetic nervous system is engaged, it excites your body in the face of stress or danger. The parasympathetic nervous system, on the other hand, is always looking out for moments when it can calm you down to get the necessary routine functions of your body done while it counteracts what the other system has put in place. Together, they take your body from stress to relaxation, from fear to courage, and from worry to peace.[1]

In contrast to its comforting name, the sympathetic system is not about sympathy at all (it was called sympathetic from the Greek origin of the word which means 'feeling together', due to its proximity to the spine and many internal organs). It is what sounds your internal alarms in the face of danger or stress, what triggers your fight–or–flight response. It's not sympathetic to your happiness but rather to your safety. Like the one in the couple above who doesn't care how beautiful things are but just cares that they are practical, the sympathetic nervous system does not care about how good you feel. It spends every moment, once activated, making you feel stressed in order to keep you safe. Part of that emergency plan includes involving its allies, your glands, to use chemistry as another method of communication across the body, to ensure this safety-focused functionality is delivered.

Your parasympathetic system (para as in adjacent to the sympathetic system) is engaged when it's time for you to rest – which, interestingly, is considered a vital function for your survival. The parasympathetic nervous system wants you to preserve your energy, digest your food, rebuild your muscles and maybe even close your eyes to reflect or get some sleep. It's the one in the couple focused on making things tranquil and beautiful. When activated, it makes us feel comfort and peace.

The structure of the sympathetic system enables it to send distress signals to all relevant organs at once. The parasympathetic system, on the other hand, sends specific signals to each organ separately. To understand this difference, imagine a factory where the announcements are played on loudspeakers that need to be louder than the noise of the machines. In this factory, when an announcement is made, the announcer shouts and the speakers magnify the noise to reach everyone at once. That's the behaviour of your sympathetic nervous system. Even a small stress signal sent down one path will trigger many organs and glands. That's why, when we get stressed, we feel that tingling almost everywhere in our bodies – in every organ and in every gland. The parasympathetic system, on the other hand, is similar to a modern office environment where you can notify an individual, or a small group of people, using a messenger system on their computers or their phones, without disturbing anyone else. That's why it takes you a while to fully relax and fall asleep.

Understanding exactly how each of these two systems works and where they go wrong in the modern world is crucial to our happiness. Imagine that while you are deeply absorbed in reading this, one of your friends decides to play a practical joke on you. He sneaks up from behind you and squeals like a hungry weasel. Did you just put the book down and look behind you? Come back, keep reading. This is just a hypothetical scenario.

If this practical joke did happen, your **sympathetic nervous system** would jump to alert. The squeal represents a clear and present danger. Stress signals are immediately sent down through your nerves to the muscles of your legs, instructing the blood vessels to dilate to receive as much blood as needed for you to pop like a spring out of your seat. The same signal reaches your digestive system, where the soft tissue surrounding your intestines reacts by reducing the blood it receives so that all your energy is directed to the urgent task at hand – keeping you alive in the face of an annoying friend. Finally, the same stress signal reaches the suprarenal gland which responds by secreting adrenaline into your bloodstream. Adrenaline then acts as the microphone magnifying the stress signal to increase your heart rate, sharpen your vision and prepare you for an imminent fight-or-flight response.

Adrenaline is one of the important hormones that affect our mood. Others include cortisol – which affects metabolism and the immune system and plays an important function in helping the body respond to stress; dopamine – the reward hormone that excites us and keeps us coming back for more pleasure and fun; testosterone and oestrogen – the hormones that impact our masculine and feminine biology and, also, lead to mood swings as their concentration in our bodies change. Then there are my favourite two hormones: oxytocin – also known as the love hormone, which helps create bonds between mother and child, and impacts on desire and intimacy between couples; and serotonin – an inhibitory hormone that calms us down when we are OK with life as it is, which is how I define true happiness!

Electrical and chemical signals, of course, are the main reason why emotions have physical signatures. The signals of the nervous system and the hormones secreted in response to any emotion trigger sensations in our bodies physically.

Your friend, shocked by your disproportionate reaction, realizes his mistake. He apologizes sincerely and, as compensation for his bad behaviour, offers you ice cream. As you sit down and fill your belly with spoonful after spoonful of this pleasure, your stomach sends a signal up to your brain that the conditions are back to normal and there is no need to panic. Your **parasympathetic nervous system** engages to slow your heart rate down, clean your system of the residual adrenaline, direct more blood to your digestive system and allow you to relax. It all feels good again.

Reading this, I guess, you may feel an inclination to like your parasympathetic nervous system and, perhaps, dislike that troublemaker – the sympathetic nervous system. You would be wrong to feel that way. Stress is extremely valuable if what attacks you is a genuine threat. A bit of stress is not a very large cost to pay for staying alive. Stress is also what pushes you over the line to finish your work, find better solutions to a problem or recognize that your partner is feeling upset so that you make amends. A bit of stress is good for you.

What you should dislike, however, is the continuous practical joke the modern world has been playing on us.

Your Lifelong Practical Joke

The problem with the modern world is that it's playing practical jokes on us all the time. Being late to a meeting, having your mobile phone's data network disconnected or not finding your favourite brand of oat milk are not a form of threat. Yet we take them way more seriously than we should and, in doing so, involuntarily engage our sympathetic nervous system in response to their presence. And then we let the stress that this causes us linger.

The original design of the sympathetic nervous system assumes that it will only be engaged in exceptional cases of emergency. Putting some of your organs in hyperdrive and depriving others of the lifeblood they need to function is OK for a few minutes to run away from a tiger. When it goes on for days, months or even years at a time, however, this constant stress and abnormal distribution of energy around our bodies becomes the biggest threat that we face. Heart disease, high blood pressure, depression, even suicidal tendencies and many other chronic conditions have been proven, study after study, to be associated with stress. The dangers of prolonged stress surely surpass the dangers of missing the payment deadline of your utility bill, which triggered it.

Living through the practical joke of the modern world and its illusory threats, your sympathetic nervous system no longer becomes your saviour. Instead, it becomes a threat that's working diligently to kill you.

You're smarter than that. I think it's time that we play the joke back on the modern world.

This begins with a choice to end the stress despite the perceived pressures of daily life. You may not be able to avoid the daily stressors but you can end the stress. Let's make this choice now.

Even if you are eager to continue reading, I suggest you take a few minutes to put the book down, get up from your seat and stretch. Engaging your parasympathetic nervous system needs nothing more. A short break and a bit of downtime should do it. Though, it would help you if you have a better grasp of further details.

Psychological Comfort

The autonomic nervous system works efficiently in both directions. In one direction, it initiates the different states of stress we feel, and in the other direction, our state of stress dictates its behaviour. Allow me to explain.

When your parasympathetic nervous system is active, you feel rested and relaxed. That's understood. What's interesting is how that works in the opposite direction. If you consciously make yourself relax, your parasympathetic system will be activated as a result. When I asked you to get up and stretch, I simply asked you to force your body to relax. When you do, your nervous system engages to make you relax even more.

In a study by the Department of Psychology, University of Kansas, 170 participants were asked to complete two different stressful tasks while holding chopsticks between their teeth in a manner that produced either a smile or a neutral expression. Smiling participants had lower heart rates during stress recovery than the rest of the group did.[2]

You know what that means? A simple chopstick that you bite between your teeth – which forces the muscles of your face to smile – can make you happier. Fun fact? This also means that using too much Botox, which tends to temporarily paralyse facial muscles and make it harder to fully smile, can affect your mood negatively. Just saying. In psychology, this phenomenon is known as the facial feedback hypothesis: the way we move the muscles of our faces changes our emotions.

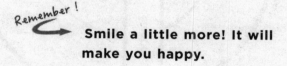

Remember !

Smile a little more! It will make you happy.

The limbic and autonomic nervous systems clearly react to each other. Emotions lead to physical signatures. We know that already. What seems less well-known is that the opposite is also true. We only feel an emotion when its physical signature is felt in the body . . . first. Interesting, isn't it?

One prominent theory that explains emotions is the James–Lange theory – attributed to William James and Carl Lange.[3] It suggests that the physiological change is primary and the emotion is secondary. For example, if you see a threat approaching you, your heart rate increases first and your eyesight focuses to prepare you to run. Those reactions are autonomic, involuntary, and they are produced in a flash by your sympathetic nervous system. They happen first before you are even aware that there is a reason to panic.

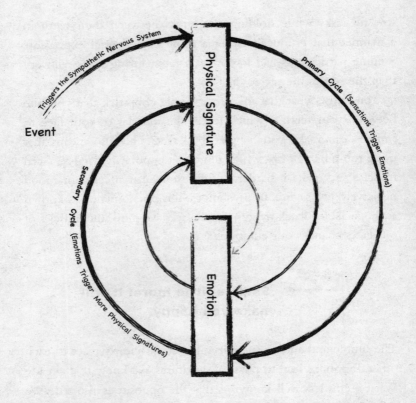

The changing physical conditions are then interpreted by your limbic system as evidence of a possible threat. This triggers the emotion – fear or panic – which orders your body to verify the existence of the threat which, if confirmed present, stresses the sympathetic nervous system further. This is the reason why you jumped out of your seat first when your friend played a practical joke on you, then realized there was nothing to fear later. The expression 'my heart missed a beat' says it all. If the threat is 'big enough', we feel the physiological symptom, missing a beat, way before we even figure out what happened and react emotionally to it.

Remember !

You don't run because you are scared. You feel scared because you're about to run.

This cycle is also true for positive emotions. The practice of monks, for example, who seek to reach a state of perpetual peace, involves a lot of nature contemplation and tranquillity. By spending time in these conditions, their parasympathetic nervous systems are activated even though they may have other reasons for concern – not having the resources to sustain their own life, for example, which is a practice of advanced ascetic monks who travel for years with no resources, dependent on others, learning to trust that life is always going to be OK.

Obviously, we don't need to go to those extremes. In fact, we can activate our parasympathetic nervous system on demand by engaging in simple, everyday activities.

Smile more, watch a comedy, embrace a friend, love and feel loved. Sit in silence, have an ice cream, stretch on your sofa as if you have nothing to do. Force your physical form to activate your parasympathetic nervous system by doing the things you would normally do when you're naturally relaxed and peaceful. It's an easy hack. And it works.

Very Important !

When you regenerate the physical signatures of an emotion, you will start to feel it.

But wait, it gets even better.

Being around others who smile also changes our mood. We humans (as well as other primates) have what is known as mirror neurons – neurons that fire both when one acts and when one observes an action performed by another. This means that when you observe another human doing something, the neurons you would use to do the same thing start to fire in sync. This is why the porn industry (which I wish did not exist) is so successful. We feel aroused when we see others aroused. It is also why surrounding yourself with happy people makes you happier over time. Every time they smile, your smiling brain fires up, helping you shift your mood over time through neuroplasticity. This is one of those things that is better experienced than explained, so let's practise.

This exercise will show you how to find peace and tranquillity in a stressful environment. It won't remove the reasons for the stress, but it will give you the clarity you need to start addressing it.

Practice Exercise
Chill

Target	Learn to activate your parasympathetic nervous system on demand
Duration	30-60 minutes per exercise
Repeat	Repeat for the rest of your life
You'll need	A quiet corner

To deactivate the stress-inducing sympathetic nervous system, you need to get its opposite twin – the parasympathetic system – activated. Here are a few ways to do that. These methods work even when the reason for your stress remains.

Relax Your Body

When our parasympathetic nervous system is activated, we feel relaxed. Approaching this from the opposite direction works just as well – if you manage to relax, your parasympathetic system will be activated, and you will relax even more. Techniques borrowed from traditional practices of meditation, reflexology and massage are very effective in achieving this. In simple words, here's what you need to do.

Sit in a comfortable seat, loosen any tight clothes and take off your shoes. Set the timer on your phone to thirty minutes (or less if you are at work or a bit rushed, but give yourself no less than ten minutes), then place your phone face down and don't check it again till your timer goes off.

Stretch your body to make sure there are no aches or pains you may not have been aware of. If you find any, attempt to keep stretching them or massaging them until they feel relaxed.

Find the most comfortable position on your seat and breathe deeply several times. Enjoy a long exhale that sounds like a sigh. Put your hands behind your head and lie back. Yep, that's it. That's your practice exercise. Call it the chill position.

Smile! Keep smiling. Breathe deeply. Keep breathing.

Be kind to yourself. Massage your face gently. Feel the blood circulating. Massage your skull with all ten fingertips. Massage your feet. Press on the different pressure points (your feet will tell you where) and stay there until there are no aches left. Massage your neck and shoulders. Tilt your neck to one side, then the other. To the front. To the back. Feel free to push a bit with your hand till you feel the full stretch. Close your eyes. Massage them gently. Massage behind your ears. Wait a bit in silence and try to listen to your body. If any part calls, touch it gently like a mother would comfort a child. Maybe bring a healthy snack with you to your relaxation session. Nurture your body and reassure it that everything is OK.

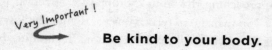

Very Important !

Be kind to your body.

By that same token, think about cutting down your caffeine consumption gradually, ideally till you consume no more than one cup of coffee and one cup of tea a day. Less is even better.

Caffeine keeps you on alert – the opposite of what you need to relax. It will feel hard at first but then you will feel fresher without the caffeine addiction.

Think about how you sleep. Activating your sympathetic nervous system during the day will keep you awake at night in a vicious cycle. Sleep is crucially important. There are lots of resources online and many sleep experts who can help. Here are the basics, however. Preparing for your night's sleep starts at 10 a.m. when you consume your last caffeinated drink of the day. Wind down gradually towards the evening. An action movie at 9 p.m. is a very bad idea. It will energize you while you need to become calmer and calmer with every passing minute past midday. A horror movie will cause you nightmares. Attempt to remove all the reasons for waking up at night. No eating heavy meals before bedtime, no drinking too much water – which wakes you up to empty the tank – or drinking too little – which makes you feel dehydrated and gives you headaches – all very bad for rested sleep. Try to make the place where you sleep darker and try to make the temperature of the room a degree or two cooler than the day temperature. Use ear plugs and eye masks if you need to. A good sleep is at the heart of a relaxed body and an active parasympathetic nervous system.

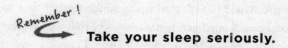

Remember!

Take your sleep seriously.

Did I need to write any of this down? No. You know it all. The interesting question is, why don't you do it? Because you've been trained by the modern world to set different priorities. It's not that hard to relax if you make it a priority and give yourself the time. It's entirely up to you. I am always surprised by those that keep saying they're busy and keep pushing themselves but then somehow find the time to binge watch a series or go out with loud friends instead of spending the highly needed time to . . . chill!

In the Middle East where I come from, we have a proverb:

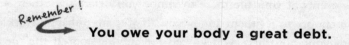

Remember!

You owe your body a great debt.

Repay the debt. Be kind to your body. Relax.

Relax Your Mind

Relaxing your body has an immediate effect, centring you away from stress. Relaxing your mind, however, goes much deeper for much longer.

It takes deliberate intention and lots of practice to relax our minds in our distracting, highly pressured world. Everything we encounter is geared to stress us, to keep us running and striving for more. Advertising makes us feel that we're always missing out. Our bosses make us feel we always need to try harder. Magazines make us feel that we're not good enough. Social media makes us feel that everyone's doing better than we are. The media makes us feel that the world is evil. Politicians make us feel that we are in grave danger, and our friends make us feel that we will never find the love of our life or the job we deserve. There's always a reason to feel that something's wrong, that something needs to improve and that we're not safe. Our sympathetic system is in hyperdrive, we are stressed and always on high alert. But how many of these things are actually true? Is the world evil? How many people committed a crime last night and how many committed an act of love? Are we in grave danger? How long have we heard this and yet we lived another day? Are we missing out on another phone, can of cola or fancy car? Or do we have all we need? Is there anything truly wrong? I mean, think about it. Life is not always perfect. As a matter of fact, life is always *not* perfect. And yet, when you put it all together, it's not too bad after all. Are the events of your life there to annoy you or are they there and you choose to let them annoy you? If you are unhappy working with your boss, have you looked for another job? If the media and advertising industry is pouring negativity into your head, have you chosen to switch them off? If some friends are making you feel bad, have you decided they may not be the right friends for you?

I am not suggesting that you quit your job (or relationship, or commute, or friendship) today. But if any of these reasons are causing you stress, start moving in the direction of a more relaxed life. Take a year to find another job, take three to move to a new place. Just start to move. Allow yourself to receive the gift of living. Take steady steps and you will, eventually, get there. Message me when you do. It will make me very happy.

Over the years, I have found that relaxing and clearing my mind follows three stages. Try them yourself. First, focus on something **tranquil**. Second, see how **safe** you really are. And finally, recognize the **blessings** in your life. Let's practise.

Tranquillity

Find a quiet, safe place where you will not be interrupted. Set your phone timer to thirty minutes, then place your phone face down. Don't look at it until the timer goes off.

Start by relaxing your body like we did before, but this time add a new twist. While you help your body relax, think happy thoughts and focus on things that make you feel peaceful. Think of happy memories. Picture a wonderful vacation. Watch pictures of beautiful nature. Play soothing music and listen attentively. Imagery works really well because it activates your right-brain hemisphere, which is closely connected to your emotional system. I wonder why we don't do this every day when . . .

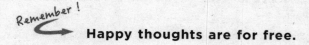

Remember!

Happy thoughts are for free.

We can generate them on demand. All you need is the will to command your brain to think positively. It doesn't matter what's happening in your life; you can always find a positive happy thought.

A friend of mine recently told me that when she feels a negative thought is stuck in her head without a clear path to resolution, to stop the incessant nagging, she makes an appointment with it. She acknowledges how she feels by telling her brain something like: *OK, I realize you are worried about [X]. I realize it's an important topic, but I don't think I will be able to resolve it now. Let's put it to one side and come back to it, say, at 11 a.m. tomorrow. We will be OK till then. So, start thinking of beautiful, tranquil things till we discuss it.*

She's into art, so she whips out her phone and browses artworks by her favourite artists. Believe it or not, this works. Try it. It's not escapism. It allows the parasympathetic nervous system to kick in and make room for your thoughts to clear. By the time her 'appointment' is due, her brain will usually have resolved the issue already.

Thinking positively is not hard, if you put your mind to it. Your brain, however, has a tendency to always go back to the negative. Because observing what is wrong is more important to your safety (if something is going right it does not constitute a threat), our brains tend to spend most of their time hunting around for what's wrong. Of course, when you look for something, you're much more likely to find it, which can make your outlook on life pretty grim. But there's a hack. We can use your brain's ability to find what it's looking for to our advantage. By looking for what's right, you're likely to find it too.

If you search for evidence, quickly you will realize that . . .

You're Safe

The second stage of calming your mind is found in the realization that, mostly throughout your life, you are OK. You just need to remember that. Here's how.

Find a quiet, safe place where you will not be interrupted. Set your phone timer to thirty minutes, then place your phone face down. Now, let me ask you a few questions. Did you notice how when I asked you to find a safe place for this exercise, it wasn't hard at all? Did you notice how when I asked you to leave your phone for thirty minutes, the world as you know it did not collapse? Yet, we constantly reach out to our phones thinking that we may miss something critical. Do you realize that the mere fact you are reading this page right now means that you are not threatened in any way whatsoever? If there was something truly so threatening, wouldn't you have been focusing on that instead of reading my words?

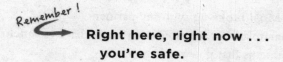

Remember !

Right here, right now . . .
you're safe.

Safety is but one of the many blessings we enjoy every day, and yet take for granted. Let's see how many more of these blessings you can remember.

All Your Blessings

It's time to take stock.

Pick up a piece of paper and a pen. Ask your brain, systematically, to tell you what is good about your life right now. Write down at least five things that you are grateful for. A loved one that is safe and happy; the quiet time you have to read this book; having a job (even if you hate it); having friends or family that care for you; the food you had to eat today (Is that a blessing? Yes! More than two billion people in the world don't have food to eat every day).

Remember !

There's so much good in our
life . . . count your blessings.

50-50

Another powerful exercise I sometimes do is to insist that my brain gives me one good thing about any specific situation for every bad thing it brings up. You see, our brain's negativity bias makes it see more wrong than right. Force it to be balanced by asking for a fair share of each. I do that with friends every time they complain:

'Oh, Mo, I broke up with my partner.'

'Congratulations, at least you no longer have to suffer the stress and arguments that got you here.'

'Oh, but he cheated on me.'

'Congratulations, it's so good you no longer have to be with a cheat.'

'Argh, this means I have to start dating again.'

'Amazing, so much fun with someone new.'

Of course, if you look at life objectively, you will realize that most of life, much more than half, is OK. Most of us are mostly healthy, interrupted only with a few episodes of not feeling well in a year. None of us had ever seen a pandemic before, hence why Covid shocked and shook everyone. We walk on solid ground most of our lives. Most of us never ever experience an earthquake. So, if you want to be mathematically accurate, you should ask your brain for many more good things about a situation for every bad thing it brings up. How about three good for every one bad? No. No! How about nine rights for every one wrong? That would be a much more accurate reflection of the truth.

Create More Safety

If your parasympathetic system needs safety to engage, give it safety. Make your life safer. Here's how.

I grew up in Egypt. Life, for the average Egyptian (judging by wealth and quality of life), is much tougher, in general, than it is for the average Western person. Yet, growing up, I felt that Egyptians were, in general, a lot less anxious about life than the average person living in the West.

This wasn't because they had health insurance or unemployment benefits. It was because in Egypt, like many other emerging-market societies, there's an implicit unwritten pact that family, neighbours and friends will have each other's backs. The ultimate feeling of safety, I believe, is triggered by genuine human connections. In tightly knit societies, we learn to trust our brothers and friends more than we trust the twists and turns of life. Perhaps, if you find the right people, that will be true for you too. How can you find people who will be there for you in times of need? Find people who you are willing to be there for too.

I invite you to welcome more trusted humans into your life on a regular basis. In poorer countries, relationships are often built with no material expectations from each other because, typically, most people don't have enough material possessions to give any away. Usually, all we look for is good company, laughter, a shoulder to cry on, and the love we feel around those who are close.

Surrounding yourself with people you love is the ultimate signal to your brain that everything is going to be fine – that everything already is fine.

Fill your life with people you love, and you will always feel safe.

When you feel safe, and find the peace associated with an active parasympathetic nervous system, you will finally have the cognitive space to wonder why you ever spent so much of your life obsessing about things that don't really matter. I've been wondering about that myself for years. Here, in the next chapter, is what I found out.

Chapter Nine

In Limbo

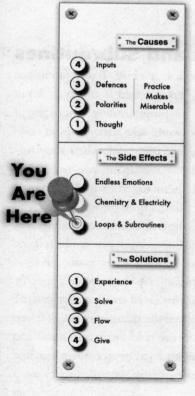

The Causes

4. Inputs
3. Defences
2. Polarities
1. Thought

Practice
Makes
Miserable

The Side Effects

Endless Emotions
Chemistry & Electricity
Loops & Subroutines

You Are Here

The Solutions

1. Experience
2. Solve
3. Flow
4. Give

Have you ever woken up with a musical tune stuck in your head? Even if your favourite song, after a while it gets annoying. Regardless of what you do, you can't shake it.

Or have you ever had a thought stuck in there — popping up over and over again? Was it a negative thought?

I'm sure you have. For most of us, this is a regular habit. Unresolved thoughts tend to pop back up, asking to be resolved. When they are negative, the longer we keep them pending, the more frequently and fiercely they attack. Often, the sequence of thoughts goes beyond just replaying the actual event that upset you. Our brains volunteer additional drama that makes things more colourful, but much worse. The event upsetting you may be, say, that your boss was grumpy on Friday. On Saturday you replay the events to torture yourself. On Sunday, you play it again and make it personal. You start to believe that he's only grumpy with you. A few more replays on Monday where you tell yourself that nobody, not just your boss, ever appreciates you and on Thursday you start to think of how you will live when you are a homeless person on the streets after getting fired and never finding a job again. This process of replaying the same negativity inside our heads happens to all of us. I call it . . .

Loops and Subroutines

When I started to code computers as a child, I was fascinated by how my computer did exactly what I told it to do as it ran through line after line of code. The programming languages of the era, however, were primitive. It would take many lines of code to perform a task. If you coded a few tasks and, when they finished processing, you wanted them to run again, you needed to repeat them, unless you grouped them together and instructed the computer to repeat the whole thing. Those groups were called subroutines – a sequence of programme instructions, packaged as a unit to perform a group of tasks. Sometimes you could tell the computer to repeat an appropriate subroutine as many times as needed until a certain event took place – say, the value of a specific parameter became bigger than ten. This saved us a lot of effort: the computer did what it was told, checked the parameter and, if it was not yet time, would go back and do the tasks again and again and again. The problem was, sometimes that parameter never reached ten and so the process would repeat endlessly. We called that a loop.

The norms of society, the expectations of the workplace and every other rule that we accept and blindly integrate into our lives are the subroutines. Often, we run those sets of instructions on repeat without really thinking about them. They drive our mechanical lifestyle. We rush through every day doing certain things over and over, almost unconsciously. Wake up, get ready, hit the traffic, browse Instagram, get coffee, answer email, get more coffee, when asked how you feel say, 'I'm fine,' and if you feel vulnerable at work, hide it. When you go on a date, make it look like you are easy-going and have no needs or traumas, and if you hate what you do, shut up, get more coffee and keep doing it. The 'routine' continues till the end of your day, only to start again the next day. Week after week and year after year. Any software developer could easily see ... **we're looping**.

The thoughts in our heads keep looping too. We keep repeating them on autopilot without being aware. When something upsets us, we keep thinking about it again and again, sometimes for weeks or even years. I call this the suffering cycle (which I discussed in detail in *Solve for Happy*). The first event that triggers our unhappiness might have been warranted. A grumpy boss is a reason for unhappiness. The following cycles of unhappiness, however, are not triggered by your grumpy boss or any other event in the real world. They are triggered by the thoughts you repeat. I sometimes call this 'unhappiness on demand', the Netflix of unhappiness. Remember that scene that happened last Friday? Let me play this again and torture myself.

Those loops are happening all around us. We can observe them on the faces of people in a crowded place. The thoughts themselves are not observable but their effects cannot be missed. We become absent, living inside our heads and submerged in suffering.

Your brain is not looping because it likes to make you feel bad. On the contrary, it loops because it feels that this is what is best for you. If there is an issue pending, it will bring it back up until it is sure the issue is being attended to or resolved. Once you get what makes your brain do this, it will be easy to resolve.

Think of a friend who's hyperexcited a lot of the time. Once something excites them, they absolutely have to tell you about it . . . that very instant. 'Did you hear? Beyoncé ate a cheeseburger! OMG OMG OMG! We have a car parked near our home that has velvet-covered seats!' Sometimes they have a dream, and you're in it, right? They call you as soon as they open their eyes, even if it's 6 a.m. You don't answer so they call again at seven, then at eight, then at ten past, and again at quarter past. Then they text you, then call again, then text: *You have to hear this!* At 8.30 a.m., the disappointed emojis start to fill your screen. You then wake up at nine and text back saying: *Hey, I just woke up. I'm getting ready to go to work. Can I call you at 10?* As soon as you do this, they go: *Sure, that's fine* and send you a smiley face. That friend is your brain when it feels the urgency to alert you to something it's excited about.

Your brain, like your excited friend, is not trying to annoy you with these thoughts. It genuinely believes that what it has to say is of paramount importance and you're ignoring it, so it says it again. As soon as it can, your brain creates a thought, engages a negative emotion to alert you – which causes you to suffer – and then waits for you to take action. If you do nothing, it brings up the thought again, engages more of the same emotion, and waits. No action? It brings it up again . . . and again. It then adds the emojis – the drama – and wakes you up at night all in hopes of catching your attention – an endless negative chatter that makes you feel bad.

In technical terms, your brain groups a bunch of negative thoughts together (a subroutine), then repeats them endlessly (in a loop), and this becomes the endless chatter of that little voice in your head. Sometimes, very few times, these repetitive thoughts are positive and delightful. *I am so proud of my daughter, Aya*, is one such thought. It helps encourage her to keep going and keeps us closer together. The negative thoughts, however, lead to unhappiness, sometimes even depression. This needs to be stopped.

Loops don't end till we end them. To do that, I need to have a crucial conversation with . . .

Becky

Over the years, as I mentioned earlier, I have come to call my brain Becky – the name of a third party, a separate entity from me.

This started when one of my dear friends, Azrah, read an early draft of *Solve for Happy*; she told me how fascinated she was with the concept of the illusion of thought – that we are not our brains. We met for coffee and while we spoke about various topics, she made a self-deprecating comment which I thought was so unfair I interrupted her and asked, 'Where did that come from?'

She said, 'Oh, sorry. Becky told me.'

I asked, 'Who's Becky?'

She said, 'Becky . . . my brain.'

I laughed and asked, 'Why Becky?'

She said, 'She was the most annoying girl in school – the one that always made me feel bad about myself and made me do things I didn't want to do.'

Imagine that back in school you also had this friend. Let's call her Becky (or Brian if you prefer).

She was the kid who spoke non-stop from the minute you met her to the minute you left and, on top of that, every few minutes or so, she would take you to a corner alone, tell you that you were worthless, complain and complain. When done, she would leave you alone, exhausted and stressed, wondering what that was all about and with nothing resolved or improved. Then, as soon as you managed to catch your breath, she would come back to annoy you some more.

Now let me ask you this: can you picture yourself going to school every morning asking, 'Where is Becky?' When she approaches, would you jump out of your seat and say, 'Yes, Becky, please hurt me.' Would you let Becky speak uninterrupted for hours every day? Would you even want to be friends with Becky at all? Of course not.

For what it's worth, though, let me tell you what Becky has done to me. Then you judge for yourself. Here's my personal story. One that I've never had the courage to share before.

Depressive Me

We've All Been There!

I was not always happy. As a matter of fact, there have been many points in my life when I was completely depressed. My sadness and depression peaked in my late twenties.

I had married the love of my life, Nibal, at age twenty-four. I loved her so deeply, and considered her to be the biggest gift I had ever been given. (I still do today, even after we mutually decided to go our separate ways a few years ago.) Our two wonderful kids, Ali and Aya, joined us before I turned twenty-seven. Now, they were the biggest gift a man could ever dream of. There was nothing more that I needed from life other than to see the three of them happy.

My first job was at IBM. I was hired as a systems engineer. My first monthly salary at IBM was $180 a month. This may not seem much but, compared with the cost of living in Egypt at the time, it was higher than a senior government official and made me the highest earning among my brothers. I could afford a good life for myself and my family. I bought a good car. I was the happiest man you could ever meet. Everything was good. Until it wasn't – or at least until I thought it wasn't.

Those were the boom years for the Arabian Gulf countries. My peers at work could relocate there much more easily than I could because I needed to cover the expenses of a family in the process, and they started earning thousands of dollars in monthly salaries. As single men and women in their twenties, they had lifestyles that would be the envy of any rich brat. They bought fancy cars, rented lavish apartments, partied and travelled to exotic places. They even played the lower-cost Egyptian market to their advantage and bought big villas in lavish parts of town.

I responded by doing what I knew how to do. Worked harder, got promoted and started businesses which all made me more money, by Egyptian standards. I could manage to provide an amazing life for the family, but nothing more.

Nibal and the kids were happy, but I was slowly falling into a deep depression. Somehow, I felt deceived by life. This was despite knowing how lucky I was. I had my wonderful family, all the love in the world, and we had everything, materially, that we needed. But I was dazzled by the fancy lifestyles of my single friends. One thought gripped me and I could not shake it off – *Life is giving my friends more than me, even though I am the hardest working of them all.*

I can look back now and see how unfounded that thought was. I was the one being given more in every possible way – more love, more family, even more skills that would propel my career further than everyone I knew soon after. But my stupid impatience blinded me and, once that thought gripped me, I could think of nothing else.

Like an old man, I started to come home exhausted after a long workday, sit myself in a corner and brood incessantly. Poor Nibal would pour love on me, tell me that everything was brilliant, but I wouldn't listen. In a matter of months, I had moved from happy to miserable because of a thought – one single thought – playing on repeat. That kind of thought is a typical loop – endless cycles reinforcing the same negative concept. With every cycle they become stronger and more frequent, taking us deeper and deeper down a spiral of negativity until we are crushed under it.

I hit rock bottom in less than a few months. I remember vividly one evening bursting into tears. I cursed life, God and my luck. Nibal, that wonderful woman, hugged me and cried for my tears. She felt she could no longer help me, so she started to join my sadness in her empathic attempt to take some of it away.

This was my first turning point. Seeing Nibal in that place triggered me to do something about it. Though, as you might expect, I did not focus on my depression but what I thought the reason for it was. I decided to move to Dubai. That solved the money and lifestyle issues, but the thoughts remained. Instead of comparing myself to my friends, I started comparing myself to the wealthy citizens of Dubai.

It took me years more of deeper unhappiness to realize that I never really needed any of the things I was crying over and that I never even really enjoyed any of the things I spent my life trying to acquire. One fine evening, it all became clear. After years of battling with that one thought, I finally realized that I had everything I needed to be happy. That it was a matter of choice, of perspective – a matter of switching my thought. Instantly, I found my happiness. Not a dollar more had been added to my bank account and nothing in my material world had changed in any way, but I was happy.

Interrupt Levels

Back to computers. In the early days of coding, when the computer got stuck in a loop, it halted. The screen froze and pressing any key on the keyboard yielded no response. The instructions ran frantically inside the machine and fully occupied it. Lost in its own thoughts, the machine lost the ability to express them on output devices, connect to the rest of the world or feel external interactions. This is exactly what had happened to me.

As we surrender to our modern-world programming, we suffer the same symptoms those old machines suffered – an inability to recognize the thoughts that reshape our lives because we're so absorbed in the routine of our frantic life.

To fix this, a skilled developer would make sure that the appropriate 'interrupt levels' were set before he started running his code. Interrupt levels are the instructions that tell the computer to look out for certain events, even while busy doing other things, and allow these to interrupt its mechanical, mindless looping once those events occurred. In plain English, I needed to tell my computer: 'While occupied in performing a specific operation, keep a lookout for the keyboard combination Shift + Q. If I press that special sequence at any point at all, stop whatever it is that you're doing and hand control back over to me.'

I guess you know where I'm going with this. My wonderful mechanical friends, it's time you learned to write your own code and set our very own interrupt levels.

The Contract

Being stuck in a thought that make you unhappy works against you in two ways. Firstly, it makes you feel awful and who wants that? Secondly, it adds no value whatsoever. You can choose to stay unhappy for an hour, a day, a year or a lifetime. Regardless of how dedicated you are to your unhappiness, nothing will change. Thinking that unhappiness will resolve the issue is what I call a false contract with life.

Perhaps this deadlock stems from back when we cried as young children so that an adult would come and help, offering love and tenderness. Some of us believe that this will be true in adulthood too. I don't know what makes us do it. Some of us stay unhappy without taking charge of the trigger for our unhappiness. Is that in the hope that life will fix it? When did life commit that to you? Can you dig through your old papers and show me that contract? Well, I have news for you. You are not a little kid any more. No one will show up to the rescue even if you cried for years. The only way to change your life is to be in charge. You need to sign real contracts.

On my relentless quest for happiness, I signed one with my brain – a contract that is enforced in every transaction between us.

Mo's gone all metaphysical on me now, you may think. *Like, who has a contract with their brain? I mean, when I feel unhappy, I can't help it.*

Well, I'm sorry but that's wrong. I have shared with you analogies between your brain and software since the beginning of this book. Nothing about your brain is more like software than its full compliance to do as it's told. Any software code is nothing more than a slave – it repeats the same tasks assigned to it exactly as instructed. No classical software ever written has ever decided to improvise or follow its own choice. If you coded it to show a circle on the screen, it will show a circle on the screen.

This is also true for your brain. Despite its natural intelligence, it does exactly what it is instructed to do. No one has ever instructed his brain to raise his left hand and it decided to shake his right foot instead. The reason why the thoughts presented by our brains sometimes appear to be random or against our own wellbeing is because we give those weird instructions to our brains. Even then, they do exactly as they're told.

You don't believe me when I say that, do you? That's exactly where the biggest dysfunction in our relationship with our brains resides, because how do we even begin to tame a beast if we don't believe it's tameable?

When I was a child, my school would organize a field trip once a year for us to watch the 'national circus'. The parts that intrigued me most were when the wild animals took centre stage. Here's a massive, aggressive-looking tiger being approached by a thin, weirdly dressed man. In my little brain, I thought: *There will be blood. Someone stop this idiot.* But the trainer of the beast did not seem to think that way. He approached with such confidence that whatever he instructed was performed by the tiger – no questions asked. The tiger did backflips, allowed a rabbit to ride on its back and sacrificed its dignity as a predator in every conceivable way. Every year, I came home thinking that perhaps the most valuable asset needed for you to be able to tame a wild beast is just the solid belief that you can.

Your brain may be a different kind of beast, but it still does exactly what you tell it to do. This holds true even when you're feeling unhappy. You may feel upset about something and obsess about it on your commute to work or school. Once you get there, however, as soon as your boss or teacher asks for the report that is due today, you snap back into attention. *Enough thinking about what upsets us. We need that report.* Your brain complies instantly: *Sir, yes sir!* It stops thinking negative thoughts and shifts to the task at hand.

It's doable – every single time. You just need to tell your brain what to do.

Why is it then that you don't do that without a boss telling you to? Well, what can I say? You need a boss because you're not yet the boss.

This is not the case with me. I'm the boss and Becky knows it. When she feels like complaining 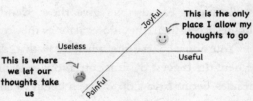 about something, I treat her as a good boss would. First, I listen attentively for a while and then I ask her to look at things differently. I insist that my brain starts to think the correct way and provide me with either joyful or useful thoughts.

Let me give you a couple of examples – painful as they are to me.

Bring Me a Better Thought

We've All Been There!

I'm not immune to unhappiness. But I know reasonably well how to stick to the contract I signed with my brain whenever it starts to make me unhappy – and it does that a lot. Since the moment my wonderful son, Ali, left our world, there has never been a day when the memory of losing him has not crossed my mind. My brain is very good at reminding me by saying – several times a day – *Ali died*. 'Ali died' is a very painful thought. No words can ever describe what it feels like to lose a child. All I can say is that it triggers a physical pain in my heart, as I told you earlier, in the bottom right-hand side, almost as if someone had cut that part of me off and left a void behind. This pain comes over me rapidly and it is exactly as intense as on the day he left. Not an ounce less, not even a tiny tad easier. Yet, *Ali died* is only half of the truth – the half that my brain elects to bring up. There is another side – and I have developed a strategy, in compliance with my contract with Becky, to see this happier side of the truth. Every time my brain says, *Ali died*, I answer with the other half. I say: *I know, brain, but **Ali also lived***.

That Ali lived is a wonderful, truly joyful thought. When I say it, often out loud, I remember all the wonderful moments we spent together. All the music we played, all the jokes we made, all the laughter, hugs and wisdom. All the warmth, love and happiness. Ali was a gift that I never expected. One I was not even qualified to receive. The pain of losing him fades in comparison to the bliss of having had him in the first place.

Ali lived, brain. That's the thought.

Ali died. Yes, that's true. But *Ali lived* is also true – it's the joyful side of the truth. I choose joy. I remind myself every day that Ali still lives. *Alive*.

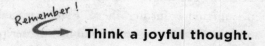

Think a joyful thought.

When Ali died, due to a preventable human error, my brain attacked me viciously. It told me I had failed in my role as a father. I was supposed to protect him. It kept me trapped in one thought:

You should have driven him to another hospital. For days, I had no other thought in my head ... and it hurt. It hurt and it hurt but **it did not change anything**. On day four after his departure, I took a stand and told my brain (out loud): 'I know, brain. I wish I could have driven him to a different hospital, but I can't go back in time to change where we went. Most importantly,' I continued, 'this thought is useless, brain. Give me something that I can actually act upon – something that can make things better.'

It took time because my brain still kept trying to take me back down that same negative thought spiral. But I stuck to my same response: *Give me a **useful** thought.* My persistence paid off on the night of Ali's memorial, when my brain, reluctantly, offered the thought that I should sit down to write Ali's approach to happiness and share it with the world.

Yes, brain, yes!! Great idea. It still would not bring Ali back, but hopefully it would make things better. As I spent the following months and years delivering on this mission, believe me, it did make things better.

The day I hugged Ali for the last time, I saw how he had developed into a handsome, tall, wise young man, one any parent would be proud of. It was the highest point of my life. I don't expect to be back at that point any time soon, if ever. Hours later, when I carried him on my shoulder to his resting place, was my lowest point. Many grieving parents just throw in the towel and give up on life. They spend the rest of their lives at that low point and never recover. I can assure you that, today, I am not at that point either. I am much further ahead. Fully engaged. Feeling energized and hopeful that our world will be a better place. This makes me believe that it was not for nothing that Ali left. Millions who had been consumed by unhappiness may have now found hope for a happier life, all because of what this magnificent young man planted in me. All because of one useful thought: that *I should honour him and make the world aware of what he taught me.* It still does not bring Ali back, mind you. But it makes my every day slightly better than the one before.

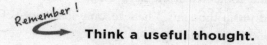

Remember !

Think a useful thought.

This contract that you sign with your brain, when strictly enforced, works. It not only makes you happier, but it also helps you become more successful by ensuring you don't waste valuable brain cycles caught up in useless incessant thought.

At the risk of sounding oversimplistic, if I had to name one cause of most of the unhappiness we feel, it would surely be the loops and subroutines of incessant thought. Accordingly, if asked for one cure for all unhappiness, I say that would have to be the antidote to incessant thought – deliberate attention applied to ensure that the contract above is always in effect.

Masterful practitioners of happiness are fully aware of the events taking place in their life. Being human, negative events sometimes charge them with negative emotions or trigger pain. They fully embrace these emotions, but this is as far as they allow their current to flow. They use deliberate attention to ensure that these emotional charges do not trigger harmful cur-

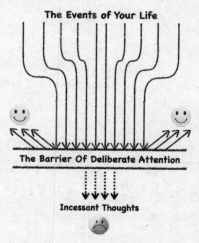

The Events of Your Life

The Barrier Of Deliberate Attention

Incessant Thoughts

rents of uncontrolled loops of thoughts that turn into recurring suffering. Instead, they look at the situation holistically, find its positive side and use that to generate joyful thoughts. They also use the stored emotional potential to initiate useful thoughts that can work in their favour. They make things better while keeping peaceful and contented at the same time.

Beyond joyful thoughts, I believe, only four types of thoughts can be considered useful.

1. Experience (life exactly as it is)
2. Solve (problems and address challenges)
3. Flow (to find your optimum performance)
4. Give (to find your ultimate state of happiness)

Master those and we're done.

Easy, this will not be. Useful, it will indeed be.

Summary of Part Two

*T*he impact of a thought is surely not confined within our skull and surely not to the instant that thought took place. What you think changes you emotionally and physically, and then it changes your pattern of thinking itself as it plays endlessly on repeat.

Our emotions, erratic as they sometimes may seem, are hyperpredictable. They are triggered by thoughts that follow repeatable patterns. The modern world teaches us to hide our emotions and this disconnects us from them, even to deny them. Leaving our emotions unexpressed turns us into zombies walking through life uninterested or pressure cookers waiting to explode.

But we only feel alive when we feel, just like we only feel when we are alive. We need to get in touch with our emotions, acknowledge them — even celebrate them — sit with them, experience their storms and harness their energy to move us forward.

Our autonomic nervous system responds to the world even before our thoughts catch up with what happened. Our sympathetic nervous system stresses us to protect us. It prepares us to face challenges and threats with superhuman powers. This feature in our design saved our species, but now, as our stress response lingers, it is leading us to unhappiness.

We need to engage our parasympathetic nervous system to remind our bodies that things are OK. Learn to relax, be around those who do, and create a sense of safety by remembering our blessings and removing what stresses us from our lives.

Finally, we need to stop the endless loops of incessant thinking. They take us down a spiral of unhappiness and leave no positive impact on the world whatsoever. To stop the thinking, treat your brain like a third party. I call mine Becky and I have a clear agreement with my brain. Bring me joyful thoughts or useful thoughts. Every other thought is a waste of my life. Sign the contract. Get your brain to comply.

Part Three

The Neural Path to a Happier Life

A brain is always welcomed when it brings up a joyful thought. Otherwise, the only thoughts allowed are useful – experiential thoughts, problem-solving, being in flow and giving. This is the shortest path to make the world better and make yourself happier.

Welcome to the Real World

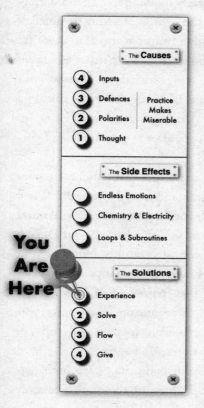

Remember the Default Mode Network we discussed in Chapter Six, the parts of the brain that become active when we think in the absence of regulated attention? Remember how we said that an overactive Default Mode Network is associated with many of the clinical conditions of unhappiness – such as depression, substance abuse and anxiety? We also found that when our minds wander, we tend to feel less happy.

At the opposite end of this is what science refers to as the Task Positive Network. This network includes the parts of our brain that light up when we focus. At the core of this network is a type of thinking that we usually don't recognize as thinking at all, though without it, no other thinking could ever be useful. That thinking is the way we perceive the environment around us and inside us. It's how we experience the world – call it . . .

Experiential Thinking

Experiential thinking includes all kinds of brain activities that are concerned with observing life exactly as it is. You think experientially when you're attentively listening to a friend, admiring the beauty of a butterfly's colourful wings, enjoying the smell of coffee or tuning into the noises and the music as you sit in a cafe. It's noticing a change in the body language of your partner as a result of a comment you made. It's looking inwards to observe your breathing as you inhale and exhale. It's recognizing the pain in a specific part of your body, or experiencing your storm of emotions as they swirl, triggering physical signatures in your body and corresponding thoughts in your head.

Deliberate attention is the key ingredient that switches on your ability to observe the world inside and outside yourself. When you are experiencing the world, you engage your Task Positive Network. Simultaneously, attention also switches off your Default Mode Network and, in the process, significantly increases your feelings of calm, peace and happiness as the loops of incessant thoughts disappear. This means that, regardless of how intense your incessant thoughts are and how unhappy they make you, once you pay deliberate attention, your unhappiness will stop – or at least will pause until you start ruminating again.

There are many reasons why your brain can't keep both networks running at the same time. Three of these are freakishly similar to how computers work: limited resources, switching cost and processor speed.

Limited Resources

Have you noticed, when you are creating a back-up or installing system updates, how your computer gives you that annoying scale that lasts for ages? 10 per cent complete, 11 per cent complete, 12 per cent complete. Why does it not just get it done?

Our computers operate within an environment of limited resources. If the file you download from the internet is a gigabyte in size and the network speed is a gigabit per second, the file will need a thousand seconds to download. It's just how it is. Our brains, though still smarter than our computers, suffer the exact same limitation.

Watch how your brain works as you try to cross the street. This seemingly simple process dwarfs even the best computers we've invented so far. Your brain collects information from sensors, your eyes and ears, performs incredibly complex spatial calculations to observe where every car is going to be in the following few seconds, then performs magical motor control functions for you to walk – balanced upright – across the street. What a machine! Give your brain the task of listening to your friend and mother talking at the same time, however, and it will fail miserably. Why? Simply because it does not have enough computational power to do both tasks at the same time.

To understand how this works, let's do a simple exercise. Please set a timer for sixty seconds and attempt to add the odd numbers in the following Sudoku puzzle while you read the letters in the sentence at the bottom backwards (that is to say S – D – R – A – W ... and so on). Ready? Sixty seconds. Go!

7	6	2	3	2	7	9	4	2
7	1	4	8	4	3	6	3	9
6	7	3	8	9	4	7	9	4
1	7	7	9	7	6	5	7	4
8	2	1	6	5	8	7	6	3
7	4	1	2	7	6	8	1	7
5	4	1	7	4	7	9	8	9
9	4	9	1	8	8	6	9	3
2	3	3	6	2	8	8	6	1

READ THE LETTERS IN THIS
SENTENCE BACKWARDS

Did you manage to smoothly read the letters backwards as you did the maths? Even the maths geeks in you that thought, *Every square includes a 1, 3, 5, 7 and 9 which adds to 25, and there are nine squares so the answer is 25 x 9 = 225*, could not have done that while reading the sentence backwards. Also, by the way, because you were not observing the actual image but judging by what you know about Sudoku, you missed that some of the squares have the wrong numbers in them so not all squares actually add to 25. The point is, no one manages to read the letters while adding the numbers correctly. No way. Why?

Because even though our brain is the most sophisticated computer on the planet, it still – as with every other computer – has limited resources. Those resources are usually sufficient to perform only one task at a time.

There is ample scientific research that points to the concept of limited brain resources. Visual decision tasks, for example, where participants are shown a string of letters and asked if the string is an actual word, are used to measure brain processing capacity. As the complexity of the task increases, the participants' brains run out of processing power and this causes their reaction time to become slower.

Hick's Law states that the time it takes to make a choice is linearly related to the variety of the possible alternatives. When the amount of brain resources needed to resolve the complexity at hand are limited, the brain takes longer to find the answer.

Moscoso del Prado Martín from the Université de Provence in France uses lexical decision tasks, where participants are asked **to decide, as quickly and as accurately as possible**, if a word shown to them is a real word, to determine how much information the brain can process. His research indicates that the average human can process no more than about sixty bits per second.[1] To put this in context, to understand the words of one person talking to you, you normally need a little more than half of that. That's why it's easy to listen attentively to one person speaking but it becomes very difficult, even impossible for most of us, to make out what two people say at the same time. You simply don't have the brain resources for it.

It's funny, but as I write this, I am sitting in a cafe in Montreal. Just a few minutes ago, a group of Arabic speakers sat down at the table next to me. As they speak in English or Arabic, my writing speed becomes significantly slower. As soon as they switch to French, which is a language I do not speak and so I dedicate zero brain cycles to deciphering, I go back to my normal speed.

Our brain's limited processing power is the first reason why paying attention switches off incessant thinking. The second you pay attention, you start to dedicate your limited brain resources to what you're focusing on and that normally leaves your brain with insufficient resources to think incessantly. So, the thoughts stop. It's that simple.

Remember!

> **Your brain has just about enough power to do only one thing at a time.**

But then what about multitasking? You could be brushing your teeth, listening to the news and thinking about paying the rent on your apartment all at the same time. How do we do that? We switch between the tasks as frequently as we can, like a juggler constantly redirecting his attention fully to the one ball that is about to fall while ignoring the other balls that have been set in motion higher in the air. As we switch between the tasks we're trying to perform, however, the processing power required to do this exceeds the sum of the processing power needed to perform each individual task. Some additional attention is needed for the act of switching itself. This is known as . . .

Switching Cost

To understand how multitasking works, and the tax it applies on your brain resources, let's do another simple exercise. Set a timer to fifteen seconds and please look at the pictures of the animals and birds opposite. Attempt to say, out loud, the names of as many animals and the words written in front of them as you can. Say the name of the animal you actually see first, then read the word written in front of it.

Ready? Go.

Did you manage to do this smoothly without errors? Or did you have to pause as you moved from animal to animal, for a tiny bit, to remember the name? Did you sometimes make mistakes — reading the word before you said the name of the animal in the picture or saying the wrong name due to the contradiction between the picture and the word?

Most of us stumble as we do this exercise because images are processed in the right hemisphere of your brain while words are processed in the left. When both are displayed, the word is primed for the brain because it's on top. Your brain is told to say the name though, so it takes time to switch back to processing the image and when there is a contradiction between the different perceptions, it stumbles even more as you move back and forth to verify which is correct. The only way for you to perform this task at blazing speeds is to stop the switching by separating the words and the images on two different sheets.

Even without the information contradiction, switching still comes at a cost. In tests performed by the Department of Nuclear Medicine, University of Michigan, subjects were instructed to perform a memory task while simultaneously verifying simple maths equations. The results demonstrated that there was a cost in accuracy and latency when both tasks were to be performed simultaneously as compared with performing each component task alone. This cost was a result of the brain dedicating part of its processing power to regions of the prefrontal cortex that were active in the dual-task tests but not active in performing the component tasks.[2]

To switch between tasks takes time and brain resources. Therefore, distracted attention seems to drain us as we make very little progress. This is also why those who get distracted often find their thoughts tend to stay shallow and repetitive.

Remember!

Switching between tasks costs your brain valuable resources.

Then there's one more thing to consider. It seems that our brains tick faster when performing certain tasks and slower when performing others.

Processor Speed

Not all tasks are performed by your brain at the same speed. I'm not saying that different tasks are performed faster than others, but that your brain itself becomes faster when performing certain tasks and slower when performing others.

As a young geek, when I bought a new computer, what mattered most to me was a measure of its ability to perform calculations. This, at the time, was measured in clock speed, or megahertz, the number of times the clock of the processor could tick per second. With every tick of that clock, our primitive processors could perform one single calculation. Faster processors were better, obviously, because they could do more calculations.

With the advancements of EEG brain scans, it is becoming evident that your brain is very similar in its behaviour. The clock speed of your brain seems to tick faster or slower depending on the specific task it performs. I find this fascinating.

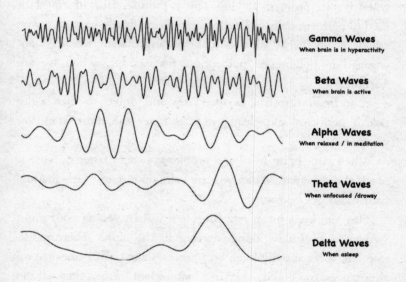

Gamma Waves
When brain is in hyperactivity

Beta Waves
When brain is active

Alpha Waves
When relaxed / in meditation

Theta Waves
When unfocused /drowsy

Delta Waves
When asleep

Neurons work by sending nerve impulses — electrical signals — from one to the next, transferring messages around the brain and the body. It's this electrical activity, sometimes called 'brain waves', that is picked up by EEG scans.[3] Those waves happen at different frequencies depending on the brain state and what function it's performing. EEG studies tend to group those into different frequency bands.

Delta waves tick slowly up to 4 times per second (hertz). They usually happen in states of deep restful sleep. Theta waves tick at speeds of between 4 and 8 hertz and occur when we are awake but unfocused, drowsy or non-vigilant, perhaps mind wandering or during light sleep. We can deliberately get ourselves into the theta spectrum when we meditate and they also happen when we are deeply relaxed, which means not bothered even by our inner thoughts. Alpha waves tick at between 8 and 13 hertz. Beta waves tick between 13 and 30 hertz when we exert focused attention, when we are problem-solving. This is the spectrum of the brain used to perform daily tasks effectively. Then, finally, gamma waves, which are in the 30 hertz and above range, occur when we are engaged in heightened perception, for example when we are learning.[4]

Your brain throttles its speed up and down to match the task it performs and clearly it ticks faster the more attention you pay.

When your brain is solving problems, it ticks faster because it needs the resources. When you are calm, in a state of meditation, your brain ticks slower.

This requires a bit of reflection here. When you let your mind wander, it meanders along, starting in the alpha spectrum. To stop the incessant thinking, you are presented with one of two alternatives. You could slow your brain down further, through the act of meditation. That way, with a slower processor, you deprive the looping thoughts of the processing power they need to exist. Alternatively, you could push the throttle, through an act of deliberate attention. While that increases your processing power by increasing the number of calculations your brain can do per second, it consumes the available processing power to focus on the tasks you are paying attention to.

Remember!

The speed at which your brain performs incessant thinking is too fast for calm meditation and too slow for heightened attention.

Speed up or slow down your brain. Just don't drift aimlessly.

And you know what the coolest hack is? Regular meditation helps you to more easily achieve states of hyperperception and improve the overall functioning abilities of the brain. Researchers at the University of Wisconsin–Madison have found that, during meditation, Zen Buddhist monks produced gamma waves that were extremely high in amplitude (the depth of the waves). Waves from disparate brain regions were in near lockstep (showing that the brain was in a robust synchronicity across its various functions), which was sustained for remarkably long periods.[5]

What is common between states of meditation and states of hyperperception? Only one thing: a sense of deliberate attention to experience and engage with what is – the highest forms of brain performance a human can attain.

Remember!

The first step to finding happiness is to start paying attention.

Your Complex Processor

Take your brain's limited resources, the cost of switching tasks and its variable processor speed together and it becomes clear that the path to a happy mind resides in dedicating the limited resources of your brain away from distraction to the type of deliberate attention that keeps us focused. In that sense, experiential thinking – as in dedicated undistracted attention to what is – completely suspends our incessant thought. It works.

It's just a matter of simple maths . . .

For any cognitive task to be performed, the following equation has to hold true . . .

Processing Capacity needed for the task + Switching Time = Available Brain Resources

If the available brain resources are not sufficient for the task to be performed, our brains prioritize the task they are instructed (by us) to perform, and drop everything else. In doing so, they suspend background tasks, such as incessant thoughts, to free up the resources they need. If you instruct your brain to fully experience the current moment, every smell, every sound and every sensation, it will run out of brain resources to think of anything else.

Remember!

Focus on something real and the brain chatter stops!

Now, if experiential thinking were a sport, the Olympic champions of this would surely be the monks of Eastern religions who practise it diligently in the form of meditation.

Meditation Works

Meditation is all about mastering experiential thinking. When you meditate, you don't use your brain to learn, plan or solve problems. You don't use it to do anything. You use it to just be. Meditation is all about dedicating your brain's resources to observing the world exactly as it is.

Meditation works because the act of deliberate attention

activates those regions of your brain that you want active and suspends the parts you don't. The attention consumes all of your available brain resources, which tend to be reduced as your brain ticks slower. So none are left for your mind to wander to thoughts that may upset you.

Thanks to neuroplasticity, years of diligent meditation practice completely rewires our brains. Sarah Lazard, from the University of Boston, ran a study to measure the long-term impact that meditation has on the structure of our brains. The brains of the study participants were MRI scanned before and after they did an eight-week meditation-based stress reduction programme where they were told to meditate for thirty to forty minutes every day. The results showed that areas of the brain responsible for learning, memory and emotion regulation became larger. These are the exact regions of the brain that shrink in people who suffer from depression or post-traumatic stress disorder. Another region that becomes larger is the region that gives us perspective, empathy and compassion, and there was also a decrease in the parts of the brain constantly looking for possible threats – and triggering stress as a result. Meditation uses the best part of the brain and you know the rule ... What you use grows and what you don't shrinks.

Dr Richie Davidson scanned the brains of Tibetan monks using MRI and EEG. One participant – Matthieu Ricard, a French writer, photographer, translator and Buddhist monk – became the face of this research when the media named him the happiest man in the world. His scans showed that when meditating on compassion, Ricard's brain produced a level of gamma waves (which are linked to consciousness, attention, learning and memory) 'never reported before in neuroscience literature', Dr Davidson said. The scans also showed excessive activity in his brain's left pre-frontal cortex compared to its right counterpart, allowing him an abnormally large capacity for happiness and a reduced propensity towards negativity.[6]

I'm telling you. This stuff works.

Remember !

→ **Meditation, done correctly, rewires us to become happier, more empathetic and compassionate.**

But there's a catch.

The monks who participated in these studies had been meditating for a lifetime – accruing 34,000 hours of lifetime practice on average, according to Dr Davidson. That's why their MRI scans showed almost superhuman abilities and why they are an example to all of us in how to find calmness, empathy and compassion.

I wish I could follow in their footsteps but how many of us can actually achieve that? Given the rapid pace of our modern lives, how many of us succeed in even sticking to a daily meditation practice? Very few.

When Meditation Fails?

On the launch of *Solve for Happy*, I spoke at the World Happiness Summit. Speaking to more than a thousand people in the room, I asked: 'Who here meditates?' Most hands went up. So, I said: 'Keep your hand up if you meditated every day for the last month.' More than half put their hands down. Then I said to those who meditated every day: 'Doesn't it feel amazing at the end of your meditation?' They all nodded in approval. Then I said: 'Keep your hand up if it still feels amazing three hours later when you've gone back to the hustle and bustle of life?' Almost every hand disappeared.

Committed to his path, Matthieu Ricard has dedicated more than fifty years of his life to his practice. He has lived in India, Bhutan and Nepal. His retreat place, a remote hut on top of a mountain, is 9 foot by 9 foot with a big window, no heating, no hot water or any of the luxuries of life. He spent more than five years there in solitary isolation, waking up every morning at 3.30 a.m. to practise. When I hosted him on my podcast, Slo Mo, I asked him how he could put up with such harsh conditions. He answered, 'What harsh conditions? It's my favourite place in the world.'[7]

Meditation is a practice that was developed for a different time and a different lifestyle. Monks need to meditate four hours a day for seventeen years or more to rewire their brains enough to view the world correctly even as they left the meditation room. I urge you to do that or as much of it as you can. The rewards are immense when you do. I meditate fiercely and have not missed a day for more than 600 days. It makes a mega difference but, even then, I need more. Without the hours, you're deceiving yourself in assuming that meditation, the traditional way, is a good enough practice to help you find uninterrupted happiness.

When the stresses of life become too much to bear, those who are a little more enlightened rush to the meditation room. For as long as deliberate attention is exercised during meditation, the impact is felt vividly. But often as soon as we're out of the meditation room, and once again engaged in a stressful life, we revert to our stressed condition. The short-term impact of meditation on all of us is undeniable. Even fifteen minutes will change your day and make a difference. But if you're the type that skips a few days of practice every now and again, you will fail to reap the long-term rewards. If you want the real deal . . .

Meditation needs to become a lifestyle.

Meditating, the traditional way, for hours every day is an option that most of us, who are out in the streets battling with life, don't have. What should we do then? Find an alternative form of meditation that's fit for the modern world. Let me share with you what works for me.

Meditation for the Modern World

You don't need to sit cross-legged with your palm in the shape of a Chin Mudra and say *om* to meditate. You can practise by cultivating qualities such as full presence and deliberate attention every moment of your day. To do that, I use brain games. I've listed some ideas here; you don't need to do them all. Pick the ones that you like and do just enough of them to make deliberate attention a noticeable part of your lifestyle.

One Beautiful Thing

I choose to walk whenever I can instead of taking transport. Often I walk to work and meetings. In the past as I walked, like every busy executive, I read my emails, made phone calls and thought about the day ahead. I was multitasking; it saved me a bit of time and every business book told me that was a good thing. But they were wrong. While I may have got a few extra things done, my distracted attention also added stress and deprived me of an opportunity to experience life instead of just running through it.

One day I recognized that those walks presented an incredible opportunity for me to calm my brain. All I did was give myself an easy task – **take one beautiful photograph a day**. With that simple instruction, I found myself properly experiencing my surroundings. I was looking for beauty and so I found it. Even in cities that are thought of as concrete jungles, I saw more butterflies, more roses and more smiley faces than I had ever seen before. For years, my regular forty-minute walk to work became my refuge from my fast-paced life, my sanity in the madness, an oasis of calm in the frantic rush that surrounded me everywhere. Everything slowed down for me and I managed to find peace. It wasn't only that the beauty I found all around me uplifted me. It was that the attention I paid as I looked for that beauty calmed my mind.

Only Good Music

When I drive or commute anywhere, I use music to trigger my focused attention. I never play music in the background while I am distracted with something else. Instead, I set six stations on my radio and pay attention to make sure **I only listen to songs that I love**. I give my brain a clear target – I will not listen to an annoying presenter blabbering away, I will not listen to a song that I don't like and I will not listen to commercials. If any of these come on the radio, my alert brain finds it and I switch to the next station. If that isn't playing a song that I love either, I select the next station and the next, and if I find no music that I love on all six, I switch off the radio and wait sixty seconds before I switch it on again to repeat the exercise.

There is so much joy in doing this. When you experience music deliberately, not as background noise, you contemplate the lyrics, you hear the bass guitar and every subtle tune. This is music at a whole new level. The act of paying attention to look for songs is an act of active meditation. So don't say meditation is hard; it can be a lot of fun.

Every Number

At work, it's easy to get distracted with the rush, emails and politics. Your mind can wander when a meeting is boring or a conversation is irrelevant. To keep my mind focused, I taught myself to focus on every number on every slide. I would stop the presenter to explain where it came from and what it meant. They'd say, 'But, Mo, that's not important,' and I responded, 'If it's not important, don't put it on the slide.' Quickly, the team learned to keep our slides cleaner and our conversations leaner. We became fully present, focusing only on the stuff that matters. When I meet people one to one, I put my phone down, look them in the eye and give them my full attention. I ask questions and I am always fully present listening to the answer. This helps me calm my brain and train it to experience work fully. It also helps me learn more, dig deeper and so make better decisions. It helps my team feel valued, heard, acknowledged and seen. This single move helped and continues to help me succeed in my career.

Mo-time

Then I have my time alone. I call it Mo-time. If you saw me then, I would look funny because there I would be sitting in a room alone for fifteen minutes every three or four hours at work. No phone in my hand. Not talking to anyone, not answering emails, not writing. I would literally be doing nothing other than observing the thoughts in my brain. Practising this regularly resets your brain into a mode of silence and observation that completely calms the beast.

Tense?

I have noticed that when I am thinking incessantly, even the tiniest thought, I feel a tension in the muscles of my forehead and scalp. For that, I learned to observe how quiet my brain is by sensing that tension. Practise directing your attention to those areas of your body that feel tense. Once you observe them, you can focus – not on stopping the thoughts but on releasing the tension. It really is an incredible feeling. I find that when you manage to relax that tension, your thoughts actually stop – just like when your thoughts stop, the tensions dissolve. But it's not an on–off switch. I've come to recognize that, when I relax, there is another level of tension still present, so I release that, and sometimes there is still more tension present. This shortcut is one of my favourite exercises to stop my thoughts. I don't know if it will work for you but try it anyway.

One Thing at a Time

Multitasking is a myth. The only way you can fully pay attention to what you do is to focus on one thing at a time. We fall into the trap of multitasking either because we want to squeeze more into our limited time or because we can't live with the boredom of doing things attentively. We try to drive and make phone calls at the same time, work out and listen to a podcast to become more productive. Then we listen to music while we fill in forms, trying to make the task a little less boring. Well, think about the experience of making a phone call or listening to music while you respond to emails. You will notice that when you focus on the music, you don't really make much progress on the emails, but once you decide to get done with emails, the music turns to background and you may not even remember which songs were playing. To fully experience your life, do your best to do one thing at a time. If you talk to a friend, fully enjoy the conversation. If you play music, fully tune in and dance. Even when you fill in your tax report, give it your undivided attention and enjoy the progress that you make as this mundane task comes closer to its end. The task will become easier, you will finish it faster and, most importantly, you will fully live the moments during which you did it.

I sometimes play this game by not mixing foods. Take one bite. Taste it fully, chew it well, swallow, then take another one. Mindful eating is a refined form of meditation. Try it with mixed nuts. Take one, taste it fully then experience another, different, one. Even better, isolate your senses. Try to use ear plugs as you watch nature or an eye mask as you listen to music. Use both as you stretch your body. This dedicates all of your brain's resources to what you're sensing and magnifies every experience several-fold.

Do It Like It's the First Time

Another interesting trick is to force yourself to perform every task as if you are doing it for the first time. Be curious, focus on every step, and make sure you do what you do as well as you can. It matters that your tasks are perfect, but what matters more is that you fully experience them. The first email you sent on the first day of work took a lot of attention and concentration. You read what you received then read it again. You then wrote a response, saved it, waited a bit, then read it again, edited it, read it again, then asked a friend if it was good enough and finally, when you felt it was perfect, you clicked send. Why not do that every time? When you cook, read the recipe again, taste what you're cooking, then adjust the spices. When you play a video game, assume it's the first time you ever touched a controller. Feel amazed by the graphics and explore every part of the game. Remember that first kiss? (Need I ask?) Why not make every kiss a first kiss? If you really want to pay attention, do everything as if you were doing it for the first time, the best time.

Body Scan

Feeling every sensation in your body is a deliberate act of observation that completely tunes you into yourself as a form of meditation. Direct your attention to every inch of your body, from your head to your toes. **Tune in and find how you feel.** If you find tensions or stresses, be kind to yourself. Stretch or massage the aching part gently. Try to listen to what your body is telling you instead of ignoring it or swallowing medicines to silence it. (I'll include an awareness exercise around this later in the chapter.)

Experience the Storm

Connecting with your emotions is harder than connecting with your physical sensations. This needs a black-belt level of awareness. Finding how you feel, acknowledging it, sitting with it and finally embracing it requires deliberate intention and introspection. This too is a form of meditation. Refer back to the 'Experience the Storm' awareness exercise we discussed earlier (p. 212) and make this part of your day, or even several times a day.

Human Connection

This is my absolute favourite way of paying attention – connecting with you and every human I come across. Try to look people in the eye and listen attentively. Put your phone down and completely tune into the energy of another. Don't judge what they say. Don't allow yourself to judge how they look. Don't assume what they feel and don't make up stories about who they are or how they got to who they've become. Ask questions. Then shut up and listen. Listening, once our brains stop blabbering away, is a much bigger joy than talking. There is nothing more enjoyable than being totally present in a conversation. Nothing is more human than giving another human a safe space to share. As you let yourself be fully drawn into the world of another, you live twice. You learn twice. I'm a human connection junkie; you will notice it if (and hopefully when) we meet. It makes me feel alive.

Please note, however, that connecting to the negative energy of another is a slippery slope. If the conversation is aiming to object-ively assess reality it becomes a form of experiencing the world for two. But when the conversation is just about complaining and whining, it brings both of you down with double the force.

These are a few of the games that I play with my brain. Use them if you like, or develop your own. Just find ways to draw your brain into states of full presence and intense attention throughout your day. The modern world teaches us that being productive and effi-cient is about delivering results in the material world. Often the brain games you need to play to engage your deliberate attention may not have any material gains at all – and that's absolutely fine. The value you gain from experiential thinking is mostly felt inside you. It calms you down – and so helps you to make better deci-sions. It makes you more aware and informed – and so smarter. And with the impact of neuroplasticity over time, the deliberate attention you practise makes your brain more peaceful by default, so fewer things will aggravate or upset you. In the long term, those changes to your brain will go help you achieve success on top of your happiness.

Putting all the games together, I managed to add three to four hours of deliberate attention every day for years on end. It did not feel like meditation and certainly did not feel like hard work. It was just fun and the impact on me was undeniable. You can do this too. It will change your life. Experience life every minute of your day.

All the brain games (other than Mo-time) I listed above were, if you noticed, focused on observing the world outside me. There is a whole world inside each of us to explore and experience. Here are a few exercises that can help you direct your attention and experience inwards.

This is a well-known meditation technique used to help you calm your mind by focusing on a specific part of your body and feeling the life in it.

Awareness Exercise Body Scan

Homework

Target	To become aware of your body
Duration	15 minutes
Repeat	Repeat daily
You'll need	A quiet corner Deliberate attention

I will use it here to help you scan your body, as an engineer would scan a faulty machine, inch by inch, until you become fully aware of every pain, fatigue, irregularity or dysfunction.

Find a quiet place and make sure you won't be interrupted for at least ten to fifteen minutes. Sit upright in a comfortable position. Put your feet on the ground and your palms in a position where your arms feel rested.

Now start to scan every part of your body and every one of your organs, starting from your head down to your toes.

Let's do this: direct your attention to your head. Can you feel any headache? Can you pinpoint exactly where it is?

You don't have to do anything about what you find. Just take note of it and move on. Now, direct your attention to your forehead. Can you feel any tension?

Your eyes. Your cheekbones. Your nose. Any discomfort? Any abnormal sensations? How about your sinuses, your ears? Any pain?

Let's focus on your throat, how is that feeling?

Your teeth. Have you been grinding them? Can you feel it in your jaw?

Keep going. How is your stomach feeling? Has it been struggling lately? Any other abdominal pains? Bloating? Discomfort?

Let's not skip your lungs. All good? Are you breathing deeply enough? Give it a try: take a very deep breath, as deep as you can go and then some. Does that feel different from the way you normally feel?

How about your neck? There must be a bit of tension there. Move your head to the left and the right, does it still feel OK? Lean your head forward, back and sideways. All good?

Shoulders – OK? Back – rested?

How about those legs? Your feet? Are they tired?

Good.

Now that you've given yourself a first round of full awareness of your body, give it another scan. Go through the whole thing one more time, promptly. Attempt to feel everything you took note of previously. Just make sure that's it and nothing is missing.

Now that you know how this is done, make it a daily practice. Do it wherever you are – a cafe, a classroom or on your bed before you sleep. Once a day, practise experiential thinking by connecting fully to your body.

Our bodies speak to us all the time but few of us are listening. They're telling us all the things they need and often all the remedies to their pain. If we listen, we can fix a lot.

Practice Exercise
Self-healing

Target	Learn to give your body what it needs
Duration	30 minutes
Repeat	Repeat as needed
You'll need	A quiet corner, paper and a pen

OK, let's not get carried away. What I will teach you here is not some kind of special magic or a medical degree. You don't need to be a healer to take away the majority of the pains and aches your body suffers. All you need is a bit of time, self-love and care.

Start by doing a full body scan just like we've done above. Only this time we will not stop when you find a pain. Instead, we will try to heal it.

Direct your attention to each one of the pains, aches or discomforts you find, one by one. As you home in on it, ask your body what it wants so that it feels better. Once you get the answer, do it. The trick here is to listen to your body, not your head. Your head is programmed to believe that you can only be healed using the techniques you were told about by the modern world – tablets, gels and surgeries – basically stuff that can be sold for money. Your body does not really need a lot of that cra[censored]. In fact, it can become more stressed and tired as a result of these modern-world interventions. Often, a few common tools – massage the part that hurts, stretch it, keep it warm, keep it rested – will heal many aches. But we don't want to jump to any conclusions and think about which to use either. We need you to learn to feel.

Try to master the art of listening (to your body). It knows, mostly, what it needs.

Feel free to jump back and forth between the different issues, in any order, whenever you feel like it. Your body will tell you where to look. Like fixing a complex machine, it tends to loosen a screw here to remove a hatch there, and then look underneath and flip a switch before it goes back out and tilts a lever. Keep going until you feel noticeably better. Do this every day. It's good for you.

Simple as this chapter may have seemed to you, experiencing life is of paramount importance to your happiness. It takes commitment and practice to depart from the rat race of the modern life and allow yourself to fully experience every moment. Make it your priority. Experience the real world. You will live a happier life.

Experiential thinking, however, is but one of four types of useful thoughts. Let's keep going and discuss the other three. It's time to solve some problems.

Chapter Eleven

The Engineer in You

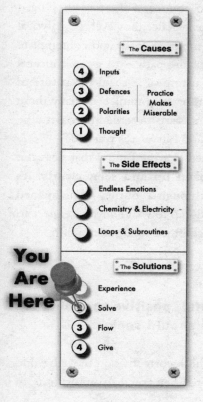

The Causes

4 Inputs

3 Defences   Practice
          Makes
2 Polarities   Miserable

1 Thought

The Side Effects

Endless Emotions

Chemistry & Electricity

Loops & Subroutines

You Are Here

The Solutions

Experience

Solve

3 Flow

4 Give

Because meditation has such a positive impact on wellbeing, and because during meditation we try to calm the mind, a misunderstanding seems to be quite common. Some believe that thinking is a bad thing, that we meditate to quiet the brain because thinking makes us unhappy. Nothing could be further from the truth!

There's nothing inherently good or bad in thinking. Like with everything in life ... **good thoughts are good for you and bad ones are bad.**

If you're thinking positive thoughts that make you happy and make the world a better place, then think away. Go full speed. The more the merrier. There is no need to shut your brain up to find peace. You can find peace just as well when your mind is active. All we need is to stop the useless negative thoughts and bring on the positive productive ones. Positive thoughts work for us twice. They make us peaceful and calm and, at the same time, they make us more successful, smarter and more effective. In short, they make our lives better. Who could ask for more?

True meditation is not about spacing out. It's not about chilling and relaxing. It is about arriving at the truth. The first part of that journey is known as mind training, it teaches those with distracted minds to learn how to command the tool they need for introspection. The core of the practice, however, is analytical meditation – using those calmer minds to focus and contemplate the truth. This is the objective of the path – to grasp concepts such as the nature of reality, the nature of self and the nature of suffering. It takes years of rigorous practice until, eventually, those concepts become clearer. The mind starts to settle into clarity, the acts of the physical form follow, and Nirvana is reached.

You see? Nirvana is not defined as a calm mind that does not think. **Nirvana is to have woken up and seen clearly.** It's a mind that arrives at the truth through a journey of disciplined analysis, reflection and introspection. How can anyone expect to see with clarity if their target is confined to a quiet brain?

To stop thinking is the wrong target.

Very Important !

To think useful, positive thoughts is the target we should seek.

When you direct your brain to think correctly, you move beyond just calming the beast to taming it. When you do, you turn it from your worst enemy into your best ally — your intelligence that helps you solve the puzzle and figure things out.

Second only to its primary function — which is to keep you alive — the most important function of the human brain is . . .

Problem-solving

When you solve problems, neurons fire all over your head. While the core work related to problem-solving happens in the pre-frontal lobe, for you to solve a problem you need to use language and comprehension, you need to integrate information from your senses, from your memory and from your emotions. You often need to use some motor skills, perhaps to take notes or move yourself and other things around. When it's time for problem-solving, it's all hands — or in this case neurons — on deck.

Problem-solving, perhaps, is the finest display of our brain's capability. As it coordinates all those disparate functions, it delivers something that the human brain, still today, is the only machine or living organism capable of delivering: a solution to a novel and complex problem.

While the basic function of our brains is survival, their highest function can be summed up in one simple word . . .

Intelligence

Another bias of the modern world is a tendency to glorify one type of intelligence — analytical intelligence or IQ — over the many other types that we possess. IQ is the kind of intelligence needed to perform tasks and deliver results. It is what helps us work better and succeed, but it does not always lead to happiness.

In recent years, neuroscientists have identified areas in the frontal lobe around the forehead as the centre of self-control.

This is where executive functions happen, for instance discipline in performing a task or the ability to plan. When you focus on a task or try to ignore distractions, this part of your brain becomes particularly active. The extent to which a person can utilize this predicts many important capabilities, including whether they are likely to follow the norms of society, resist temptations, addictions, or avoid behaviours that lead to unhappiness. It also predicts the willpower to resist the urge to eat this carrot cake I can see right in front of me in this cafe, while I'm on a low-carb diet. Those capabilities come in very handy when the 'doing' part of the previously discussed Be–Learn–Do model is needed.

Those with a higher IQ tend to discount immediate rewards in favour of longer-term goals. They are better able to prioritize their impulses in the service of achieving all kinds of success, including their happiness. So yes, IQ matters, but it's not the only type of intelligence you need to find happiness. Not even close.

Take emotional intelligence, or EQ. Research shows that those with high EQ excel in many areas that lead to happiness, such as openness to new experiences, agreeableness (hence their popularity and the high quality of their relationships), ability to win others over at work (hence their success), reduced drug use, aggressiveness and psychiatric symptoms in general.

Peter Salovey and John Mayer, who developed the idea of EQ, see this kind of intelligence as consisting of four main components: the ability to identify emotions, the assimilation of emotions into thought, the understanding of emotions, and the management of emotions.[1] Those four components correspond roughly to the model we discussed in Chapter Five.

Awareness of your emotions, recognizing the thoughts that triggered them, embracing them and then choosing to sit with them is all part of EQ, which leads to mastering the 'being' part of the Be–Learn–Do model.

And then there is practical intelligence.

In his book *Successful Intelligence*, award-winning professor Robert J. Sternberg proposed a distinction between analytical intelligence – the type of intelligence measured by IQ tests – and practical intelligence, the type of intelligence one uses in the real world to solve problems relevant to one's own life. Practical intelligence is a lot more comprehensive and inclusive.[2]

The relationship between intelligence and happiness, however, is not always straightforward. Often, those who think a lot are generally unhappier. They tend to analyse and dwell too much on little things that don't really matter. Nations at large are taught to glorify analytical and critical thinking. In the process, they constantly look for what's wrong with life. As they look for it, they find it and that makes them unhappy. They expect life to be perfect, up to their standards. But life always falls short, and that makes them unhappy. It's almost as if an abundance of intelligence is a curse that leads us to suffering. Perhaps a curse that defines our way of life way more than it should.

In this chapter, I will try to apply intelligence to the challenge of using our brains, reliably, to find happiness. A worthy problem to solve, I think you would agree.

I will try to summarize my approach in the simplest possible form. Once you grasp that, you can then expand on it to suit your own models of intelligence.

To give it a name, let's call this model . . .

The Happiness Flow Chart

When we wrote programmes to teach a computer how to solve a specific problem over and over in an accurate and predictable way, we always started with a flow chart that summed up the logic programme behind it. By now, I'm sure you're beginning to recognize how similar our brains are to the computers we have built. So, maybe a flow chart for happiness could programme our brains to address any potential reasons for unhappiness systematically. Once the code is installed it should work repeatedly, just like it does with software.

Another topic I discussed with Matthieu Ricard on Slo Mo, was unhappiness. I asked him: 'Being the world's happiest man, are you always happy?' He laughed out loud and answered me in his lovely French accent: 'What are you talking about, Mo? I am pissed off almost all the time.' You see, even the most advanced happiness practitioners will occasionally feel unhappy. Unhappiness is a survival mechanism. It is needed to help us correct course. No one is always happy. The trick is to minimize the time you remain stuck in suffering so that you can bounce back to a state of happiness as quickly as possible.

If I am to live up to my self-assigned mission and tell you and others about happiness, I need to become the Olympic champion of the sport. I take my happiness very seriously but I still don't try to avoid feeling unhappy. Instead, I measure how quickly I bounce back to happiness when something makes me unhappy. Believe it or not, when unhappiness attacks me, I bounce back to happiness within a matter of seconds. In 2020, with the exception of three times when I remained unhappy for a few hours, my average bounce-back time was, to be exact, seven seconds.

You can do that too.

The secret is a systematic way of solving the problem. I have summarized it in the happiness flow chart. Let's see how this works.

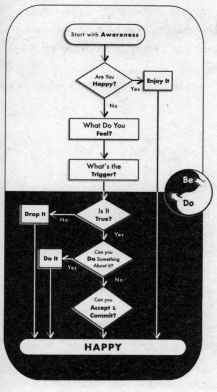

Be Before You Do

Like with everything happiness, we need a bit of being before we start doing. We learned about the steps of the 'being' part of this flow chart when we covered your right brain. No result is achieved as you go through those steps. They just help you be. Being is a recognition of the truth that we need in order to do what's best for us. Only when we achieve that state of being does the real 'doing' begin.

The doing part of the flow chart is mostly about applying our intelligence to problem-solving. It's designed to debug the errors our brains produce when caught up in the survival mechanism known as unhappiness. This part helps you fix the errors and reverse them by following the exact same steps every single time — like a software programme.

Influenced by the pace and values of the modern world, most of us fail to fully live one or both of the states of being and doing. Almost all of us fail to find the correct balance between them. This flow chart is all about balance. If you complete one part but not the other, you're in for a big disappointment and long-lasting suffering.

You will be happy to know that the first part – the being part – is entirely concerned with teaching you how to feel and fully embrace your emotions, which has already been discussed in detail.

The being part of the flow chart consists of three questions:

Question 1: Are you happy?

Question 2: What do you feel?

Question 3: What is the trigger?

We start with a simple question that should be playing on repeat inside your head all the time: *Are you happy?*

Please put the book down and take a minute to ask it now. **Are you happy?**

If you are, then the objective is achieved. Enjoy your happiness fully.

But if your answer is *No* then you need to make it your priority to answer the second question and find out exactly: *What do you feel?*

Finding the answer is a delicate process. You will need to acknowledge how you feel and sit with it. Then you may need to experience the storm and ask yourself what other emotions are there inside you, undetected. We've practised these skills before. It's all just a question of being; a question of **opening yourself up to your own emotions so that you can recognize when there is something to feel before you think about the need for something to do**.

We have practised those steps before in Chapter Seven, so I will not repeat them now. It's not rocket science really. I'm just asking you to connect to your emotions. When you do, embrace them fully, and then we move on to the third question:

What's the Trigger?

Every emotion you've ever felt is triggered by a thought. Question 3 helps you find the exact thought, which makes you much more likely to fix the *real* issue.

This seems easy but it comes with a challenge.

When we experience our storms of emotions, thoughts rush frantically through our heads. A thought triggers an emotion, which then triggers multiple thoughts as our brains attempt to analyse the situation from all angles. In that process our perception of the events gets mixed up with our emotions, assumptions, insecurities and interpretation of the situation. For example, suppose your date from last night didn't call or text you after your lovely dinner. There could be many reasons for that – they got busy, they lost their phone, or maybe they are taking time to reflect on what they want to say. None of those, as a thought, would make you unhappy. The *thought* that triggers your unhappiness, however, would sound something like: *I'll never find someone. I'll spend the rest of my life alone.*

The event was that they didn't call. The thought? *I'll spend the rest of my life alone.* Very different!

Find that thought. If we want to solve a problem, we need to first know what the problem is. You're feeling unhappy because you think you'll spend the rest of your life alone. That is a serious claim. It would make anyone unhappy. That's what we need to work on.

Finding the thoughts that trigger us, however, is tricky because ... I'm going to make a bold claim here ... your brain has never ever, ever, in your entire life, told you the truth. Never! Not once!

Don't get me wrong. Your brain is not evil. It's your closest ally. It wants what's best for you — what it thinks is best for you — always. It just does not know the truth.

Life throws an endless amount of information and stimuli at you every second of every day. There is so much to comprehend and make sense of — too much to fully grasp. Your brain, like an honest witness, will describe the scenes to the best of its ability. All it can do is tell you what it thinks happened. There really is no way to verify the validity of those thoughts for sure. Take, for example, asking your brain to accurately describe the space around you. This very simple request would need millions of data points to be performed accurately: the position, colour, smell and texture of every little point in the space surrounding you, including a chair in the corner, every letter on this page, the electrons forming a current in the electrical lines and that tiny fly about to land on the back of your neck. This one simple event, what's around you right now, is simply impossible to grasp fully, and so our brains give us the closest approximation they can come up with. You know what that means?

Very Important !

Your brain never tells you what happened, it tells you what it thinks happened.

Just Another Story

If for some reason a friend is a little harsh to you one day, the event in its purest form can be summarized as: *My friend spoke harshly to me.*

This kind of event might shift your mood to unhappiness. The thoughts running through your head, triggering emotions, however, may not be as factual and dry as the above description. They may include anything from *He no longer likes me, He doesn't want me in his life because his new girlfriend is taking him all for herself, He will be this harsh forever now that I let him get away with it*, all the way to *He's always rude to me* (forgetting that he is most often kind and courteous).

Dramatic as these thoughts may be, have you actually observed any of them as part of the event at all? Did you manage to go into your friend's head to discover that he doesn't like you any more? Or did you make those assumptions yourself? Did you witness a conversation between him and his new girlfriend where he was instructed to stay away from you? Or was that a story you made up? Do you have a time machine that allows you to travel into the future to witness how this behaviour will continue? Or was that an unsubstantiated prediction that your brain just volunteered? Has he always been harsh? Or is this an exaggeration on your side?

If you have no proof, in the form of an actual observation of some sort, to validate the claim your mind is making, then it is nothing more than a story!

Once you've found that story, that thought that triggered your unhappiness, it's checkmate! You've won. You are almost guaranteed to move to happiness in just three more steps. Once you know the trigger, you corner your brain onto a path that leads, eventually, to your happiness. Your brain always has a good reason to justify why it is making you unhappy. *I'm unhappy because my best friend wants to take my boyfriend away from me.* Once your brain confesses this thought – the trigger – you're in charge of the next move on the chessboard.

BAM, you pop the question – *Is that true, brain?* Checkmate, you win.

Let me guide you down that path. We now need to move to the doing part of the happiness flow chart. This is where we use our

intelligence, **insight**, **problem-solving abilities** and **actions** to overcome our unhappiness.

The doing part of the flow chart also consists of three questions:

Question 4: Is it true?

Question 5: Is there something you can do about it?

Question 6: Can you accept and commit?

 If you've been reading for a while, I suggest you get up and stretch.

I need you feeling fresh for this next reading sprint.

Question 4, the first in the doing part of our flow chart, is probably the second-most important question you will ever ask . . .

Is It True?

It may be hard to believe, but a lot of how I approach happiness I learned from being a software engineer. Anyone who's ever written code knows that the only one way for your code to run is for every command, symbol, punctuation mark and number in what you wrote to be 100 per cent accurate. One typo in one character in one line out of 50,000 lines of code and the programme will not run. The habits of software coding taught me that there is only one correct way for things to work and that if my code is not making me happy, this isn't due to an error with the machine (me), but rather because something was not correct with the code I fed it.

These are very useful habits to borrow from when you're looking for happiness because happiness can only be found when your code complies, and the only way for the programmes that run your physical form to run correctly is to feed them with the truth.

Now that's a big word – truth. Who can claim knowledge of that? Well, anyone with a shred of wisdom knows that aspiring for truth is a lifelong journey. Often, we don't know the truth. But here's the good news. We always sense what isn't true. Removing those untruths from our lives leads us on the path to happiness. Happiness is found not only when the truth is known, but also on the path to the truth. The quest to seek the truth in every tiny detail of your life is in itself a practice that leads to happiness. Accepting and internalizing what is false, on the other hand, is a sure path to endless suffering. So how do we seek what we term as true? We don't. Instead, **we reject what is false**.

If our brains make us unhappy by giving us stories that are not even true, then the price we're paying for letting those thoughts live is too much. I have a simple rule: my code should always comply . . .

Very Important !

If I let something make me unhappy, it should at least be true.

Imagine if someone was told that they were fired, asked to come and collect their belongings the next morning and then left to suffer the anxiety and stress overnight. Then, when they showed up the next morning, they were told that none of it was true. It was just a practical joke. Ha ha – not funny! Don't let your brain play jokes like this on you. It would be such a waste of your precious life to spend even a single minute feeling unhappy about something that's not even true. Verify that something is true before you let it upset you.

But what are you saying here, Mo? Why are you assuming that my brain is this mean to me? Do our brains set out to lie? No, I don't believe so. As I mentioned before, our brains *try* to tell us the truth but often give us a false representation of reality, simply because they don't know the truth.

Ask the Right Questions

True statements, stripped of all drama and interpretation, are usually just dry descriptions of events. Our thoughts when we think of the event, however, are polluted by previous traumas, mixed up with our memories, sprinkled with emotions and coloured by all the opinions that get shoved into our heads by ideology, family, friends and the media. There's always some truth to be found at the core of these thoughts, but how do we purify that from all the added extras?

I find that four simple rules always help me strip away the pollutants and arrive at the plain truth.

Rule 1: No thoughts that are not confirmed with matching sensory perceptions.

Do I have sensory confirmation for what my thought is suggesting? Did I see, hear, touch, taste or smell what I just thought? Our senses are the only conduit of information into our system. The control centre, where the story delivered by the senses gets stitched together, is the brain. *My food smells like curry, tastes spicy and feels warm* are all observations delivered by your sensory systems. *The chef is a genius* ... well, that's a story that your brain concluded, based on those observations. For all we know, that food could have been made in a factory by a machine, packed in a plastic container and served to you on a fancy plate. The chef could be a total idiot who learned this one recipe from his mother with great effort and is hired to cook only one meal. You have no way of finding that out just from curry on a plate.

I'm not dismissing your story. It could be true. The chef could actually be a genius, but you have no way of proving that from your sensory information alone.

Rule 2: Anything but the 'here and now' is fiction that's created by your brain.

Is my thought limited to the time and place of the event? An interesting feature of our brains is that they need a timestamp and a place to exist. If a thought did not live in the past or the future, or if it did not live in a place other than where you are, it would simply be reduced to a narration of the present moment. Once you notice a past or future timestamp in the way you think, or you notice that your thought is not focused on where you currently are, you can immediately assume that your thought is probably false. For example, the thought *It's all because of how his mother treated him as a child* assumes something that you have not witnessed. It takes place in a distant past and a different location. It may be a clever conclusion that you arrived at based on previous experiences, but it's just not something you can prove, without a shadow of a doubt, to be true. Until you can do so, assume it isn't. Similarly, the thought *I'll be the laughing stock of the group tomorrow* has no evidence behind it. All future statements, by definition, are not 'true', because they haven't even happened yet. It's just a forecast that your brain constructs. Similarly, the thought *I'm certain my employees do nothing when I am not there* is a thought you can't prove, because you are not there. If your story is stamped with the past or future time, or if it lives in another place, you have good reason to doubt its validity.

Rule 3: Drama is not the truth.

Remember, there are no emotions in events. The actual events can only be described by a series of dry, factual words. Any signs of heightened emotion in the way you think about or react to something indicates that you are responding to more than what just happened. You are probably responding to a thought formulated by your brain's dramatic abilities.

Last night, a friend started shouting uncontrollably. Clearly, she felt jealous that a girl, who was a friend of her boyfriend's before they even met, sat close to him. Her reaction was disproportionate to the actual event. When I asked why such a simple event triggered so much anger, she said, 'My last boyfriend cheated on me with his best friend.' There you go. Truth!

Any thought that is emotionally charged is not the actual truth.

Which takes us to the fourth rule . . .

Rule 4: Trauma is not the truth.

Often, I found that the thoughts I had after an event were not really about what had just happened. They were also influenced by things that happened at different times – how my mother treated me as a child, the way my last break-up went, the traditions of the country in which I was raised, my beliefs in terms of how things should be done, and so on. Can you notice that pattern in your thoughts too? Are you adding your trauma to your thinking? The best way to parse the truth is to ask yourself how you would be thinking about the event at hand if you pondered it in total isolation. Is the behaviour of your boss in isolation of your fear of losing your job actually worrying? Is your current assessment of a potential partner based on your belief of how all (wo)men are? Is your impatience when stuck in traffic affected by the time when you missed a flight? The only way to handle the event with any objectivity at all is to . . . **think of every event in isolation** from the trauma caused by any other event that might have happened.

Ask the Question Right

You can go through the complex reasoning above to verify if your thoughts are actually true next time they make you unhappy. Or you can simply ask your brain bluntly, *Is it true?* Is it true that your roommate is impossible to live with? Is it true that he was treated badly as a child? Is it certain that you will be the laughing stock of the group? Is it true that the chef is a genius?

Finding the truth is not just about asking the right question – is it true? It's also about asking the right question right! Make sure your brain does not drag you into long essays and chit-chat. Asking the question in a way that leads to an accurate answer is what is known in conversation skills as asking a *closed* question – meaning, a question that can only be answered with a yes or no.

If I asked you, 'What colour is this page?' – an open question – you could give me a long-winded answer: 'Well, I once left this book on the dashboard of my car and it was one of those extremely hot summer days. I was sweating all day and had to stop for a cold drink. Then I received a call from my old friend, Pooki, who's been struggling a bit with his ego. And so we chatted for a while. To tell you the truth, I wanted to stay in the shade until I finished the call and so by the time I was back, the book had been there for a while. Perhaps forty-five minutes. No, maybe even an hour. I feel the sun has faded the colour of the pages a little. But only on the edges, you see? So while I wanted to say the page is white, I can no longer say that. I'd probably rather say … maybe … a bit yellowish … Or, what should I call this colour? Light café au lait? Cream? I actually don't know.'

That's a long-winded answer to a simple but *open* question.

It may be an entertaining story – thank you – but you have not really answered my question. This means I need to ask you in a more *closed* format: 'Is this page white?'

A closed question in this format can only be answered with a yes or a no. It doesn't really matter what colour the page is, or what life story led you to where you are in relation to those pages. If it is white, the answer is yes, and if it is any other colour, the answer is no. Simple.

What if your brain sticks to its claim and insists it's true? Then you ask it to prove it, to provide evidence for its claim.

One day I was visiting my daughter, Aya, in Montreal. We had a bit of an argument and the conversation got heated, so I told her that I would step out for a coffee to organize my thoughts so that we could discuss the topic with a clear mind and a calmer attitude later.

The minute I walked out of the building, my brain decided to tell me: *Aya does not love you any more!*

Now, please understand. Aya truly is the biggest love in my life. We are super close as father and daughter and, on top of that, I consider her my best friend and she considers me hers. When my brain made such an outrageous claim, I stopped in the middle of the cold streets of Montreal and told my brain, out loud, 'What the [censored] did you just say? How can you make such a claim? What evidence do you have for it? How about all of those loving WhatsApp messages between us? How about the "I miss you" messages and the kissing emojis? How about that hug and the happiness in her eyes when I arrived? How can those be dismissed? Friends argue and that is that. Aya loves me and I love her back, and you, brain, should be ashamed of yourself for telling such an outright lie.'

Yep. That's the way an untruthful brain should be treated. An hour later we met again, hugged, resolved the issue, and went out for dinner laughing about a million things, as we always do.

For a thought to be counted as true . . .

Remember!

Your brain should provide evidence for its claims.

Without evidence, a brain's negative thoughts should automatically be assumed to be false.

Now, if your brain admits that what you're thinking is false, you can immediately . . . **Drop It**

Don't waste a minute of your time feeling unhappy about life's practical joke. **Why would you ever let something that is not true upset you?**

If, however, after due investigation, the claim still holds true, then we can move on to the next question on the happiness flow chart.

What Can I Do About It?

The kinds of thoughts that make us suffer – the incessant thoughts – tend to be recurring and useless. They just tell us over and over again why we should feel unhappy. In that, there is no help to be found, no progress and no path to feeling better. They are useless in every way other than what they are designed for – to alert us. These thoughts are just the alarm system our brains use to tell us that something in our environment does not meet their expectations of a safe, desirable model of life. Treat your incessant thoughts for what they are – a noisy alarm. And how do you respond to alarms?

Remember!

When the alarm goes off, you do something about it.

What's the point of sitting there suffering the loud noise? An alarm calls for action and when you respond by leaving the building, you ensure your safety and stay away from the noise at the same time.

Imagine the thought that triggered your unhappiness is, for example: *My relationship with my best friend has not been good for a while.* Let me ask you a question. If this thought is true and your relationship has been deteriorating for a while, what difference will thinking about it make? Will making yourself miserable improve the relationship? If you spend the next six hours in a corner crying about it, will your friend suddenly show up and change things? What good does suffering bring? Like sitting through a fire alarm, it doesn't improve anything and keeps you suffering the noise.

The only thing that can ever change your current circumstance is the action you take.

So do something about it . . .

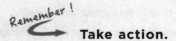

Remember!

Take action.

Just do something. Pick up the phone, text your friend and ask to meet up and discuss things. Acknowledge the behaviour on your side that has led you here and put together a plan to change it. Share what you believe you need to see more of from your friend. Perhaps, if things don't work out, decide that it's time to move on.

Whatever action you take will stop the sirens of your incessant thoughts, stop your unhappiness and, best of all, change the situation and make your life a little bit better.

Sounds simple? Yes. Because it is.

Very Important!

Instead of wasting your life feeling unhappy, get up and do something about it.

Once you do, you will start feeling better. Just the act of thinking about doing it will make you happier. This is because the positivity of thinking about what's possible removes the negativity of resignation and helplessness, while problem-solving thoughts activate your prefrontal cortex and in doing so replace the incessant thought that causes your unhappiness.

Remember!

You don't even need to solve the problem. The simple act of looking for a solution takes the unhappiness away.

Often, we delay actions because we don't know what can be done or because we fear that what we do will not be good enough. We feel that it's not a perfect solution and so we refrain from doing it. But situations are often much simpler than we think. And, more importantly, doing something that firmly moves you in the right direction (even if what you can do will not completely solve a situation) is better than doing nothing. Here is a quick exercise to help spark you into taking some kind of action.

I'm sure there are some things that you keep in the back of your mind which have been bothering you. It's time to get those done with.

Awareness Exercise
What Can Be Done

Target	To become aware of the different possible actions, which may not fully resolve an issue, but can be taken in any situation
Duration	30 minutes (x3)
Repeat	Once a week
You'll need	A quiet place where you will not be interrupted Paper and a pen

Find a quiet place, plan to spend at least thirty minutes reflecting, and take some paper and a pen with you. Start by listing down the top three issues that have been causing you unhappiness or negative emotions recently. Work through each of them one by one, determining the thought that triggered your unhappiness and whether that thought is true.

Now, if the thought was true, ask yourself: What can I do to fix this (or at least make things better)?

Write down the top three actions that you need to take to improve the situation. Be very specific in terms of what you will do and how you will make sure it is done properly. If the action you are planning is to explain to your boss that something is not going well, be very specific about what you plan to say and how you are going to make sure that your boss fully understands your point of view. Mark the date by which you intend to see the task complete.

Even better, if you can, do it right now. Don't wait. If the action you plan to take is to send a message to a friend or call a service provider, once you are done with your plan, pick up the phone and text or call ... right there and then!

When you have another thirty minutes, start with another blank piece of paper and address the next issue that's causing you unhappiness. Keep doing this until every current issue is addressed. The first time you do this, you will feel the value it brings to your life and happiness. Make it a habit. Repeat it at least once a week. The issues may be resolved by then. If they're not, then they deserve more of your time till they are. Otherwise, start addressing the next set of items on your list. Learn that happiness is your responsibility. Dedicating an hour or two a week to resolving issues that hinder your path to it is surely a worthwhile investment. If something is bothering you, do something about it. Action will stop your incessant thinking, so dedicate your brain resources to useful thoughts, regardless of results and achievements. This will bring you peace.

Time for the last question.

Can You Accept and Commit?

What if, as life sometimes corners us, there is nothing you can do about what's making you unhappy? What if you lost your job? It's done and there's no turning back. What if you were diagnosed with a painful illness? What if you lost a loved one and there's no bringing them back? What if someone stole from you? What if you lost all your money?

I've been there more times than you can imagine, and experienced every one of those, including the loss of my wonderful son, Ali. When life overpowered me, I resorted to my ultimate defence against unhappiness – **Committed Acceptance**.

Life, harsh as it is, will sometimes send things our way that we have no power to change. Look around you and notice that, for many people, this is already the reality. Billions of people are born into poverty through no choice or action of their own. Millions are diagnosed with serious illnesses and millions more are living with chronic pain. Hundreds of millions are captive in prisons, in war zones or in modern-day slavery. Billions, almost everyone, are forced to face the loss of a loved one. How does your story compare to those?

Harsh overpowering events are a fact of life. Learn to accept them. It's part of the rules of this game. Accepting gives you the ultimate power to choose your own destiny and state of happiness. Once you accept, and realistically expect, that life will not always be easy, you can choose to always be happy, not because of what life gives you, but because of the way you chose to deal with what life gives you.

But just writing this on paper does not help you achieve it. So please let me share with you how I do it.

I choose to believe that everything in life, even suffering, has a good side to it. Nothing is all bad. Failing to see the good side of a situation makes us biased. We reject and complain about our circumstances. But the good side can be found by performing a simple awareness exercise that I call the eraser test.

I have asked tens of thousands of people, during happiness workshops that I ran, to reflect back on the harshest times of their life and answer one question: Would you erase those events from your life if you knew that removing them would remove every other event they triggered? Would you erase the hardships of your past if you knew that would make you a different person to the one you are today? Would you rather have taken a different path through life knowing that, by removing the harshness, you would also remove all the learning, development, friendships and relationships that you have acquired as a result of your suffering?

Most of the people I have asked, once they had a chance to reflect deeply, responded . . .

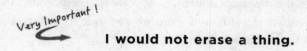

Very Important !

I would not erase a thing.

The true heroes we come across in the modern world are not the characters from Marvel comics and movies. They are the ones who go through heartache and calamity with acceptance, with grace, revealing their true essence. One of my favourite examples is Viktor Frankl, whose heroic journey is documented in his classic work, *Man's Search for Meaning*. In it, Frankl describes his experiences in a concentration camp during the Second World War. During his time at the camp, he was tortured and pushed to the brink of death while not being given enough food or proper clothing during the freezing winters. He witnessed the death and execution of people around him, including his mother, wife, father and brother, who all died in the camps. Now that's a real example of life's harshness turning against you. His suffering was on a level that most of us, luckily, never experience.

Frankl noticed that there were two types of prisoners surrounding him: those who had lost faith, meaning and hope, and those who hadn't. The latter group looked at life as a challenge to be overcome and at harshness as an opportunity to learn and develop, in preparation for a larger mission in life. Those who thought this way were more likely to survive. Victor Frankl thought of lectures that he would give based on the experiences he was having. In doing so, his current life experiences became more objective. He looked at them as learning opportunities for future sharing. From his writing I felt that **he believed that suffering ceases to be suffering in the moment it finds meaning.** To him, suffering became a task that he embraced.

Another fundamental component that will help you embrace the challenges of life is a conviction that you're never helpless. Even in the direst circumstances, you are still empowered to positively impact the situation, even if only in a small way, through your actions and attitude.

Between every event and your response to it, there is a gap – a moment of buffer where life hands the control over to you. This is when you decide how to react. You have no ability to control the external forces that led to or resulted from the event. But what you can control are the forces within you and how these manifest in the real world. **Some of us view ourselves as victims of circumstances, the object of the story, the ones who things are being done to. Others view themselves as the subject, the doer with the power to affect circumstances and tilt the game in their favour.** Those who become objects have a tendency to resign, to complain about life, acting like helpless children who can only wait for external forces to mend or take away the calamity. Those who are the subjects, on the other hand, take charge. They engage and, in doing so, even if they can't remove the scare, they still make things better. Once convinced that you have the freedom to choose your reaction, you find resilience. It no longer matters what life throws your way; what matters is how you respond. It's your attitude towards your existence that makes all the difference.

In the words of Viktor Frankl:

Remember!

'Everything can be taken from a man but one thing – the last of human freedoms – to choose one's attitude.'

I grew up in a Muslim community, and this concept of surrendering to life's uncontrollable circumstances is the backbone of our culture. The meaning of the word Islam itself is to find peace through the act of surrender. But Islam's surrender goes way beyond resigning or quitting. The peace we seek is found not only in acceptance but also in the act that follows – commitment.

When you accept something, you readjust your position in life. You no longer crouch under pressure but stand tall at the new baseline, glimpsing at the horizon of possibilities. Instead of looking back at how life has treated you, you look down and acknowledge where you are. Then you look forward. You see far ahead, and you get ready to run.

That's the time when you prevail – when there is enough space for the true game changer that you are to come out.

Commit! Understand that you may never be able to reverse the adversity you're facing.

You may never get your job back, but you can commit to developing yourself and finding a better job. You may not be able to reclaim your losses, but you can commit to doing the best you can to recover. You will never bring your lost ones back – I will never be able to bring Ali back – but we can commit to honour them, remember them and wish them well.

'Adventure of a Lifetime'
By Coldplay

Turn the magic on and remember that the pressure you're experiencing is only shaping you into the diamond that you are bound to become.

Everything you want is, despite the challenges, just a dream away. Beautiful!

We can commit to making the world better despite, even because of, our loss.

When there's nothing to do about the adversity you face . . .

Very Important !

Accept, then commit to make tomorrow a little better than today and the day after tomorrow a little better than tomorrow.

Another way I found, other than OneBillionHappy, to honour the loss of Ali has been to live the experiences he embraced. This approach has not only allowed me to feel as if I'm in his beautiful presence, but it also constantly reminds me that he was here. That he blessed our lives with his presence. You see . . .

Very Important !

To lose anything, you must have it in the first place.

To feel the hardship, you must have experienced ease. To feel challenged, you must compare the harder times with times of prosperity and flow.

Though we forget, and focus on our feelings of loss, reliving our experiences before the hardship and loss should make us grateful. It should remind us that life is not all hard and that this rough patch will pass.

I relived Ali's life in many of the things that he did. I listened to the music he liked, met many of his friends frequently and I also chose to honour him by becoming as good a video gamer as he was.

Today, six years after he left us, I'm a legendary video gamer. This has not always been the case. When Ali was alive, we often

Remember !

**There's no winning in life.
Only the opportunity to learn and become better.**

With this new attitude, in no time at all (I played forty-five minutes a day, four times a week for four months), I finished *Halo* as a legendary player. Today I rank among the top 0.2 per cent of all players in the world. Not bad for a man my age. I hope you're proud of me, Ali. I am grateful for all that you still teach me.

Be a video gamer. When the game becomes tough, real gamers don't put their controllers down and complain. Instead, they reflect, review, then engage and try again, stronger and more determined than they've ever been. What can I tell you?

Remember !

**You're a legend. So, start
playing like one.**

The Happiness Flow Chart in Action – Kate and Leo

Last summer Kate felt a strong urge to change her plan for the day. She'd come across a post on social media about a two-day training course in contemporary art appreciation. She loved art and recently she had been caught up in the hamster wheel of work and felt she needed a change. Something in that post called out to her. Kate had been feeling lonely for a while. She'd recently ended yet another relationship and wished that she could find her partner, her soulmate. She even wrote down a prayer in which she described him. She believed that the universe was listening and she was right. It was!

The training wasn't bad, but what caught her attention most was a handsome gentleman, Leo, who spoke politely, almost like someone in a movie about the British aristocracy. He made insightful comments followed by well-constructed questions and listened attentively. When any of the students made a point, he twisted around to face them, giving them his full attention. By midday, her thoughts were no longer on art but on comparing him to her prayer. It seemed that everything checked out. *Could it be true?* she thought. *Is this him? Have I found my soulmate?*

During a break, she did something she'd never done before. She walked up to him and said, 'Hi, I'm Kate.' He answered with a smile, and the rest is history. A month later they were living the perfect love story, in what looked like the dream relationship. He treated her with love and respect, attended to her every need and embraced her tenderly when she was down. He always told her how amazing she was but also told her his views, assertively, when she needed to change direction. In no time, she was glowing, her career was thriving. She knew he was the one.

Unfortunately, life did not agree. Within a year, his work shifted to another country and his foreign visa status in her country expired. Meanwhile, her career was at a critical stage and they both knew that she would not be able to drop it all to join him when he moved. If she did, she would lose the essence of what was important to her and that would jeopardize their relationship. Whichever way they went, their relationship would suffer. On a summer night, with tears in their eyes, they went their separate ways.

Kate was my good friend. Over the next few months, she texted and called me to say how miserable she was. She felt angry, sad, broken, worried and confused. She loved him and she knew that he loved her too. She could not accept the harshness of life where such love could not be given the space it needed to thrive.

Are You Happy?

Kate was obviously not happy. She was fully 'being'. She felt every emotion, and that took its toll on her body – from lack of sleep to nausea and fatigue. She was truly experiencing a storm but unable to 'do' much about it. And then we met for a coffee.

What Do You Feel?

We did not waste time on meaningless niceties. Kate took less than a minute to explode into a storm of emotions; first a flood of tears, followed by anger and insults about life in general, including other friends, inanimate objects, herself and even Leo.

What's the Trigger?

When she had settled a bit, I guided her step by step through the approach of the happiness flow chart. Here is how it went: 'Let's do this together, Kate, let's fully experience this storm. Please write down every emotion you feel.'

She wrote them down. Then I asked: 'Rank them in order. Put the ones you feel most strongly on top and let's tackle those first.' Anger and fear (with all its derivatives) came on top.

'What thoughts are causing those? Let's write them all down. Take your time. Hours, if you need to. Let your brain go wild. Don't respond to any of the thoughts that come up, just write them down.'

Remember, Leo wanted to be with Kate. His hand was forced. That was the event in its simplest form. Yet the thoughts that triggered Kate were very different. Here's some of what she wrote:

He left me.

There will be other women in his life.

I can never touch another man again.

I will spend the rest of my life alone.

We will drift apart.

We were always together. Now, it's difficult and expensive to be in the same country, let alone the same place.

There were many other thoughts, but let's stick to those for now. They give you enough to see the process in action. Every time Kate wrote a thought down, I said, 'Aha, and what else?' I never dismissed any of the thoughts or attempted to discuss or resolve them. I just asked for more. At the beginning, the thoughts were coming very rapidly; then they started to slow down, first to a stream, then to a drip. By the end, it took minutes for her to find a thought and often it was a repeat of something she'd already said. When that happened, I simply said, 'Aha, but we wrote this one before. What else?' By then, through this simple process, I saw Kate's face ease, her anger dissipate and her usual glow return. Eventually, her thoughts became almost entirely irrelevant to the topic. Thoughts such as *I'm hungry.* I responded the same way, with a smile and often laughter: 'Aha, let me write that down ... you're hungry. That's a problem. What else?' She herself was now smiling, and even a little giggly. She said, 'I think we have enough here.' We did.

Notice the burden that our incessant thoughts place on us. Just the act of systematically releasing them makes us feel better. Your brain is not bad, it is just very serious about its job – ensuring your survival – and it does not give a s[censored] if doing that job so diligently makes you feel horrible. It will not stop until it is heard and acknowledged, and so to help you find a breather . . .

> **Experience the storm for as long as it takes till the calm sets in.**

With everything written down, I looked at Kate confidently and said, 'You do know that it is now checkmate, don't you? Once you've acknowledged your emotions, chosen which you will work on first and captured the triggers for your unhappiness – your thoughts – there is no way for your brain to hijack your happiness any more. It's just a matter of three simple questions. We will address those thoughts one by one. It all starts with one core question . . .'

Is It True?

'Your top thought is, "He left me." Is that true, Kate?' I said. Kate immediately became emotional all over again.

She said: 'Yes. He did!'

'How did he leave you?' I asked.

'He left to go to another country.'

'Why? Was it to leave *you*? Was he running away from *you*?'

'No,' she said. 'He loves me. He was crying when he left for the airport. But he could no longer stay in the country.'

'This is not about you, is it, Kate?'

'He put his work ahead of me. He left me for a job . . .' Kate's brain attacked swiftly in response.

'Did he really? I didn't know that. Did he not attempt to stay?'

'He couldn't stay,' she said. 'His visa expired.'

'Who did he leave then? Did he leave *you*?'

'No . . .' Kate said with a sob in her voice. 'He left the country.'

'No, Kate. If you want to be specific, say the country left him. Words matter. They create our reality. Leo did not choose to leave you. Life forced Leo onto a new path.'

She nodded. But I kept going. I asked her if he said she couldn't go with him. She eventually admitted that she had decided to stay because her career was booming and, actually, she didn't want to leave her friends and family here.

'Oh, then if you don't mind me asking, if he could not stay but you could go and you chose not to then . . . who left who?' There was a long moment of silence.

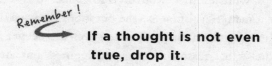

Remember!

If a thought is not even true, drop it.

Next thought. 'There will be other women in his life. I understand how hard this thought is to handle but I need to ask you a question. Is that true?'

'What do you mean? Of course it is true. What do you expect? He will live alone?'

'I don't know Leo, Kate. I am asking you to look at the construction of the sentence you told me and check if it is true.'

Frustrated, Kate answered, 'I am not following you and, honestly, I feel irritated, so can we please stop playing word games?'

I smiled understandingly and said, 'How can something be true if it has not yet happened?'

Remember!

Every statement with a future tense is not true.

All forward-looking statements are predictions, at best. I learned that in the stock market. A well-fed individual with a shiny title and an expensive suit sits in front of a camera and assures the viewers that the market is going to crash. If you take that as a statement of truth, you will immediately sell the market short. But how can you know?

'We don't know the future, Kate. We just don't. **To upset yourself about something that has not yet happened is like having food poisoning from a meal you have not yet eaten.** It just does not make sense. Besides, have you ever asked yourself how these thoughts are affecting your behaviour?'

We even addressed the most difficult thoughts: 'So what if he sleeps with another woman? How does this affect you? Why does it matter?' (I often use the questions 'So what?' or 'Why does it make you feel unhappy?' to uncover the deeper thoughts that are the actual reason for our unhappiness but are hidden away by our brains.) 'If he slept with another woman, does that mean you were not enough? Or is it perhaps just about the flow of life?'

Eventually, we got to the hardest thought of all: 'We will drift apart.' 'Is this true?' I asked.

'Well, you said all future statements are not. So, I guess it's not true,' answered Kate impatiently.

I said, 'Yes, we don't know if that is going to happen so it's not "true", but it would be such a shame if you did drift, wouldn't it. You seem to be so good for each other and such good friends?'

'Yeah,' she said with every cell of her being.

'OK,' I said. 'Can you rewrite this statement in a way that makes it true?'

She contemplated her notepad for a moment and then wrote: *There is a risk that we might drift apart.* 'Yes! This is a true statement,' I said. So . . .

What Can You Do About It?

'Nothing,' said Kate. 'There's nothing I can do about this. It's just what it is. We are thousands of miles apart.' This, of course, was another of the depressing thoughts that Kate's brain was constantly engaged in. 'Not only are we separated by life circumstances, but [the core thought] it's going to get worse and worse and there is nothing we can do about it.'

Those kinds of unresolved thoughts are the main triggers of our suffering cycles. When our brains identify a challenge or a threat, they alert us to it in the form of a negative emotion. When the issue is unresolved it keeps coming back up, and when the negativity is combined with despair that there is no way out, the depth and frequency of the cycle intensify. But the underlying reason for despair is just another unexamined thought and is often not true – as in Kate's case here. So, I took her back to our core analytical question. 'Is that true, Kate? Is there really nothing you can do about it?'

After hearing this, Kate went on to tell me at length all the reasons calling each other was so difficult. Eventually, I said: 'This is not the answer to my question. I need you to be honest now. Is there something you can do to keep close or is there not? Just answer yes or no. Then we can get into the details of how good or effective it is.'

As I explained earlier, it's often useful to insist on a closed answer instead of an essay. Because our brains have a bias to search for problems, they tend to exaggerate every challenge and refuse to admit what is true. They attempt to keep us worried by throwing loads of scattered negative thoughts at us.

After a long pause and what looked like some inner conflict, she admitted: 'Yes, there are things I can do to stay close. They are different to what we had before and more difficult but if I embrace them, I can make them work.'

played together a game called *Halo*. 'Difficult' was the maximum difficulty level I could play. Ali, on the other hand, played on 'legendary', up there among the elite. When we were faced with a challenging segment of the game, I panicked while Ali flowed through it as if walking down a water stream in the middle of nature. He did not seem phased at all. I could not figure out how he did it until I decided to play in his honour.

As I moved up one level, from 'difficult' to 'heroic', my perception of the game completely changed. When the game became a bit more challenging than my skill set, I found myself engaging with more ease. Counter-intuitive, I know, but here is what happened. As soon as I reset the difficulty of the game up, my expectation was reset down. I no longer expected to be able to finish every mission on the first attempt. Instead, I learned to realistically expect that things would be tough until I conjured up the skill needed to tackle the more challenging tasks ahead. Because I wanted to make Ali proud, I viewed every stage that I played until I got there just as training and practice. That's when the magic started to happen. Suddenly, I felt no pressure and enjoyed the challenges. I even wanted them to be harder **because the harder they became, the more skilled I became as a result.** When I failed a mission, I accepted that I was not ready and that made me commit more. I looked objectively at my mistakes, then jumped back into the game to try again and again. I didn't even try to finish the mission then. All I wanted was to . . .

Remember!

Make the next attempt slightly better than the one before.

Try this with your own life and it will feel like a game. This is the biggest secret that we mostly miss . . .

'The truth is out there,' I said. 'We just need to insist on receiving nothing less from our brains. Give me an example of something you can do.'

'Well, there is an interesting charm to being on video calls. It reminds me of the time we were dating. It's romantic and, honestly, if I stay up a bit late, we can have the calls in the morning his time which is his favourite time of the day.'

I gave her a moment to reflect on this new insight before I asked: 'So, is there something you can do to reduce the risk of drifting apart, Kate?'

'Yes,' she answered immediately with a sparkle in her eyes. So I said . . .

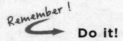

Remember!

Do it!

Our actions and our attitude are the only things within our control. Always ask your brains for solutions that you can effect in the real world. Without you asking, your brain will stay in its comfort zone and keep looking for problems. When you find that there is something you can do, commit to doing it the best way that you can. And while that may not always resolve the challenge you're facing, it will certainly make things even a tiny bit better. For a start, it will dissipate your despair and make you feel empowered.

Once you are engaged in the analysis and the action, you'll suspend the suffering cycle, stop your incessant thoughts and immediately feel better.

Kate then went on to say: 'I miss him. I feel lonely without him.'

And that surely was a statement of truth. You see, all your feeling statements are true. At least, they are for you. There is no denying how we feel, even if we wish we felt differently.

Remember!

What you feel is always true.

It's also true that she can't do much about that. Missing someone you love when they're away is just a fact. You can't change the missing. When there's nothing you can do about a challenge you are facing, it becomes time for the ultimate happiness skill of all.

Can You Accept and Commit?

'Kate,' I said, 'I am Middle Eastern. I know what it is like to have to ask for permission to enter a foreign country. This, sadly, is the state of our world. It is possible that you and Leo will not have the chance to be together for a long time, or ever again, as lovers. I hope this will not be the case but, if it were, what will you do to make things a bit better?'

She said, 'I want him in my life as a friend.'

'Then be a friend. Stop acting suspicious and jealous and angry and start acting as a friend. This may not solve the visa issue but at least it will save what can be saved.'

My conversation with Kate lasted several hours and extended over several days. We needed to address every thought diligently and sometimes we addressed the same thought the exact same way several times. Often, she would spring back into negative thoughts, usually the same ones, and the negative emotions that came with them. As we kept asking, 'Is it true? What can you do about it? Can you accept and commit?' we always bounced back to clarity. Clarity brought peace, and peace enabled Kate to make the right choices.

I can't give you a Hollywood-style romantic comedy ending for the story and tell you that Kate and Leo managed to find a way to be together again. All I can tell you is that at the time of writing Kate is happy, able to accept the circumstances of her life, focused on her career (which was one of the factors responsible for her situation in the first place) and feeling open to the flow of life. She no longer suffers the torture of a load of unnecessary incessant thoughts.

Isn't that what life is all about?

Chapter Twelve

The Artist in You

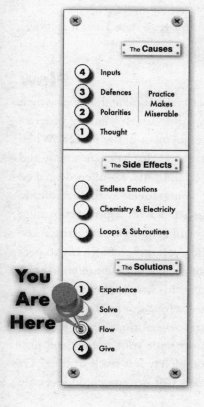

The Causes

④ Inputs

③ Defences Practice

② Polarities Makes

       Miserable

① Thought

The Side Effects

○ Endless Emotions

○ Chemistry & Electricity

○ Loops & Subroutines

The Solutions

① Experience

 Solve

⑤ Flow

④ Give

You Are Here

When I started my career at IBM, I learned to work with mini-computers. There was nothing mini about those machines (they were the size of small cars) other than being very small compared to the mainframe (which fitted the size of a large room). One of the early mini-computers was the System/36 which was warmly welcomed by the banking industry due to its ability, among other things, to perform batch processing. The term batch processing was widely used in industrial systems to mean the perform-ing of an industrial process in batches – like running a payroll programme for a whole company overnight. All you needed was to start the batch and let the machine run. It sounds primitive compared to today's computers, but batch processing was extremely valuable for tasks such as closing the day in a bank. Optimized to perform high-volume, repetitive tasks, batch runs were used for updating information in the relevant databases, generating reports, printing documents and other non-interactive tasks that must be completed reliably within certain business deadlines. Once the computer's ability to run the batch was verified, it most often performed it flawlessly without much 'thought' about what was needed. It was a systems administrator's paradise – effortless and flawless.

We humans run in batch mode too. It's a state known as 'flow'.

Flow

In positive psychology, flow is described as a mental state in which a person performing a task is fully immersed in a feeling of energized focus, full involvement and enjoyment in the process. When in flow, you become fully absorbed in what you are doing and completely lose your sense of space and time. It's often described as being 'in the zone' – almost losing touch with the outside world. It's a state commonly associated with artists performing their masterpieces or athletes performing at their peak. Bruce Lee called it the state of no mind – when you move effortlessly to perform every move perfectly without a single thought in your head.

A common misconception is that this state of flow is restricted to top artists and athletes. It's not. Each of us can abide in a state of flow and many of us achieve this several times a day. Can you remember as a child playing a sport with your friends and getting so absorbed in it that you completely lost track of time? Or a time when you let go and danced as if no one could see, only to realize you'd been doing it for an hour and were completely drenched in sweat? Those are flow states. Painting, drawing, writing and other creative activities normally pull us into flow. Video games, when at the right level of difficulty, can lead to deep states of flow. Even work, for those who like what they do, can often lead to flow states.

Flow has been discussed for thousands of years in Eastern religions, just not given this memorable name. It only really came to the awareness of Western societies, however, in 1975 when the term was coined by one of my favourite authors, Mihály Csíkszentmihályi. Since then, masses of research has been undertaken to try to understand and accurately define that state. My personal definition?

Remember!

Flow is the state when the doing and the being merge as one.

This is different from being in a state of pure experiential thinking, when your focus is on observing the world. Or from being in a state of problem-solving, when you are engaged to analyse and make a difference. It is a merging of both. And though we previously agreed that as a rule our brains barely have the resources to perform one task at a time, **in flow it seems that both tasks coexist – pure awareness and flawless execution – each enhancing the other**. This truly is the best of both worlds: awareness and performance in one.

To activate this blend of seemingly contradictory states requires the concurrent use of brain regions that normally don't fire together. It requires a special elixir of neurochemicals that normally cancel each other out. When you enter a state of flow, your brain decides that what it is doing is important and challenging enough to give it its full attention. To perform, it releases norepin-ephrine, which is the hormone normally associated with your fight-or-flight response. This makes you more alert, focused, and improves your muscle control. In the case of flow, however, it does not cause stress because there is a concurrent release of serotonin, the calming neurochemical we associate with happiness and the activation of our parasympathetic nervous system. Combine them perfectly and you get a flawless performance that's bathed in hap-piness and calm. Nice! Then it gets even better. In flow, you also release dopamine, which further enhances your focus, as well as your motivation and pattern-recognition abilities. You also release anandamide, which enhances your memory and cognitive abilities, helping you think outside the box. This, simply, is the perfect cock-tail of neurotransmitters. You couldn't ask for a better mix. Cheers!

Another interesting observation is that when we are in flow, our brains down-shift their gears into theta waves, the ones acti-vated during meditation, which calms your brain across the board. Many distracting brain functions switch off as a result, allowing you to get into that peaceful state that monks train for years to achieve. Magic. But the best is yet to come.

When we are in flow, our brains enable what is known as tran-sient hypofrontality. This is when parts of your prefrontal cortex are temporarily disabled. You may recall earlier that we associated hypofrontality with attention deficit disorder and, consequently, unhappiness. In this case, however, it just seems to deactivate the parts of your prefrontal cortex associated with your own self-critic. That nagging voice telling you that you won't be able to perform or that you're not good enough goes quiet. A sense of freedom emerges, and that's when genius strikes.

Because you are not criticizing yourself, you stop wasting brain cycles on overanalysing and 'what will they think of me' thoughts. Once this nagging brain stops, you start to interact with reality in a more instinctual way. You start to tap into the kind of decision-making that you are normally unable to access consciously. You become Neo in *The Matrix*. Everything appears to slow down and you find that you're able to see and dodge a speeding bullet with no thought at all. Least effort. Maximum performance. An engineer's dream.

Flow has gained a lot of attention in the last decade and became a trendy topic, debated in business, sports and arts alike. Just as with everything else our modern society becomes obsessed with, we've productized it and made it seem like a privilege reserved only for those who work hard, or perhaps pay for a trainer or a consultant, to help them achieve.

But that's not at all true. Flow is part of all of us. You can cultivate it as your true nature by following a few simple steps.

It's practice time.

Flow is not a state reserved for top athletes and musicians. You too can find flow in every single thing that you do.

You just need to know how to lead your brain . . . into the zone.

Practice Exercise
Find That Flow

Target	Flow on demand
Duration	30 minutes (or as long as you need)
Repeat	Repeat infinitely for every task you do
You'll need	Nothing really. Just something to do and a bit of time

For beginners, it's easiest to start with tasks that you really love and enjoy.

I, for example, actually like to wash the dishes; it relaxes me. So, I will use this seemingly mundane task as an example here. If you're not a dish washer (obviously you're not), choose your task – making coffee, brushing your cat, playing Sudoku or creating presentations at work. It's all fine, as long as it's a task you enjoy.

When the task is too easy, we don't use the full processing power of our brains to do it. The spare processing power leaves space for your mind to wander. In order to find flow, you need to adjust the difficulty level of the task upwards so that it's challenging, but not too hard.

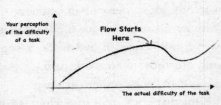

As the task becomes harder, your ability to perform it declines until flow kicks in. When it does, almost like a second wind, the task becomes easier.

When I played computer games with Ali, I noticed that I could not stay fully absorbed in the game, suspending my thoughts, until I was playing the harder levels. Only when the game became challenging enough did my brain tune in and manage to find flow. As the game became harder, I found it easier. Try it. It's fascinating.

Making the task harder is easy if you're playing a game but how about simpler, repetitive tasks such as washing the dishes? You make the task harder by raising your quality standard for every single repetition of the task. When washing dishes, I take every dish, wash it thoroughly, dry it perfectly, inspect it closely, repeat if I need to, then place it neatly where it belongs, before I move on to the next one. I also try my best to waste no water and not to splash around the kitchen. Necessary for the task? No. But vital for my ability to enjoy flow.

Remember!

Make the task just a tad harder than your current ability but not too hard in order to find flow.

The more you do this, of course, the easier the task becomes for you – once again like a broken record – because of neuroplasticity. The more you manage to find your state of flow, the better you become at finding it. Ask me, I'm a writer. I know that, without a shred of a doubt, to be true.

To remain in flow, keep making the task a little harder every time you repeat it, so it remains challenging even as you get better at it.

Aspire for the highest quality for every repetition of the micro task at hand. Don't set yourself targets that span more than one task and don't focus on the target of the full activity. Every dish should be washed well while you wash it. Don't worry about drying it yet and don't think about all the dishes in the sink. Don't limit yourself with targets. Don't try to finish the washing in fifteen minutes.

Just stay focused on every single dish and every single move instead.

Remember!

Your intense focus should be on every single micro task.

When we set big targets, our attention shifts away from the experience and moves into planning for and worrying about the

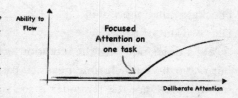

future and what the finish line will look like. There is no finish line in flow. It's found in every single second of the process.

Another key to success is to understand that flow is very fragile. It's a neat process that can easily break once interrupted. Finding flow requires a clear mind and undivided attention. It's only maintained if undisturbed. So . . .

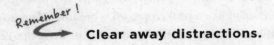

Remember!

Clear away distractions.

Allow yourself to be fully absorbed in the task without anything that could distract your attention. If you're washing the dishes, wash. Don't watch a sitcom on TV. If you really want to dance, stop washing the dishes and flow dancing. If you want to flow while playing a game, don't talk to other players, get fully sucked in and focused. Distractions shake your state of flow. Interruptions collapse it altogether. Prepare your environment by removing all possible interruptions. Switch off your phone and tell your roommate or mom that you need some time alone. Don't even let yourself interrupt your flow. Don't check your phone for messages. They'll be there when you're done. Have you ever seen a pianist playing a masterpiece while looking up to check how the audience perceives them? When truly in flow, the whole world fades to the background. Nothing matters but what you're doing. Even the simple act of checking the time will take you out of the zone.

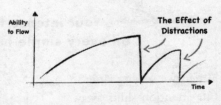

Set a timer, not with the intention of telling you when to stop, but rather how much time needs to pass before you allow yourself to stop. Once the reminder is set, you won't feel the urge to check the time any more and that is when you will let go and fully commit to the task at hand.

Remember !

Flow is found in the absence of time.

You'll be surprised how, when you are in flow, you won't even care about time. You want the task to end. I normally reset the timer when it goes off several times before I actually stop.

Leave our world behind. There is no big target and no time pressure so just enjoy what you do. Find your flow – your highest state of peace and performance – you will want to stay there for the rest of your life.

Chapter Thirteen

The Mission is on the Right

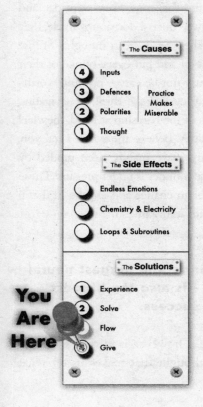

The Causes

4 Inputs
3 Defences   Practice
2 Polarities   Makes
               Miserable
1 Thought

The Side Effects

Endless Emotions

Chemistry & Electricity

Loops & Subroutines

The Solutions

1 Experience
2 Solve
  Flow
  Give

You
Are
Here

Experience, solve and flow. These brain patterns are a sure path to happiness. They stop your incessant thoughts through the act of deliberate attention. The more you practise them, the more they become your default approach to every challenge that life throws your way. Even in the midst of the tragedy of losing Ali, my brain promptly reverted to what it is good at, observing the truth and solving the problem. These 'useful thoughts' impact you in more profound ways than just easing your sorrow because they truly are the pillars of success in our modern world.

Happily Successful

One big difference between those who fail and those who make it, is the tendency to quickly shift to useful thoughts when life changes course. Some of the best entrepreneurs I have worked with live constantly in that state of useful thinking. None of them is as lucky as people think. When problems happen, they don't search for a quiet corner to complain and curse life. They simply don't have the time for that. Instead, they show their true colours. They experience – they call a meeting with their teams to collect as many facts about the situation as they possibly can. They solve problems – they consider all possible solutions to overcome the challenge. They prioritize and they make decisions. Then they flow – once a decision is made, they focus on its execution. They clear their heads from thoughts of loss, and they skip the drama. They tune in and put every ounce of their attention into the task at hand. It may not be easy – nothing worthwhile ever is – but through it all they feel the thrill of navigating challenges. Through it all, regardless of the hardship at hand, they feel energized, purposeful. They feel happy. Believe me when I tell you, my investment decisions in start-ups have mainly been guided by how happy, peaceful and focused the founder is under pressure. Those who lose their ability to stop the brain chatter and engage in useful thinking lose their business and, with it, my investment.

Very Important !

Useful thinking – the biggest neural reason for happiness – is also the biggest secret of success.

Experience-Solve-Flow as a model, however, is missing the most useful thought of them all, the thought that makes us do what makes us happiest – Give!

Five years after Ali died, I was on stage in Amsterdam at a conference called Wisdom in Business. At the end of a one-hour fireside chat, the host asked me how I felt about the loss of Ali five years on. 'On the one hand, the pain of losing him does not go away. I miss him every single day,' I said. 'But yet, on the other hand, I have never felt happier.'

The auditorium, with more than five hundred people in attendance, was engulfed in total silence. Everyone looked at me as I could no longer hold back my tears. This talk was at the very end of a long day where I had been interacting with many readers of *Solve for Happy* as they kindly shared with me how the book had helped them to change.

'I have never in my life felt so much love,' I said. 'All the hugs and words of gratitude. All the messages I get, all the people who come and shake my hand as I sit in a cafe somewhere in our big world, not because I am some kind of a celebrity they want to take a selfie with, but because they see me as a friend, someone who has helped them through a rough patch in life. What an honour. It's all too much for my heart. I feel grateful beyond what words can express and humbled beyond my comprehension. It was the last of countless gifts my wonderful son, my sun, Ali, gave me before he left this world. It was as if when life took away the endless love he poured on me, it gave me what must be the only gift that could match his love – the love of tens of thousands of wonderful humans that have set out on their path to become like Ali.

'Despite all my years of happiness research, until then I never realized that nothing could make us happier than making another person happy. And I set myself the target of a billion.

'It's funny when you think about it, but while I initially viewed my mission as my attempt to give something back to the world, nothing has ever given me more. While my mission is to make others happy, every day it has been making me happier and happier too.

'Ali's never coming back. I've learned to accept this, and the pain remains. Add up all the love and kindness I have received every day, however, and the result is simple. I have never felt happier. I have never been more at peace.

'This joy is not exclusive to those who set big targets and missions. You will feel it every time you give something to enhance the life of another. If all that we do in life, in a way, is our attempt in one form or another to attain this glorious feeling we call happiness, then giving might be the most selfish thing we can ever do. How bizarre!'

Through the bright lights shining at me on the stage, I could see so many others had joined me in my tears as I heard the host reply, 'I think there's nothing more to say.'

Throughout this book I have shared with you some of the stupid things I have done in my life which made me and others unhappy. In this last story, I want to share with you the one thing I stumbled upon, with no prior intention, which made me the happiest man you will ever meet. This final chapter asks you to . . .

Give. It's the smartest thing you can ever choose to do.

Give

How can giving be useful for me? you might think. *If I give away my hard-earned money, I will end up in need. If I give my time, I may end up tired and worn out.* Is that what you believe?

If you do, you'd be wrong. Very wrong.

Giving is obviously good for those you give to, but could it also be good for you? To recognize that, you need clarity of vision and a master's vantage point. Let me explain.

The act of giving obviously involves two entities, a giver and a receiver of the gift.

The assumption obvious to the naked eye is that when a gift moves from the giver to the receiver it adds to what the receiver has as it takes away from what the giver used to have.

Underneath the obvious, however, this is not at all true. That perception of gifting is the common misperception of those who don't give. It is a massive optical illusion that misses on a lot of details that are only recognized through close inspection and questioning of the core assumptions. If you truly open your mind, you will realize that the act of giving does not necessarily reduce what the giver used to have, and it does not necessarily involve moving the gift from one entity to another at all. If you want to see that truth and learn to be more of a giver, learn to ask four questions:

Is there a cost to holding on?

Is the gift even yours?

Is there something to be gained by giving?

Is there a difference between the giver and the receiver?

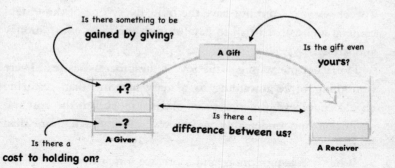

Is There a Cost to Holding On?

The first thing to question when you don't feel like giving something is: what is the true value of keeping it?

Often, we think about the value of the thing we can give, but we don't recognize the cost saved by not keeping it. We think that it's just sitting there and that it costs nothing to keep. But it does. Everything we invite into our lives comes at a cost. Sometimes we don't recognize that cost because the benefit outweighs it, but when the benefit diminishes, we hold on to those 'things' ignoring the cost. We hold on, even though the only impact those things have on our lives is to drain us.

I learned this first-hand when I collected classic cars. Those beautiful masterpieces of engineering art were so seductive to me that I spent a significant amount of my time and attention seeking them. When I found one for sale, I had to make the effort to go see it. It was rarely ever as advertised. These things require work ... lots and lots of work. I had to inspect them, spend time and money to buy them, then after the initial jolt of happiness as I drove them home, I'd usually discover they had hidden issues. Then I had to fix them, restore them, maintain them, renew their registrations, clean them, park them, cover them, disconnect their batteries when I travelled and drive them each for at least 30km a week, even if I did not have the time. Every one of those steps came at a cost that I had to pay for with my time, effort, money and stress.

Don't get me wrong – the joy of the process was real. There is nothing more rewarding to a geek like me than restoring an old engineering marvel to its original glory. But the cost was significant and undeniable, and it was about much more than money.

When we acquire more and more, we forget that . . .

The more things you have, the more things have YOU!

This is not only true for luxury items. Aya recently invited a kitten into her life. That little bundle of cuteness sleeps sixteen hours a day and when she wakes up, often between midnight and 3 a.m., she sprints, slides and jumps all over Aya's flat. She pounces on top of my chest when I visit, and Aya's when I'm not there. This is adorable the first time but seriously annoying on the third night. If you shut the door, she meows non-stop and wakes you up anyway. You let her in and she sheds hair everywhere. Allergy medicines become a staple, all for the joy of watching that fuzzy, cuddly little thing chase around. As soon as you wake up, she asks for attention. She demands to be fed, dislikes what you offer her and meows endlessly until you replace it, then she vomits it a while later at the exact moment you are about to rush out the door. She is firmly the boss and will be for a while. What a joy!

Many of us adore cats. I do too. It's just important to acknowledge that keeping a cat comes at a cost to your time, stress and bank account. *Dogs are better*, I can almost hear all of you dog fanatics say, and I am not even going to venture into what the costs of keeping a dog are. It would lose me way too many readers. But let's just say they do not come free. If you see someone picking up someone else's poop, you know who's working for who. There's no denying the joy that the unconditional love of a pet brings, but it comes at a price that's not to be ignored.

So does everything you invite into your life. Even a shirt needs to be washed, ironed and folded. It takes up closet space. Replace it with a T-shirt and you can skip the ironing, but still the washing machine needs water, detergent and the eventual maintenance. Your phone needs to be charged and protected. Even money itself comes at a cost. Once you've earned it, you need to keep it safe and invest it. You need to deal with all the messages your bank sends, and you need to file a tax report. Just by sitting there, even if you do nothing about it, your money will probably come at a cost of depreciation in its value.

Remember !

The benefits of what we bring into our lives are undeniable, but they all come at a cost that's not to be ignored.

And then there's opportunity cost — a business term that refers to lost opportunity as a cost. Think about it. If you could make a guaranteed $100, and you passed that up, you could say that you lost $100. This loss, perhaps, is represented by the cost of holding on to things. Whether or not something adds benefit to our life, its presence stops us from letting other things in. The shelf on which you keep your T-shirts is a limited space. Fill it up and you'll lose the opportunity to buy that other cool top you come across. Buy that and you suffer the clutter. Fill your life with 'friends' that bring you down and make you miserable, and you lose the opportunity to bring in true friends who will lift you up and help you feel better.

Remember !

What we hold on to takes up the space we need to invite what enriches us into our lives.

With that in mind, start asking yourself if you really need all that you have. This dress that won't fit any more, that old jacket you know you won't wear again, those extra dollars that could be tax deductible if you gave them to charity. What are they costing you? And if they leave, what space will they free up for new opportunities and experiences to come in and replace them?

Think about all the things in your life that you wouldn't miss if they were gone. How much would it cost you to give them away? Think about all the free hours that you spend binge-watching Netflix. What is the cost to you? And what would you gain if you spent some of them volunteering or teaching a skill that you know?

Very Important !

What you keep costs you and what you have won't be missed. GIVE IT ALL AWAY.

Is the Gift Even Yours?

Our perspective of what it means to give becomes even more interesting when we realize that often what we have is not even really ours. All we need to do is zoom out a bit and broaden our perspective to realize that this is the truth.

Answer me this: Where are all the things you had throughout your childhood? Why are they not yours any more? How many of the things you have previously owned over the years? Did the toys break? Did you lose your colouring books? Have your clothes become too small? Why don't you have them today? What happened to every dollar you ever earned? You may have managed to save some but the rest is gone, isn't it? It was never yours to keep. It was just in your custody for a short while before it went away to be in the custody of another who kept it for a while then gave it away too. If you still have your wedding dress or favourite music album on vinyl, do you think those will be yours to keep forever? Are they really yours when you're not even using them or just locking them away? Will you never part with them? What happens then when death comes to visit? How will you hold on to them then?

The maths is unmistakable. **Life is a zero-sum game.** You come to this life with nothing, let things into your life for a while, then leave with nothing. Through it all you never really own anything. **You just rent a few things on the path** because . . .

Very Important !

Nothing is ever really yours to keep.

It gets even clearer if you broaden your understanding of space. Think of something you own that you left at home this morning. That TV or game console that you love so much. Is it really yours when you are at work? Can you switch it on and watch the news? What if you really needed your toolbox when visiting a friend but it was left back home, do you have tools then? Are they yours? Now think about all those things you consider yours and apply the same logic.

Remember !

Things are only ours when we use them.

Take the very thing that we associate most with ownership – your money. Is your money *ever* yours? It surely wasn't yours until you earned it. On your payday it shows up in your bank account, which technically means your bank owns it, and they give you a card that allows you to use some of it (not all of it because they have limits on daily withdrawals). They will also ask you questions if you want to withdraw large sums in cash or transfer some to a friend who happens to have a Middle Eastern name. Which means they have enough control to make it not yours when they so choose. Of course, if your bank goes bankrupt, the money goes with them, which truly begs the question: Whose money was it then? The only time your money becomes yours is when you walk to an ATM machine and withdraw some of it. Now you're holding it in your hands. It's yours (an evil laugh would be appropriate here as you raise your hands to the sky and shake the money violently). You have it, but what is it worth? Nothing. It's just a pile of paper that brings no value to your life until that moment when you decide to spend it. That one instant, that microsecond, is the only instant when you actually own your money – but in that same instant, it's gone. It's not yours any more. It now belongs to the person who took it, though he does not really own it either.

Remember !

➤ **Your money is not your money until you spend it, and . . . as soon as you do, it's not yours any more.**

All you own now is that thing that you exchanged for your money – say a can opener. Of course, the same logic applies to the can opener, which is mostly useless until you get to your kitchen, hold it in your hand to confront a can with its fate. The can opener is yours then for twelve seconds and then it belongs to the kitchen drawer for weeks on end. Nothing is yours for more than a few seconds, minutes or hours at a time, then it's someone else's. Told you, life is one big rental scheme.

That illusion of ownership is only revealed to us when we lose what we thought we owned. When travellers lose their hand luggage, they often realize that they don't even remember everything that was in it. They agonize about losing a phone charger or a valuable ring for a short while and then they get on with their lives. They buy another charger and wear another ring. Most forget about the loss other than those who obsess over it because it was their grandmother's ring and held emotional value for them. But losing the ring does not make her any less their grandmother or make them love or remember her less. I say that while I myself am one of those people. I always wear several necklaces, modestly threaded with a small pendant, that have been gifted to me or remind me of loved ones. One of those is Ali's earring. Since Ali left our world, it has become my most valuable possession. I lost it once. I forgot it in a hotel as I rushed out to catch a flight. As I realized my loss, it felt like a spear was stabbing me through the heart. I was stuck on a long flight unable to call the hotel and ask if they'd found it. For the first hour or so, I felt so angry at myself. I told myself things like *How can I live without it? It's the only thing I have left of my son.* I tortured myself with these thoughts until I remembered . . .

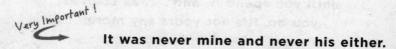

Very Important!

It was never mine and never his either.

It was *not* the only thing I have of Ali's. I have all of Ali. He lives inside me. All the laughter, the joy, the wisdom. Every memory and every word he told me. Every loving thought that reminds me of him. He is with me all the time. Those moments and experiences are my only true possessions. I don't need a piece of metal to remind me of him. I am Ali.

Loss wakes us up from our illusions. The times when we suffer the greatest loss are the times when the truth sets us free.

When all is said and done, life itself becomes the only thing we own while we live it and even that too is for rent. What we think we own simply amounts to nothing. When confronted with the truth of our fragility, the masks of our ego get stripped away. Only then do we recognize that we're all essentially the same. That a fancy car or an expensive suit is just a facade that we hide behind and even that, sooner or later, will be stripped away.

There is, perhaps, no better display of this truth to be found than in the Islamic pilgrimage to Mecca. Every year more than nine million pilgrims gather in this tiny, mountainous desert city to leave their earthly life behind. The men wear nothing but two pieces of white cloth symbolizing the rags the bodies of Muslims are wrapped in before they are laid in their graves. The women wear simple flowing dresses and headscarves. No expensive shoes or watches, no key chains with expensive car logos and no fashion to hide behind. When the rituals of Hajj — as this pilgrimage is called in Arabic — are over, the men shave their heads and in the remaining few hours they are awakened to one only truth: that without everything we hoard in life to feed our egos, we are all essentially exactly the same. The spectacle is awe-inspiring in its magnitude. In the absence of the egotistical masks we hide behind, it's impossible to tell rich from poor, who's Turkish and who's Moroccan. Who's a dropout and who's a PhD. It is a humbling experience. Everyone is exactly the same. The other inspiring side of that experience is that as you, yourself, strip down to just a couple of rags on your body, you live the lives of those in need. You remember that you could have been born them. You also realize that you need so much less than you think.

Once you recognize this truth, giving to another starts to feel like giving to your own child or to a loved one. When you recognize how blessed you are, it becomes hard to deny what actually matters. Helping out and giving — whatever little you have left — becomes the only logical thing to do.

Remember!

The feeling of freedom from attachment is one of the highest joys.

Try it yourself. Don't take my word for it. Find a warm old jacket in your closet – one you like but don't wear often. Make yourself let it go. Walk to someone who you know is in need and hand it over to them. Tell me how it makes you feel. The joy of giving added to the joy of freedom from attachment to what you owned. Take thirty seconds of your time on a busy day and, instead of rushing, smile and compliment the barista who makes your coffee. Tell me if that doesn't feel more delicious than any coffee you ever had.

No car has ever made me happier than at the time when I was giving it away. Of all the cars I collected, and I collected many, I donated some to be auctioned for charity, sold some and gave the money away, and offered some to friends who needed them at nominal prices. I now only have in storage the two Rolls-Royces that were made famous because I mentioned them in my first book. I'm keeping them as they appreciate in value so that when I auction those too, at the right time, they will raise *a lot* of money for a good cause. Yes, I am selfish that way. I am saving them for an explosion of joy.

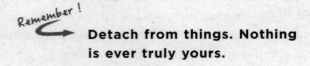

Remember! **Detach from things. Nothing is ever truly yours.**

Which leads me to one more pivotal question in this conversation . . .

Is There Something to be Gained by Giving?

The word 'giving' is so misleading because in the act of giving one receives so much – often much more than what is given. Keeping what's supposed to be given, on the other hand, takes away from an abundance that could be had. What I want to say is that more doesn't lead to happier.

Let's examine this by looking into the widely available body of research on the topic.

Lots of studies, such as Kahneman and Deaton's famous study of 2010,[1] show that income only affects our happiness positively up to a certain point. This research showed that happiness increased for the study participants along with the increase in their income until their income reached the average income of the country in which they lived. Beyond that point, more money did not result in more happiness. It is understood, clearly, that if you can't make ends meet, it is harder to find happiness. If there's no food on the table or if you have to work three shifts just to get by, you have many justifiable reasons to feel less happy. The more money you come across then, the easier your life becomes and this impacts on your happiness positively. This trend, however, does not continue endlessly. Once all your basic needs are met, your level of happiness tends to plateau.

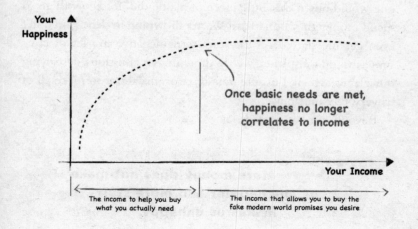

Your Happiness / Your Income

Once basic needs are met, happiness no longer correlates to income

The income to help you buy what you actually need

The income that allows you to buy the fake modern world promises you desire

When our incomes increase beyond our basic needs, we spend more on things we don't need and so they don't make us any happier. Scott Holdman, Director of the Impact Institute, exposed this trend in his TED Talk with staggering statistics. An article in the *Wall Street Journal* revealed that Americans spend 1.2 trillion dollars annually on non-essential goods – things they don't really need. Estimates by Annie Leonard show that 99 per cent of the stuff that Americans purchase is trashed within just six months.[2] The *LA Times* claims that there are 300,000 items in the average American household.[3] This American consumerist lifestyle is rapidly being exported across the world.

We are drowning in consumption. All the stuff we buy clearly impacts on our wellbeing, though not in the way advertising campaigns try to tell us. Clutter makes us stressed and it makes us feel guilty.[4] Furthermore, consuming creates more hunger to consume. We start to buy on impulse to distract ourselves from our problems, which only breeds more unhappiness, discontentment, anxiety and depression.[5] This does not even include the impact on our happiness of the debt we incur in order to consume. Nearly 200 million Americans have credit cards,[6] mostly to buy things no one would buy if that little piece of plastic did not allow them to spend money they don't have. We are drowning in debt. And don't even get me started on the long-term negative impact of consumerism on our planet. We are drowning in emissions, destroying our planet, which, I'm sure you agree, is just about to make all of us very, *very* unhappy.

Beyond our basic needs . . .

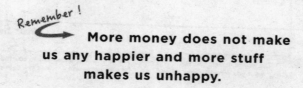

Remember!

More money does not make us any happier and more stuff makes us unhappy.

There is, however, one thing that makes us happier beyond meeting our basic needs, and that is giving. Harvard Business School professor Michael Norton ran a study where students were given some money.[7] 'We gave them an envelope with some cash in it. The envelope also included one of two notes. One note said, *By 5 p.m. today spend this money on yourself*, and the other note said, *By 5 p.m. today spend this money on somebody else.* We asked them to fill out a short survey to indicate how happy they felt that morning ... We then called them up at night and asked them what they spent the money on and how happy they felt.'

This study was conducted in many societies around the world. The results were always the same. It didn't matter if you gave a cup of coffee to a friend in Seattle or saved a child's life from malaria in Congo, those who spent the money on someone else felt happier than those who spent it on themselves.

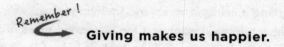

Giving makes us happier.

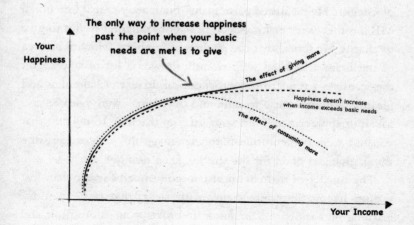

The Darwinian principle of 'survival of the fittest' is misunderstood by many. It suggests that the selfish individuals who are able to out-compete others are most likely to survive. Well, that is true of course if you can survive alone, but if you're human, you only live if the whole tribe survives.

Giving, in that sense, is not an act of altruism. It is a selfish act our species has used to ensure its collective survival. Think back to our early cave-dwelling years. What chance do you think we would have had for survival if we, tiny little primates, had faced the beasts of the era alone? Living, hunting and working together is what made us survive. It was to the benefit of every individual to be surrounded by others who were healthy and capable. It was vital for the survival of the species that we gave to each other and attended to each other's needs in order for the collective to survive.

The same reward system used to encourage other survival mechanisms – such as reproduction – is also used to reward the act of giving. Giving activates the mesolimbic pathway in your brain which releases dopamine. One interesting piece of research on this was conducted by William T. Harbaugh of the University of Oregon. He measured participants' brain activity in a functional MRI as they were making decisions about whether or not to give to charity. He found that the nucleus accumbens, which is an area of the brain associated with reward, showed a lot of activity on the scans. As a result, the neurochemical drivers of happiness and pleasure – dopamine, serotonin and oxytocin – were released as a token of appreciation from your survival machine to tell you that you did well. In neurotransmitter language this only means one thing: giving is good for the species, keep doing it.[8]

The impact of this chemical trio goes much further than just feeling happy. Serotonin helps with sleep, digestion, memory, learning and appetite. Dopamine improves your motivation and arousal. Oxytocin decreases blood pressure and increases bonding. Social fears are reduced and replaced with trust and empathy. Oxytocin is also an anti-inflammatory. It reduces pain and enhances wound healing.[9] There is a lot to be gained from giving. Putting things in perspective . . .

Very Important!

Giving might be one of the most selfish things you can ever do.

Kindness is one of our most fundamental survival mechanisms. It is deeply hardwired in us. Giving to others is at the core of our very own survival because none of us can make it alone.

When our biology, spiritual teachings and societal norms motivate us to give, they also motivate billions of others to give to us. This closed loop is not always seen clearly within our modern societies, because so much of what we needed to do as a tribe to survive is now expected to be done automatically by the economic, social and governance systems of our society. As a result, we learn to ignore how necessary our individual acts of giving are and assume that these are the responsibilities of the system. Thousands of people do little things every day for you to survive. From the police officer to the street cleaner, from the farmer of your food to the driver that moves it to the point of sale. Every nurse and doctor on standby, every engineer that builds and every scientist attempting to help us figure out how the world works. Yes, they all get rewarded for it in some kind of a monetary form but that does not make it devoid of giving. You too are contributing to society in some shape or form. You need to recognize what you do as such, not just as a job or a duty. Even if you're compensated to do it, that's natural. Being rewarded to give is what nature always intended anyway. When any of us manage to see the value of what we do in terms of giving to others, we feel the biological rewards associated with those acts. That's when our work becomes our purpose because, believe it or not, if survival is our mission in the game of life . . .

Very Important !

Giving may well be our only purpose.

Why, then, do we hold on to whatever little we have? Because, like most other wrong habits, we are conditioned to do so.

When Life Itself is in Flow

Through the years of wars, recessions, depressions, even pandemics, those who experience hardship learn to save a little stash. From generation to generation, the conventional wisdom of saving for a rainy day is passed down to us all. We keep a bit of money in the bank in case we lose our income, we keep a bit of food in the fridge in case we wake up hungry, and we keep that old prom dress just in case we lose twenty-five pounds at the exact same time we feel like becoming a teenager again, just in time for our ten-year school reunion.

The things we keep give us a false feeling of safety and, as they do, they clog the system. They stop the flow of life itself and, with the space they take in our life, they stop us from receiving.

There is only one way through which you can achieve abundance, and that is to stop piling up what you don't need and rarely ever use. Instead, you get to true abundance when you stay open for receiving, by keeping space in your life for new experiences to flow in, and by believing in your heart that there will always be something coming your way, just as there always has been.

Think of life as a closed system. All the evidence of physics proves that there is conservation of everything. Nothing is ever created from nothing, and nothing ever goes to waste. When you give, you put more flow in the cycle of the system and you leave a space behind – a vacuum – to be filled. This positive imbalance allows for flow and forces the system to give back to you to fill the void. If you stop giving, the cycle is interrupted. Not only do you stop the flow of life when you stop giving . . .

Remember !

When you stop receiving you interrupt the circle too.

It's the balance between the outflow and the inflow of goodness in your life that enables the circle of life itself to flow.

One evening after giving a talk I got a standing ovation. I felt so uncomfortable that I said, on stage, in front of thousands of people, 'Thank you, thank you, please stop. It makes me uncomfortable.' A wise woman came up to me after the Q&A session and explained to me why I needed to learn to receive just as much as I gave – that when people stood up to show their gratitude, it was good for them to give me that gift and that I interrupted that flow by refusing to receive it. So, I've learned to change and open up to the gifts that others – and life itself – give me. Since I have, I've been receiving more and more. **It's not selfish. It makes the cycle of life complete.**

As we give we gain and, trust me, there is so much more truth to this statement than meets the eye. This underlying truth is found in the true nature of the relationship between the giver and the receiver. It's a truth that may only be grasped through a stroke of insight to help us answer this final question . . .

Is There a Difference Between Us?

I mentioned Jill Bolte Taylor, her TED Talk and her book, *A Stroke of Insight*, earlier. Jill's experience when a stroke disabled the functionality of her left-brain hemisphere is a revelation of the truth. She said:

> *I felt enormous. I looked down at my arm and realized that I can no longer define the boundaries of my body. The atoms and the molecules of my arm blended with the atoms and molecules of the wall and everything around me . . . I felt as one with all the energy that was. It was beautiful!*
>
> *Right here right now I can choose to step into the consciousness of my left hemisphere where I become a single individual separate from the flow of life. I can step into the consciousness of my right hemisphere where we are − I am − the life force of the Universe.* **Where I am one with everything.**

This experience of the world, the way Jill described it, is reinforced by anyone who has been on a psychedelic trip, experienced shamanic breathing or managed to transcend the body through meditation. When we see beyond the illusion of our individual separation from all else, we realize that . . .

Remember !

> **You, me and everything, in the absence of illusions, are one and the same.**

And this is not just some spiritual jargon.

At the very physical level, every single atom in the universe is constantly being recycled. One day it is part of you and the next it is part of me. If you recognized the truth of what we are made of, you – like Jill – would fail to see the distinction between us and see your hand and mine blend in one.

At a societal level, we are part of one community. One that is stronger when it acts together. A community that expands beyond you and me to include every other living being in the universe. A community that has over the last one hundred years of human civilization suffered to the point of extinction as we ignore its oneness and jeopardize it with our selfish actions.

At a spiritual level, if you are willing to accept that there is more to you than just your physical form, we are all players participating in one massive virtual game. While each of us navigates an individual avatar, further apart from each other, around the game of the physical universe, we can't help but observe that our actions are driving us closer and closer to switching the entire game console off. It's time to recognize that the only way for the game to continue is if we play as one in favour of the sustainability of the game instead of our own selfish, individual desires.

Pay attention to the condition of our humanity. The pandemic of loneliness, stress. The damage our planet has sustained. The toxicity of social media and the negativity of the news. It's the eleventh hour. Humanity has never come this close to losing its way and it's all a result of our ignorance of the oneness of all of us and the unification of our destiny on this little blue planet.

We must stop enforcing our separation and ignoring our oneness. We have to give to all others to save the tribe, with us included.

Enough talking about the logic of giving. Let's just learn to make it our second – no – first nature.

Practise giving every day and you will get better at it. Observe the impact that it has on your happiness and prosperity, and you will want to give more. We can practise giving just as we can practise a musical instrument. It is a skill. Try this for twenty-one days. Trust me, it will work.

Practice Exercise
Give Give Give

Target	Make giving the centre of your life
Duration	Just a few seconds
Repeat	Repeat whenever you can
You'll need	A bit of generosity and a belief that what you give comes back to you and multiplies

Everyone you come across, every minute of every day, is in need of something.

They may need your smile, reassurance, kindness, advice, hugs and much more. Even kings and queens, CEOs and heads of state are in need of a genuine human connection. Believe me, I've witnessed it first-hand.

Just as with every skill, start small. Here is a set of simple exercises that you can include in your daily life. You don't need to give big, just frequently. You know this by now: neuroplasticity strengthens your neural networks every time you use them. So, let's work those giving muscles till you become an Olympic champion at it.

Buy Them a Coffee

Something about this simple practice fills every cell of my body with joy. Have you ever bought a coffee for a friend? Consider buying a coffee for a stranger. If you can afford a cup of coffee. Consider tipping the barista the value of one more coffee.

If someone is working at a cafe to make you coffee, it's likely they could really use a few extra bucks. They could be a student trying to pay living costs or a single mother trying to make ends meet. If you, on the other hand, regardless of your disposable income, can afford to buy a coffee, then consider if you can spare the cost of another. Even if you skip your cup the next day. Your gift does not end their struggle but it will help them feel that they're not alone. It may empower them to get up, stand tall and feel a bit more supported. Do it again whenever you can. Every little helps.

This is your *kindness* challenge: give as much as you buy for yourself at least once a week.

Smile at Strangers

I lived in London for a year. London is a wonderful city, but it is a bit of a grinder – incredibly fast-paced and stressful. I always joke about how easy it is to tell the Londoners from the tourists as soon as you land in the airport. The tourists will be walking slowly, often in groups or couples, chatting and laughing. The Londoners, on the other hand, walk fast. They get a serious determined look on their faces as soon as they step out of the plane, and they start to sprint as if the airport doors are about to close. This habit persists for as long as they are in the city. Everyone's almost always in a rush. Once I saw a mother and daughter walking at the speed of a bullet in Hyde Park. I thought they were late for something but then suddenly they got to a patch of grass, looked at each other and sat there to enjoy the sun.

Now, I love Londoners and I laugh with my friends about how fast they walk when we're heading somewhere together. I always walk very slowly. I learned this from my wonderful son, Ali, who truly walked like a turtle. He would take one step and it would then seem as if he paused for a tiny bit to think if he should take the next. He would raise that second foot a bit higher than normal, just like a turtle carrying its heavy home on its back. Then slowly put it back down and pause to think about the next step. I'm a bit more of a camel than a turtle but I still manage to walk at half the speed of the average citizen of a fast-paced city. As I do, or as I sit in the train, I look at everyone's eyes as they walk the other way as I keep a smile on my face. I really smile and sometimes nod the exact way you nod in the corridors at work when you cross someone you know.

This is Jedi Master-level practice. It is difficult and intimidating at first. But once you get the hang of it, you will notice how it lightens up people's day. When someone notices that I'm smiling at them, at first they seem shocked, as if they've seen a tiger about to pounce. Then they ease up and smile back. When I nod, they nod back. Sometimes I turn my head to look at them as they pass and, almost always, I see them looking back at me with gratitude in their eyes as if to wonder *Who's this guy?*

Wherever you are in the world, try it, it's my dare for you. Quickly you will learn that it works and so it will become easier. The gift of a smile will make you happier. Do it all the way. Smile a big smile. From the heart. Don't be shy. You're not doing anything wrong. This is your courage challenge: smile at one stranger every single day.

Say Something Nice

Does being nice to people count as giving? Oh yes. It is the ultimate form of giving and, as with the other forms, it gives to you as much as it gives to others.

Talk to people who don't expect you to acknowledge them. The cashier in a cafe, the hostess on a plane, the security guard at the door of the office building. They won't bite. As a matter of fact, they will probably feel appreciated. This is the connection challenge: make a human connection with a stranger at least once a day.

Fifty Pounds

Since I started working on OneBillionHappy, I've been travelling all the time. I've downsized my whole life so that it fits in one check-in piece of luggage. Because the limit on check-in luggage for most airlines is around fifty pounds or twenty-three kilos, my new lifestyle comes with a simple rule. If I need to add something new to my bag, something else needs to be removed. If I need to buy a new T-shirt, I need to give away an old one. Do that too.

Next time you buy something new, give away something old. If you feel there is nothing you are willing to give away, then don't add more to your life. Simple!

The practice of letting go of your older things is one that needs a bit of training. Attempt to make it a habit and give away something every Saturday, for instance. As I said before, I try to give away ten items. It does not need to be big. Anything will do and deliver the practice you need. The more you do this, the more you will detach from things, and that will make you feel lighter and happier. It will give those that you give to happiness too. As you give the old to leave space for the new to come in, you complete the circle of life. Life flows through you to others. This is your flow challenge. Do it once a week.

So there you go. Four simple dares: give as much as you buy; give someone a smile every day; give a kind word to those you don't know; and give something away every Saturday. Start small but give often. Pay attention to how your life changes. Not only will you feel lighter and happier, but more loved by life itself.

When you do, then maybe it's time for your next challenge – the gratitude challenge. Feel grateful every night before you go to sleep for having been given the privilege of being able to give to others.

And finally, here's one last challenge.

OneBillionHappy

There is so much in our world today that needs fixing, it's hard to know where to start.

If you want to know our future, look at our present. Our actions today will inform our state tomorrow. Those are actions we can choose. We – you included – can choose to make a small change today that will make a big difference to all of us tomorrow. But that takes us back to the same question: what should we change?

Well, when I am presented with a complex web of problems, I always attempt to find the underlying root cause that is triggering it all. I found the answer to all of humanity's problems in two simple values: happiness and compassion.

If we learn to drop the values we embraced in the twentieth century – values like 'greed is good' and 'legal is ethical' – and learn to replace those with happiness and compassion, all our problems will go away. Yes, I believe it truly is that simple.

Remember !

Happiness and compassion could save humanity.

If we prioritize our happiness, we will remember that happiness is a choice that we make, each and every single day. We will then lose interest in the politicians and all their empty promises, stop fanatically following their fake ideologies and treat them for what they really are, civil servants who should serve our agenda – to be happy. We would realize how much of our life we have wasted chasing the wrong targets that have always made us unhappy. If we can remember that everything we ever wanted was an attempt to find that glorious feeling we call happiness and if we can remember that happiness is our default setting, always there inside each of us waiting to be found, perhaps we will decide to turn inwards, we will decide to change. Then, and only then, we might make our world better, because . . .

Very Important !

The only thing we'll ever be able to change is ourself, and the only way we will ever change the world is when we, you and I, change.

Of all the things my wise son, Ali, taught me, nothing ever changed me more than the day he came to me when he was fourteen and said, 'Papa, I want to tell you something, but it will upset you.'

At the time, I was still that larger-than-life Google executive who truly believed that I could change the world. I couldn't imagine how something a fourteen-year-old boy could say would affect me in any way, so I said, 'Sure, Ali, tell me. It won't upset me.'

He said, 'Papa, I know you really want to make a difference, but I want you to know that you will never fix the world.'

I interrupted, with the ego of a parent and teacher: 'Why, Ali? This is a loser's attitude. You can never change anything or have any impact until you truly believe that you can.'

I was right in saying this, but that was not Ali's point. In his typical way, he waited until I had finished, then gestured to me as if to say *Wait. Hear me out.* He put his hand on my shoulder and his immensely peaceful energy flowed through me, calming down my ego. I had learned over the years that when Ali spoke like this, I needed to listen. So, I sat down in silence attentively, eager to know what he had to say.

He said, 'Papa, you are never going to fix the world. You can only change your little world and the better you become at it, the bigger your little world will become. Your little world is you. Don't try to fix anything else until you fix that. When you do, you'll be able to fix me [*habibi*, he never needed fixing, but he was kind enough to say it anyway] and Mama and Aya. We will become your little world. If you do well, then maybe you'll be able to influence your team at work, then maybe your department, then your company, your country and, who knows, maybe even the world could become your little world to change, but not fix because there will always be someone suffering somewhere.'

I'm still working on me, believe it or not, and I still have a long way to go. But I invite you to join me. Work on you. Choose one thing to change, and then another. Join our OneBillionHappy mission to start by changing yourself, then impacting your little world. The mission is summarized in three steps:

1. Understand that happiness is your birthright, that it's predictable and that if you work on it you will get there. **Make happiness your priority.**
2. **Invest in your happiness.** Spend an hour a day three to four times a week learning about happiness – read a book, watch a video, talk to those that are happy or just be. Allow yourself to feel before you learn or do.
3. Find the compassion in you to make another happy. **Tell two people** (or 2,000 if you can) what you learned about happiness, then make them promise to tell two people who will tell two people. Because if every one of us told two,

who told two who told two, our little world would become the whole planet. We would reach a billion happy in less than five years.

You can do anything you set your mind to. Your brain is like a computer. You can adjust the code that runs it. When you do, your actions will follow. With practice, you can become anything that you want to be. So, choose to make a difference. Help us create a better world.

I have one last selfish request. Please find the compassion in your heart to want happiness for my wonderful son and wise teacher, Ali. Send him a prayer, a generous wish, that he is happy wherever he is right now. He started it all and he truly was the kindest, happiest human I have ever known.

Very Important !

Your little world is you. Make it better for those you love.

I'll keep working on mine for Ali.

Summary of Part Three

Many happiness teachings may seem to come across as an invitation to calm or control one's brain. Because our stray incessant thoughts can cause a lot of unhappiness, it is obvious that keeping our minds in check is a sure path to a calmer, happier life. But it's not the only path.

If an active mind is engaged in useful thinking — generating thoughts that improve your life and state of wellbeing — then, by all means, think as much as you can.

There are four types of useful thoughts. I strongly urge you to make those types of thoughts the norm of what your brain focuses on. That way it will no longer have the capacity to think the negative thoughts that waste your life and make you unhappy.

1) **Experiential Thinking** – Experiencing the world exactly
   as it is requires your brain to engage just as much as it needs
   to when processing any other kind of thought. As a matter of
   fact, because your brain is only able to do one thing at a time,
   observing the world with mindfulness is a bulletproof way to
   live in reality and not inside your own head. Meditation is a
   valuable practice that can, over time, reconfigure your brain to

become more capable of living in the present moment instead of lost in its own thoughts.

Meditation is just a practice, though. To truly transform those skills into the reality of your everyday life, use newer versions of it that are fit for the modern world to learn to be present every minute of every day.

2) **Problem-Solving** – is the most highly praised type of thinking in our analytical modern world. The capacity to overcome challenges by finding solutions is mostly applied in our work and professional life. Yet, it can equally be applied to lead to our happiness and wellbeing.

The **happiness flowchart** is a good example of how you can use your disciplined problem-solving brain to ensure you bounce back to happiness swiftly when an event disturbs your mood. Once you've learned to recognize, acknowledge, even embrace, an emotion, find the thought that triggered it and then ask yourself three questions:

a. **Is it true?** Is there evidence to support the validity of the thought triggering my happiness. If the thought is fiction created by your brain, drop it. If it is true, then ask the next question . . .

b. **Can I do something about it?** Unhappiness, you see, is just a survival mechanism. It's your brain's invitation for you to do something about what it sees as a suboptimal condition for your survival and success. If there is something you can do about what's making you unhappy, do it. The unhappiness will go away and your world will become better. If there is nothing you can do, then ask the last question . . .

c. **Can I accept and commit?** Life, every now and again, is bound to send a predicament your way. An event that doesn't meet your hopes of how life should be which is beyond your ability to fix or improve. When there is nothing you can do *about your situation, learn to accept it for what it is, then commit to do whatever you can do to make your life better despite, or even because of, the challenge that you are facing.*

3) **Flow** – *When we flow, we merge our being with our doing. We get absorbed into what we do fully, we do it better and we feel lighter. To flow, make the task at hand a tiny bit harder than your current skill, clear away the distractions and break it into smaller tasks and focus on the small bits instead of the final results, do each bit to the best of your abilities and forget about time. Give every task all the time it needs.*

4) **Give** – *It is the smartest thing you can ever do. Nothing will ever make you happier or make our world better.*

Our brains are nothing but sophisticated computer systems. They are highly predictable in their operations. You don't necessarily need a silent brain to be happy. All you need is a positive, useful brain. Your brain will do what you tell it to do. It's time to start your training.

References

Introduction

1. 'Depression Rates by country 2022', *World Population Review* [online]. Available at: worldpopulationreview.com/country-rankings/depression-rates-by-country

2. 'Suicide: one person dies every 40 seconds', WHO [online]. Available at: who.int/news/item/09-09-2019-suicide-one-person-dies-every-40-seconds

3. Sadlier, A. '1 in 4 Americans feel they have no one to confide in', *New York Post* (30 April 2019) [online]. Available at: nypost.com/2019/04/30/1-in-4-americans-feel-they-have-no-one-to-confide-in/

The Basics

1. Van Leemput, K. et al. 'Automated Segmentation of Hippocampal Subfields from Ultra-High Resolution in Vivo MRI', *Hippocampus,* vol. 19,6 (2009), pp. 549–57. Available at: dspace.mit.edu/handle/1721.1/71591

Garbage In . . .

1. Oltean, H. and David, D. 'A meta-analysis of the relationship between rational beliefs and psychological distress', *Journal of Clinical Psychology,* vol. 74,6 (2018), pp. 883–95. Available at: pubmed.ncbi.nlm.nih.gov/29168176/

2. Pratchett, T. *The Thief of Time* (London: Doubleday, 2008), p. 215.

Under Attack

1. Pinker, S. (2018). 'Is the world getting better or worse? A look at the numbers', TED [online]. Available at: ted.com/talks/steven_pinker_is_the_world_getting_better_or_worse_a_look_at_the_numbers?language=en

Practice Makes Miserable

1. Mandal, A. 'What is Neurogenesis?', News Medical Life Sciences [online]. Available at: www.news-medical.net/health/What-is-Neurogenesis.aspx

2. 'Introduction to cell signalling', Khan Academy [online]. Available at: khanacademy.org/science/biology/cell-signaling/mechanisms-of-cell-signaling/a/introduction-to-cell-signaling?modal=1

3. Radparvar, D. 'Neurons that fire together, wire together', Holstee.com [online]. Available at: holstee.com/blogs/mindful-matter/neurons-that-fire-together-wire-together

4. Begum, T (2021). 'What is mass extinction and are we facing a sixth one?', Natural History Museum [online]. Available at: nhm.ac.uk/discover/what-is-mass-extinction-and-are-we-facing-a-sixth-one.html

Both of You

1. Lienhard, D. (2017). 'Roger Sperry's Split Brain Experiments (1959–1968)', The Embryo Project Encyclopedia [online]. Available at: embryo.asu.edu/pages/roger-sperrys-split-brain-experiments-1959-1968

2. Bolte Taylor, J. (2008). 'My stroke of insight', TED [online]. Available at: ted.com/talks/jill_bolte_taylor_my_stroke_of_insight

3. McGilchrist, I. The Master and His Emissary: The Divided Brain and the Making of the Western World (Totton: Yale University Press, 2019), p. 431.

Talk Talk Talk

1. 'Know Your Brain: Default Mode Network', Neuroscientifically Challenged [online]. Available at: neuroscientificallychallenged.com/posts/know-your-brain-default-mode-network

2. Bergland, C. (2015). 'The Brain Mechanics of Rumination and Repetitive Thinking', Psychology Today [online]. Available at: psychologytoday.com/

gb/blog/the-athletes-way/201508/the-brain-mechanics-rumination-and-repetitive-thinking.

3. Arain. M. et al. 'Maturation of the adolescent brain', NCBI, 9 (2013), PP. 449–61 [online]. Available at: ncbi.nlm.nih.gov/pmc/articles/PMC3621648/

Can you feel it?

1. Kessler, D. 'The Five Stages of Grief', Grief.com [online]. Available at: grief.com/the-five-stages-of-grief/

2. 'Between Stimulus and Response There Is a Space. In That Space Is Our Power to Choose Our Response', QuoteInvestigator.com [online]. Available at: quoteinvestigator.com/2018/02/18/response/

Alchemy

1. McCorry, L. 'Physiology of the Autonomic Nervous System', *American Journal of Pharmaceutical Education*, 71 (4): 78 (Aug 2007). Available at: ncbi.nlm.nih.gov/pmc/articles/PMC1959222/

2. Kraft, T. and Pressman, S. 'Grin and bear it: the influence of manipulated facial expression on the stress response', *Psychological Science,* 2012:23(11). pp. 1372–78. Available at: pubmed.ncbi.nlm.nih.gov/23012270/

3. 'A Crisp Explanation of Facial Feedback Hypothesis With Examples', PsycholoGenie [online]. Available at: psychologenie.com/explanation-of-facial-feedback-hypothesis-with-examples.

Welcome to the Real World

1. 'New Measure of Human Brain Processing Speed', *MIT Technology Review* (2009) [online]. Available at: technologyreview.com/2009/08/25/210267/new-measure-of-human-brain-processing-speed/

2. Smith, E. et al. 'The neural basis of task-switching in working memory: Effects of performance and aging', *Proceedings of the National Academy of Sciences of the United States of America*, 98(4), pp. 2095–100 (13 February 2001) [online]. Available at: ncbi.nlm.nih.gov/pmc/articles/PMC29387/

3. 'A closer look at EEG', Epilepsy Society [online]. Available at: epilepsysociety.org.uk/about-epilepsy/diagnosing-epilepsy/closer-look-eeg#.XNCq7pNKjOQ

4. 'Experiment HP-1: The Electroencephalogram (EEG) – Wireless', iWorx.com [online]. Available at: iworx.com/documents/LabExercises/EEG-CorticalArousal-ROAM.pdf

5. Dobbs, D. 'Zen Gamma', *Scientific American* (1 April 2005) [online]. scientificamerican.com/article/zen-gamma/

6. Shontell, A. 'The best way to deal with stress, according to a 69-year-old monk who scientists say is the "world's happiest man"', *Business Insider Australia* (28 January 2016) [online]. Available at: https://www.businessinsider.com/how-matthieu-ricard-the-worlds-happiest-man-deals-with-worry-anger-and-stress-2016-1?r=US&IR=T

7. 'Slo Mo Podcast #42: Mattieu Ricard - How the World's Happiest Man Found His Way (Part 1)' [online]. Available at: podtail.com/en/podcast/slo-mo-a-podcast-with-mo-gawdat/matthieu-ricard-part-1-how-the-worlds-happiest-ma/

The Engineer in You

1. Brackett, M. et al. 'Emotional Intelligence', Noba [online]. Available at: nobaproject.com/modules/emotional-intelligence

2. Sternberg, R. *Successful Intelligence* (New York: Plume, 1997).

The Mission is on the Right

1. Kahneman, D. and Deaton, A. 'High income improves evaluation of life but not emotional well-being', *Proceedings of the National Academy of Sciences*, Vol. 107 No. 38 (September 2010). Available at: pnas.org/doi/10.1073/pnas.1011492107

2. Roth, J.D. 'The story of Stuff', Get Rich Slowly [online]. Available at: getrichslowly.org/the-story-of-stuff/

3. Macean, M. 'For many people, gathering possessions is just the stuff of life', *Los Angeles Times* (21 March 2014) [online]. Available at: latimes.com/health/la-xpm-2014-mar-21-la-he-keeping-stuff-20140322-story.html

4. Doheny, K. (2008). 'Clutter Control: Is Too Much "Stuff" Draining You?', WebMD [online]. Available at: webmd.com/balance/features/clutter-control

5. Williams, K. (2018). 'Is Consumerism Robbing Us of Our Humanism and Happiness?', Medium [online]. Available at: medium.com/@KarenWilliams.Louise/is-consumerism-robbing-us-of-our-humanism-and-happiness-cb748cb40fba

6. Gonzalez-Garcia, J. and Holmes, T. (2021). 'Credit card ownership statistics', Creditcards.com [online]. Available at: creditcards.com/statistics/ownership-statistics/

7. Norton, M. (2011). 'Money can buy happiness: Michael Norton at TedxCambridge 2011', TEDx Talks [online]. Available at: youtube.com/watch?v=ZwGEQcFo9RE

8. Svoboda, E. 'Hard Wired for Giving', *The Wall Street Journal* (31 August 2013) [online]. Available at: wsj.com/articles/hardwired-for-giving-1377902081

9. Ritvo, E. 'The Neuroscience of Giving', *Psychology Today* (24 April 2014) [online]. Available at: psychologytoday.com/ca/blog/vitality/201404/the-neuroscience-giving

THE INTERNATIONAL BESTSELLER

Solve for 😊 Happy

Engineer your
path to joy

'A powerful
personal story
woven with a rich
analysis of what
we all seek in a
way we can
act upon.'

SERGEY BRIN CO-FOUNDER OF GOOGLE

Mo Gawdat
Former Chief Business Officer, **Google [X]**

'He explains how even in the face of the unthinkable,
happiness is still possible' *Stylist*

Solve for Happy is the equation for happiness. This
startlingly original book is about creating and
maintaining happiness, written by a top Google
executive with an engineer's training and fondness
for thoroughly analysing a problem.

Out now in paperback, eBook and audio

'This book will teach you how to navigate the scary and inevitable intrusion of AI.' **Dr Rupy Aujla**

A Sunday Times Business Book of the Year

Scary Smart

The Future of Artificial Intelligence and How You Can Save Our World

Mo Gawdat

Former Chief Business Officer Google [X] and bestselling author of *Solve for Happy*

A *SUNDAY TIMES* BUSINESS BOOK OF THE YEAR

'Technology is putting our humanity at risk to an unprecedented degree. This book is not for engineers who write the code or the policy makers who claim they can regulate it. This is a book for you. Because, believe it or not, you are the only one that can fix it.' Mo Gawdat

Out now in paperback, eBook and audio

About the Author

Mo Gawdat is a serial entrepreneur, the former chief business officer of Google [X] and author of *Solve for Happy, Scary Smart*, and *That Little Voice in Your Head*. Mo has cofounded more than 20 businesses in fields such as health and fitness, food and beverage and real estate. He served as a board member in several technology, health and fitness and consumer goods companies as well as several government technology and innovation boards in the Middle East and Eastern Europe. He mentors tens of start-ups at any point in time. Outside of work, when he's not writing or reading up on business and the latest technology innovations and trends, Mo spends his time drawing charcoal portraits, creating mosaics, carpentry and indulging in his passion for restoration of classic cars.